SOUL HEALING IN AFRO-CUBAN MIAMI

Also by Judith Hoch

Prophecy on the River

Soul Healing
IN AFRO-CUBAN MIAMI

Judith Hoch

attar books

First edition published in 2025 by Attar Books
Auckland, New Zealand.

Paperback ISBN 978-1-0670142-0-9
Casebook ISBN 978-1-0670142-1-6

Copyright © John McKie 2025

The right of Judith Hoch to be identified as the author of this work in terms of Section 96 of the Copyright Act 1996 is hereby asserted.

All rights reserved. Copying and distributing passages excerpted from this book for the purpose of sharing and debating is permitted on the condition that (1) excerpts are brief, (2) the source of each excerpt is fully acknowledged, and (3) such excerpts are not onsold. Otherwise, except for fair dealing or brief passages quoted in a newspaper, magazine, radio, television or internet review, no part of this book may be reproduced in any form or by any means, or in any form of binding or cover other than that in which it is published, without permission in writing from the Publisher. This same condition is imposed on any subsequent purchaser.

Cover image: *Aphrodite's Epiphany*, a painting by Judith Hoch

Judith Hoch's website:
www.judithhoch.com

Attar Books is a New Zealand publisher that focuses on work which explores today's spiritual and mystical experiences, culture, concepts and practices. For more information on our publications visit the website:

www.attarbooks.com

Contents

PART 1: Cycle of Enchantment/Disenchantment

1	At the Crossroads	11
2	My First Divination	24
3	Synchronicity	35
4	We Met in Miami	45
5	A Family Secret	60
6	I Meet Elegguá	77
7	Move a Mountain with a Toothpick	88
8	A Healing Ceremony	97
9	Ma Rufina	107
10	Set Fire to the Shrine	120
11	The Hillbilly Circus	132

PART 2: Cycle of Death/Rebirth

12	Bloody Family Battlefield	145
13	My Mother's Ghost	152
14	Preparation	162
15	Peace Meal	172
16	The Tornado and the Crossroads	179
17	The Bed of Destruction	184
18	Tree Adimú on Key Biscayne	192
19	One Night	200
20	Stephen's Pea	203
21	Lightning, Eels and Black Bean Soup	210
22	Angelita	220

References	227
Glossary	229
About the Author	231

On the Art Deco sands of Miami Beach
the headlines read:
"Cuba is On Vacation in Miami
Come Back Another Day."
— Adrian Castro, Cantos to Blood And Honey

PART I

Cycle of Enchantment / Disenchantment

CHAPTER 1

At the Crossroads

> In our eyes the roads are endless.
> Two are crossroads of the shadow.
> — Frederico Garcia Lorca

> Masks beneath masks until suddenly
> the bare bloodless skull.
> — Salman Rushdie

ONE EVENING, when I was ten years old, a skull appeared outside my bedroom window. The skull was white. Its smiling visage, deep eye sockets, empty nostrils, large forehead and jutting jaws were sharply contrasted against the black night. I had been in bed quite a while, but I was still awake because I read a lot at night in my attic eyrie. I had heard a light tapping on the window pane. By the time I pushed up onto my elbows the skull was on the inside of the glass and coming toward me.

The next thing I knew it flew near my face, brushing it with its smooth surface. I was conscious of cold, hard bone, not soft at all. It touched my forehead and cheek as it floated around my bed. My eyes focused on its face as it rocked away and looked back at me. Moving in a subtle back and forth nodding dance, it then made a direct exit through the window on the opposite side of the attic. Somehow, I knew it wasn't threatening me. But it was stupefying.

I sat up in bed for a long time, frozen, without thought. Waiting. Then, because I wasn't clear on what to do next, not because I was frightened, I flew down the steep stairway and through the small living room to find my sleeping parents and get into bed with them.

The next morning, they told me I'd had a dream. In fact, they hardly listened to my story. I knew it wasn't a dream. I was ten, but I knew the difference. My parents were working class Lutherans living in a U.S. Midwest state, and they had no context for a flying skull. Had they been Celtic, Yoruba or Mexican, to use only three examples, they most certainly would have replied differently. In these cultures skulls are symbols of the soul, the seat of a person's divine power and her connection to the divine. That skull appeared when I was so young to signal something to me that took me years to discover, because I had no one to guide me. It wasn't until I lived in West Africa, and came to know Yoruba culture, that I learned another way of viewing a flying skull without a body. The Yoruba say a divine potential is lodged in everyone at birth. This includes our destiny and high self, the Ori. If I am out of line with my Orí, I suffer. The head and skull symbolize our Ori.

The Yoruba also pay close attention to dreams which can reveal aspects of our destiny. Years after the skull flew through my bedroom, during a very vivid dream, I opened the door to a medicine cabinet in the bathroom to find it stuffed with an abundance of orange and red chicken feathers, which swelled out from the shelves like they were inflating. While I held the door the feathers floated out and slowly descended, just touching me when they came to rest at my feet.

Now I connect both these things, skulls and chicken feathers, with Yoruba spirituality, and with its offshoot, Lucumí in Miami and Cuba. Chickens and roosters are healing fowl able to carry away misfortune and illness. Skulls are a symbol of personal and divine inner truth. They also symbolize the ancestors and the dead.

I met Ernesto Pichardo, a Lucumí obá oríaté and italero (master diviner and ceremonial leader), many years ago. He was, and is, a representative of a spiritual worldview quite different from that of my antecedents. When I met him I was teaching anthropology at Florida International University in Miami and had invited him to speak in my class. I was fascinated by his knowledge of the Yoruba Orisha, which he called Oricha, and how coherent his practice was with what I had learned when living in the city of Ibadan, in western Nigeria, where I carried out research for my doctorate.

It was then that I heard about Ernesto's Lucumí lineage teachers and his long, ten-year apprenticeship with a ceremonial leader and divination specialist, Jimagua, his elder from Cuba. A Cuban exile, Jimagua brought the Yoruba Lucumí religion to Miami. Lucumí is the largest religion in Cuba. Beginning in the 1950s, it spread to Miami due to over one million Cubans joining the exile there, which has led to some calling Miami the new Havana. Subsets of Yoruba religion, like Lucumí, exist in many places around the world, from the Caribbean to Brazil, New York to Los Angeles, London to Barcelona. But Lucumí is especially established in Miami.

When Ernesto described his title of italero, divination consultant, to Lucumí clients, I knew I wanted to schedule a session with him. His religion keeps divination at the absolute center. It is not a side show; it *is* the show. No one enters this religion without a priest(ess) who divines for her. When I look back, I realize Miami was changing character completely. I know I changed after I met Ernesto. I knew that day in my class this handsome young man had something I wanted. But I had no idea what it was.

Meanwhile, white Americans were departing from Miami, and bronzed Cubans were arriving in large numbers. They swelled with the Peter Pan flights arranged by Jimmy Carter, one of which brought Ernesto to Miami when he was five years old. Spanish quickly became the street language, but not without push-back from white nativists, who promptly put their homes on the market. Their bumper stickers read, "When the last American leaves Miami, he should bring the flag."

Ernesto arrived in a maelstrom of immigration unease, which continues to this day. But immigration was the best thing ever for a city that was once boring. Miami Beach music became legendary, food trucks like in the movie *Chef* became the norm, strong little black espressos replaced American coffee, and the food was much better, with avocados, black beans, salsa, ceviche and plantain chips available most places, a welcome departure from the sandwich-burger-soup-salad of an American eatery. At the same time, there was café Americano on menus, shots of espresso diluted with water. I couldn't go past café con leche, the sweet version of cappuccino.

I was sitting in a Latino coffee shop in south Miami one afternoon when I watched the Challenger disaster on a small television set high on the wall. I had just finished my café con leche. Hearing the tragic news in Spanish about Judith Resnick and the other crew members showed me how a bond was being forged between native and immigrant, which grew stronger as, together, we watched the news story in shared empathy and shock.

Soon I could recognize practitioners of Lucumí by their colorful beaded bracelets and necklaces. Often, as I drove through new neighborhoods, I could hear African drum beats. I counted myself supremely fortunate that Ernesto and Lucumí had come to me.

Nigeria was the first country I had lived in where the government seriously regarded popular artists who commented on politics as a dangerous opposition, so seriously it imprisoned or exiled them. I was lucky enough to meet the Nobel laureate, Wole Soyinka, a Yoruba playwright and novelist from Abeokuta, who included traditional Yoruba religion in his novels and plays. The political and social satire in his books and plays led to Mr. Soyinka being imprisoned several times. After the 1970s he spent much of his life in exile. I often recommend his work to people wanting to understand the spirit of Yoruba religion and culture.

While I was in Ibadan, Mr. Soyinka kindly agreed to talk with me about my research on Yoruba theater groups. My mind had serious reservations about myself as a young white woman wanting to study Yoruba theater. I told Dr. Soyinka that I was mesmerized by his books, which drew me to traditional Yoruba religion. On my first meeting with him, in his university office, I trembled through the entire conversation. Having read all his work, I was in awe of him. Mr. Soyinka clearly understood the exciting possibilities of Yoruba religion. He did not look on it as something evil, as inferior to Christianity, or as being of no significance, as did many Nigerian intellectuals educated by the British. And as did the Spanish Catholics in Cuba and Miami.

According to Mr. Soyinka, Yoruba traditional religion is "accommodating" and "liberating" because it incorporates new phenomenon by searching for analogues in its own traditions. Most of these analogues are in the corpus of Ifá literature, which is like the mainframe computer for Yoruba peoples. According to Mr. Soyinka, contact with unknown beliefs were not "hostile" experiences, rather they were opportunities to enrich Ifá, which now has verses dealing with Islam and Christianity.[1]

I've often noticed how Ernesto does accommodating. If a traditional story appears in my reading, which includes a vignette set on a Yoruba farm, in an instant he will take the elements of the story, for example, interactions between family members, and make them contemporary and relevant to my life. In those moments, I see how I am embraced by a human range of experience that is similar to everyone's, despite differences in times and cultures.

Mr. Soyinka's ideas helped explain to me why people of all faiths seek help from Lucumí. A Lucumí priest, like his Yoruba counterpart, works for the salvation of his client, no matter what the client's belief or confession. When we finished our discussion that day in Mr. Soyinka's office at the University of Ibadan, I stood up, shook his hand, and turned to walk to the door. Before I could open it, his arm was on my elbow and Professor Soyinka was standing right beside me.

"Please," he said to me, "come and sit down. Your zipper is broken."

For a moment, nothing registered. Then I looked down at my skirt whose waistband had pooched out so far I could see my underwear. I felt behind me and sure enough my skirt had separated and my behind was exposed down a wide swath of skin and panties. My mother had made the skirt for me to save wardrobe money. It was a mistake buying the materials in a discount store! The next moment, to my complete humiliation, my zipper pulled apart completely, and my skirt opened even wider in the back and began slipping down. I grabbed the sides of the waistband in the back and pulled them together to prevent this tragedy, gratefully sinking into the chair the celebrated writer offered me. He wisely and calmly called in his secretary, then left while she and I fumbled with the horrible skirt. I left with safety pins holding it together. I confess I never returned to talk further with Professor Soyinka. My embarrassment was too monumental and crippling. It was a huge personal loss, because I could have learned so much from him.

Two years after returning from Nigeria, I moved to Miami to take a job at Florida International University. There I met Ernesto, who visited my anthropology of religion class and introduced my students to the Lucumí religion in Miami. While I had read books and articles on the Caribbean and South American African faiths, and appreciated that some descended from Yoruba religion, I was surprised to hear Ernesto talk about the Lucumí faith in Miami using such living, breathing descriptions, replete with Yoruba language. When he wrote the word Oricha on the chalkboard, I thought for a moment I was back in Nigeria. Although the spelling was different from the Yoruba spelling, it sounded almost the same, and meant the same thing: Orisha/Oricha.

Ernesto spoke perfect American English, albeit a colourful variety painted by his humour, keen observation, dynamic energy and self-assurance. He was very slim, with black hair and eyes, and very well presented, much more so than myself in my jeans and pull over. A shining gold chain glinted around his neck under a well-pressed white, open collared dress shirt. His elegance was partially planned to explode the myth of the dirty immigrant practicing a pagan religion from darkest Africa. Colonization mocked and even outlawed traditional religions almost everywhere, locals being deemed heathens suitable only for conversion. Ernesto was already, at nineteen years old, quite sophisticated and knowledgeable about this subject.

He later divulged that divination had shown him and his medium mother Carmen Pla that they would meet someone who could understand Lucumí and be an asset to them. He thought that person was me, an educated English-speaking Anglo, who could take him out of his Cuban exile world. And I felt he could take me into his Cuban world, a journey I started by listening to and dancing salsa, which we did with a group of friends at the Trailways Motel, the only Miami venue for Latino music all those decades ago.

It's hard to imagine that now, walking down the street on Miami Beach, hearing any number of live Latino bands. As an anthropologist, I was already fed up with western superiority and the damage it had caused the Yoruba nation, among many others. I was ashamed of some colleagues, whose publications and promotions led them to profit greatly from the colonized and powerless people they studied.

After listening to Ernesto in my class, I found myself thinking about him and his skills. I'd had divination sessions with a babaláwo in Nigeria, but could not understand the complex answers, diagnosis and prescription. Yoruba is like Chinese, ancient, layered and tonal. I had studied the

Yoruba language with Yoruba teachers before going to Nigeria, but my comprehension and speaking ability were very poor. I don't think anyone learned Yoruba in less than ten years of residency, studying daily.

A while after the class I phoned Ernesto and scheduled a divination session with him, a reading as he called it. (This wasn't my first reading; I'll discuss that in the next chapter.)

I was nervous when I arrived at his home. I had many questions, including wanting to understand what or who he was reading with the small cowrie shells he rolled across the table mat.

"What I tap into is not the person but the person's eledá, the soul's double in heaven," he explained.

"What is heaven exactly?" I was wary of a concept suggesting a paradise greater than Earth, only accessible after death. In my view, Earth was already a paradise, heaven and hell being Christian and Islamic constructs.

"None of us knows," Ernesto replied, shrugging his shoulders. "It's just a word to signify that deeper realm. It's here now, but not to our senses." He looked down at his shells for a moment. "The eledá, your double, is the highest thing I can reach, next to Olódúmarè, the creator behind the creation of everything."

"So, my divine self is right here in the midst of the mundane, just like I've always believed! And during divination, there will be another level of myself talking without my conscious permission, my spiritual double? If that's true, it's like a part of me can override my brain, talk to the cowrie shells, and reveal my inner truth to you," I stated gloomily.

I was stressed because I feared the divination might reveal something I would never say out loud (unless hypnotized!), and then Ernesto would know my secrets. Everyone has some guilty stuff that they hide, while privately hoping it will somehow be revealed and healed. I worried about my spirit double betraying my bad side, but at the same time I found it hard to accept that my double was communicating with Ernesto while my mouth remained closed. And besides, what *was* my relationship to my purported double? Simultaneous entertaining contradictory ideas are a specialty of mine, very confusing.

"Yeah," Ernesto agreed, smiling. "Your ego doesn't have much to say that's relevant when you have a problem. If your ego knew what to do, you wouldn't be sitting in front of me. If I'm going to divine for you and help you, I need information. Unlike Western talk therapy, I bypass your ego by getting the information directly from your spiritual counterpart. Your ego recognizes its own truth when it hears it, and then backs down from its arrogance. Hopefully, with that revelation you can understand how to return to your path."

I was caught by his words: *Your ego recognizes its own truth when it hears it.* That sentence captured me, because when I first hear an inconvenient truth I take the path of denial, which can become quite convoluted. Finally, after myriad detours, acceptance becomes easier, because it's my destiny on the line.

Ernesto also told me that the cure for anyone comes from his or her own spiritual destiny, which made honesty, in the quest for self-knowledge and healing, very important. The time it might take to correct a life path can be short or long, depending on acceptance. As I said, the Orisha have no time. From another perspective, spiritual forces have all the time in the universe and can wait. Sometimes death occurs first, before the glacial weight of bad acts and deeds can be shifted. While I was getting used to the idea I have a spiritual dimension that could carry on a conversation without my knowledge, I was also realizing that spirit and spirits were behind many Lucumí practices and ideas. In fact, I was soon shocked into acknowledging that fact.

At the time I was staying with my partner John in a small, handmade house with screen walls surrounded by Florida jungle, native pines, lush limes, mahoganies and gumbo limbos. The neighborhood, situated way south of Miami, was called the Redlands, due to the forest and farmlands. The temperature was distinctly cooler and the air fresher than a few miles north, where the city's concrete mass absorbed heat all day. There were no streetlights or urban noise, only insects, animals and a gentle breeze playing through the thick foliage. The nights were spellbindingly lovely, the faint scent of jasmine carried on the air.

One evening, sometime after midnight, we were awakened in our loft bedroom by outside noises. We could hear thumping footsteps and trees shaking. Something like a big animal was stumbling around. I was more aware than ever of the thin screen walls separating us from whatever was out there. The steps slowly came closer and closer until they were just below the veranda, which was about three feet off the ground.

John and I sat up, silent like the creature near the house. Suddenly, two loud thuds shook the wooden deck. Someone quite heavy was clumping his way around the veranda, which groaned under his weight. We listened as these ponderous footsteps approached the unlocked kitchen door. The wooden handle scraped as someone turned it to open the screen, which it did a few seconds later. The door swung shut with a reverberating bang.

Loud, shoe-clad feet stomped through the kitchen, under the loft where we were in bed. My heart was beating fast as I squeezed John's hand tighter and tighter. My extreme terror resulted from the fact there was no escape for us except down a small ladder from the loft to the kitchen, where the deranged invader was wrecking everything.

Without warning, an ear-splitting cacophony erupted. Visualize standing in your kitchen and throwing all the dishes, pots and pans onto the floor at the same time. Imagine the noise of the crash and clash of metal and pottery on hard wooden boards. That's what we heard. But not in our imaginations. Someone really was raging in the kitchen, hoping to break everything and cause enormous destruction.

There was a moment of quiet. It was broken by the dishes being shaken in the drying rack, followed by the rattling and banging of all the cabinet doors simultaneously. In the loft I felt the vibrations as the doors slammed. More metal objects hit the floor with a distinctive metallic clangor. It sounded like the metal pan lids, usually lined up in a rack on the wall, were hitting the floor, one by one, and bouncing off onto the crockery detritus of the rest of the disaster.

"I can't stand it any longer," John whispered.

He sprang out of bed and raced to the ladder, jumped down in one leap, and turned on the light. When the light blazed, the tumult stopped as if it had been a recording with an off-button. The instantaneous, deep silence was alarming. I imagined two large men standing face to face. I heard more footsteps, normal ones like John's.

Then, a huge surprise when I heard his voice: "There's no one here. And nothing has been moved."

"That's not possible. All the dishes must be broken!"

"No, nothing like that. Come and see for yourself."

I scrambled down the ladder to the kitchen. As John had reported, absolutely nothing had changed since we'd finished dinner, washed the dishes, and left them to dry. No cabinet doors were open and almost nothing was on the floor. Mysteriously, one copper lid lay on the wooden floor. I put it back on the wall.

The next day I left for the university exhausted. I didn't tell anyone about the "happening". I was sure that none of my academic colleagues, in what Pico Iyer called "an institution of higher skepticism", would believe me. That night I decided to stay at my own house in South Miami. I pleaded with John to do the same. I didn't want him to go to sleep at the little house in the woods. But he insisted. He wanted to see what would happen. Nothing could have induced me to stay there that night. I needed street lights on the corner, and the sound of police vehicles in the distance, for reassurance.

At midnight, John phoned me. "I hear footsteps outside right now."

He didn't have to tell me what occurred next, because I heard the bedlam from the dishes, pans and doors banging against one other. Two or three minutes later, all was silent. John climbed down into the kitchen, returned to the phone, and confirmed nothing was broken, exactly like the night before. The third night, there was a repeat performance: clumsy, loud footsteps around the house, an entrance through the screen door, pandemonium until we entered the kitchen, and after that the eerie nighttime silence.

The following morning it struck me that John should visit Ernesto for a reading. I was sure Ernesto wouldn't laugh like my colleagues because, according to him, disembodied spirits were his specialty. But to my surprise, when I phoned him for an appointment and described what was going on, he did laugh, for a long time.

"You Anglos," he chuckled, "are much too rational to entertain spirits. Send John on up to me and we'll see what's really going on down there."

John drove to the Pichardos' home in Hialeah. John arrived punctually to find the diviner waiting for him, curious. Ernesto ushered John into the small divination consulting room and sat across from him at his desk.

"Well, I'm wrong," Ernesto admitted after casting the shells. "There was a spirit there. It's a male spirit who once lived in the area, maybe in an old house long gone from the property. He doesn't want anything from you. He's passed by now and won't trouble you again. You don't have to do anything, and he won't return to bother you. He was only confused."

John phoned me after he left and told me the results of the reading. He said the reading felt right, and he was impressed with Ernesto's insight.

I was surprised to hear this report because John was a true-blooded, rational thinker, educated at Georgia Tech. I had wondered how he would relate to the whole experience with Lucumí and divination. Personally, I was dubious about the reading, because Ernesto had predicted that the spirit intruder had departed. Three nights in a row the spirit, which John and I now called a poltergeist, had appeared and caused havoc. We had already accepted without question that it was a spirit; for heaven's sake, what else could we call this phenomenon that we had both witnessed!

When I reflected, the word poltergeist seemed to fit what happened well. I had learned poltergeists were reported in every country, and dated back to the first century. The word poltergeist comes from the German words *poltern* ("to make sound" and "to rumble") and *geist* ("ghost" and "spirit"). Poltergeist roughly translates as "noisy ghost", "rumble ghost" or "loud spirit". That much was certain. The rumble ghost was the loudest, most raucous spirit imaginable.

When we thought back, even days earlier, small things had gone awry. For instance, a week before the stop-over from the noisy ghost, my ex-husband and his girlfriend visited us in the little house, and as they sat under the clock the hands turned around rapidly like they were being fast-forwarded, coming to a stop pointing straight up to midnight. Dismissing the clock's behavior as an electrical fault, we continued to chat. Sometime later, I walked into the kitchen and found a pan lid lying on the floor, although I had placed it behind the wooden bars on the wall and hadn't heard it fall.

At work, I continued to refrain from discussing this with academic colleagues, as I could imagine their responses: *No such thing! A hidden prankster caused the event. It was an effect of the wind. You were both on drugs and had the same bad dream.*

Maybe I had those thoughts, too. But I knew that when I examined them, none stood up.

That night, after the reading, I returned to the little house in the woods to stay up with John and see what would happen. While I didn't believe completely in Ernesto's reading, it had made me feel a lot safer, because part of me clung to his explanation that a male spirit was just visiting, and it didn't intend to harm to us.

We lay awake, waiting for the magic midnight hour to arrive, eyes open in the dark loft, listening. I heard something outside, the snapping of branches and rustling of leaves. A raccoon. Or a possum. Then the night was still. We watched awake until after two, but the kitchen stayed as quiet as a kitchen does. The clock hands turned at a normal rate, the pan lids stayed on the wall. Around four, we finally drifted off to sleep. The next night, we waited once more, but again fell asleep to the gentle sounds of nature. As the days and nights passed, we gradually relaxed and stopped waiting for the noisy ghost to return. Later, when I talked to Ernesto again, he acted as though he hears stories like ours every day.

"Judith," he laughed, "working with spirits is like drinking water to me!"

It was one of his statements I've not forgotten. I think it was his confidence and his metaphor. What is more natural than drinking water? There was no doubting that he really knew about the supernormal. He didn't have faith that there is a spirit world. He didn't think there might be an afterlife. He knew, and he knew how to portray it and work with it, because spiritual intrusion wasn't an interest, it was his specialty.

Ernesto added that he often had the task of helping clients through health and other problems caused by a confused or malevolent spirit. Misfortune in these cases happened, he said, when an unenlightened spirit was working at cross purposes to his client's life, not just passing through a neighborhood like our rumble ghost. As the years proceeded, I experienced other remarkable spirit encounters, some fortunate, some not, along with the techniques Ernesto used to address them.

Not long ago, Ernesto appeared in a dream. We were in the woodworking shop at his Miami home. It was a perfect day, with not a cloud in the sky. I was helping him mill large monterey cypress (macrocarpa) beams, which we were feeding through the saw's turning blade, splitting them into smaller posts that we stacked in a corner. I noticed the wood was exactly like the wood I had cut and sanded for the support beams of my handmade New Zealand home. A voice clearly said inside me, you are both on the same beam. In my dream I knew these words referred both to a wooden beam and to a beam of light.

Next, still in the dream, I was riding with my husband in a car away from Ernesto's home. But when I looked back, I was surprised to see the enormous Mother Tree from the film *Avatar* standing in his back yard. The tree had a fairy tale cottage built into her branches, high above the ground. This goliath tree had enormous spreading limbs and was hundreds of feet tall, like the tree in the movie. Ernesto lives in that tree, I thought to myself.

In the dream I knew I was returning to my own Mother Tree on our land in New Zealand, where over the years John and I have planted thousands of native saplings, now grown into a forest. My Mother Tree dream confirmed that trees and their connection to the light, to enlightenment, are part of the meaning of my relationship with Ernesto and the oracle.

Ernesto does not offer miracle cures for every problem, or a charm for every misdeed. Although I wish he did! When I work with Lucumí priests, it is tempting to assume they have highly developed supernatural skills that they can use to magically reverse the worst of my fortunes. In fact, although that is what I may desire, such reversals are not necessarily what my destiny needs. Rather, given my mental, physical, emotional and spiritual circumstances at any specific moment, and given the personal, familial, business and other relationships that involve me at that time, the role of divination is to direct me to the most beneficial path, the path that will lead to my higher good, and that will point out what is actually the most important thing in my life.

CHAPTER 2

My First Divination

> Shango—
> How I had longed for this day!
> But Eshu the weaver of fate
> Has confused the threads.
> Now I must wait
> For him to disentangle them himself.
> —Obatunde Ijimere

HAD NO IDEA WHY, soon after he spoke to my class, I scheduled an appointment for a reading with the nineteen-year-old Shango priest. I just felt a nagging urge to do so. Perhaps I was using anthropological curiosity as a superficial excuse, but in my heart I knew I needed wise counsel. The bottom line was most of us don't seek consultations unless something is wrong and we know it, or wrong but we don't know exactly what. We may even be afraid to think it through. An uneasy feeling makes us feel ungrounded, yet we can't identify what is really bothering us.

Hialeah, where Ernesto and his family lived, is northwest of downtown Miami. It is reached by playing race car driver on the intimidating I-95 expressway. I lived in Coconut Grove, a tropical sand-street village where artists, academics, yogis and hippies lived side by side with wealthier people. When I moved to the Grove I walked barefoot under a bower of live oaks and orchids to the market, needing my car only to drive west to the university. A couple years later chainsaws destroyed the bower of trees, the city paved the streets, developers built gilded shopping centres on top of heritage buildings, and real estate prices looked like phone numbers.

My home in the Grove was about a half hour's drive from Ernesto's. When I exited the expressway I found his residence easily. Similar to others in the quiet neighborhood, his Florida ranch-style house was fronted by a deep green lawn and tall royal palm trees. I noticed the cerulean sky when I rang the bell. Ernesto's brother Fernando greeted me at the front door, which opened with a blast of cold air. Carmen Pla, their mother, loved very cold air-conditioning.

The icy air immediately started drying my perspiration, a natural reaction to Miami's high humidity and temperatures. I couldn't arrive anywhere without a wet shirt and my eye makeup starting to run. The old saying that Miami's heat feels like an inescapable hot wet blanket was true that day. I was ready to be rid of it.

I walked into a living room comfortably furnished with soft sofas and chairs. At one end of the room stood an elaborate Orisha altar with beautiful cakes, fruits stacked in pyramids, and many large painted ceramic bowls covered with brocaded fabrics. White candles flickered on the altar, while by the doorway light shone from a dozen votives. I noticed people walking in back corridors, phones ringing, and Spanish voices answering. Ernesto was not in sight.

I was clueless regarding what the reading, my first divination, would reveal. The truth was I felt quite uneasy as I waited. It was the first time I'd seen Ernesto at home where he and his mother were the primary healers. I also did not speak Spanish, nor was I familiar with Lucumí divination. And, as an academic, I always felt I should be working, not off doing whatever I wanted to do.

After about an hour or so, Fernando reappeared to advise me that Ernesto would not be long. Finally, he walked down the hallway and into the living room. He was more serious than I'd seen him, but he greeted me with the formal courtesy I appreciate in Cuban men, charming, pleasant, asking after family, hugging. As usual, he was wearing an impeccable white shirt, his hair neatly coiffed, his fingernails manicured, with an excellent cologne scent, his general mien one of culture and refinement.

He asked me to follow him to his office at the end of the hall, where he took a seat behind a small wooden desk and pointed to the chair in front of it, inviting me to sit down. The room was spare and plain, in contrast to the living room and orisha altars where I'd waited. A pile of white cowrie shells took my eye immediately. They lay on a small desk made of dark wood. Whereas in other homes cowrie shells might be decorative objects, here they had an important purpose, the main purpose, in fact.

Ernesto had other clients waiting, and I needed to return soon to my office. Without preliminaries, he gathered a handful of cowries in one hand and leaned across the desk. He asked me to bend my torso toward him, making it possible for him to touch the shells to my forehead and shoulders. After that, he sat back and gently opened his hand a few inches above the center of the mat. Sixteen white shells tumbled out and onto the mat. He perused them carefully, then kneaded the shells with his fingers and swirled them in a circle. The shells played a soothing sound while spinning around, a gentle clacking like the tide on the shore withdrawing over a bed of cockles. Ernesto picked them up and cast them down again.

Finally, he marked his pad of paper and handed me two objects, a small white cone shell and a small shiny black stone. He asked me to put one in each of my palms and close my hands. Then I was to swap the stone and shell from my left to right hand, making sure he couldn't see them as I did so. With the shell and stone tightly held in each hand, he asked me to first show him the contents of my left hand, then my right. He noted which object was in each hand, then once more picked up the shells and dropped them on the woven straw, where they made the relaxing moved-by-the-waves sound.

When the shells were lying still, Ernesto studied them silently. He again asked me to exchange the stone and shell between my hands and hide their contents. After that, I had to show him my left, then my right hand one more time. Later, I learned that based on the Odu (divination sign) he had thrown, Ernesto was posing qualifying questions, and the stone and shell answered "yes" or "no". Is it her relationship? Is it someone in her family? Is a remedy needed? He made more notes on his pad.

After a few minutes, I shifted in my chair. I felt perplexed, because he hadn't asked me anything. Wasn't I supposed to pose a question? Despite being only nineteen, Ernesto was calm and composed. So I sat quietly but sceptically, feeling both anxious and hollow as I waited for the oracle to speak.

During this period of silence, I tried to recall Ernesto's explanation of the process on the phone the night before. He had said he would identify my first odu (divination sign) from the shells' configuration. His determination was made by how many cowries fell with their mouths upward and how many with them down. Then he would cast them again to receive a second odu, also identified by how many cowrie mouths fell up and how many down.

The second odu would be the complement of the first, so that my reading would be a composite of two odu. There were 16 primary odu comprised of a doubled sign and 240 other combinations. With two casts of the shells, they would form one of 256 possible, but different, combinations. Ernesto, as an italero using the Dilogún, could read 13 of the primal signs, but babaláwos who used the Ifá divination system read 16 signs and their combinations. He said that only rarely did he throw outside the 13 signs within his domain; but if that happened, he would call on a babaláwo associate to read the odu. Ernesto termed the first and second divination signs, the chapter and sub-chapter of a reading. The signs always operated in pairs because they were alive and changing. He said that once a primary odu principle acted or moved, it called in a reaction, the second odu principle. If one primary odu expanded or moved forward, it caused the other primary odu to contract and return, as if the oracle energy had a life of its own.

This sounded familiar to me, because the hexagrams of the classic Chinese divination system, the I Ching, with which I was familiar, worked that way too. After casting the chapter and sub-chapter of my reading, Ernesto said he would find my life situation on a spectrum of fortune and misfortune, and also determine what remedies, if any, I needed.

When Ernesto described the Dilogún, he had also given an example of one of the 16 primary divination signs, the sign of Eji Ogbe. Eji Ogbe was characterized by throwing eight cowrie shells mouths upward on the mat and eight cowrie shells mouths downward. According to Ernesto, Eji Ogbe was the first odu manifested in nature. Eji Ogbe was the sign of the East, of the Sun and of enlightenment. In addition to these core meanings, there was a body movement associated with each primary odu. For instance, if Eji Ogbe opened on the mat, I must cross my arms and hold myself, while breathing deeply and sending gratitude inside. The orisha Obatalá with his qualities of purity, whiteness and perfection was the energy of the odu. Obatalá was the creator of the body, so to praise Obatalá involved loving oneself with self-gratitude, starting with your own physical form. Ernesto said that within the physical body Eji Ogbe symbolized the head and the double organs. Harmony, balance, rationality and the ability to judge were highlighted as mental and emotional virtues when interpreting this primary odu. Ernesto explained that Eji Ogbe also taught us to greet the Sun as soon as we awaken. Thanking the Sun for life is a very good idea. The odu's teaching reminded me of Surya Namaskar, the Salute to the Sun I perform in my yoga practice. Like Eji Ogbe, each of the other 15 primary divination signs had many levels of meaning. Ernesto added that he avoids childishly literal explanations of the odu, which are found in many popular books on Lucumí.

Ernesto sat back in his chair, and my mind returned to the present. He leaned forward again and folded his hands on the desk.

"Judith," he began, "the odu created second in the cosmos, Eji Oko, has appeared for you."

This odu was one of four signs called Parent Odu, born with the unfolding of Olódúmarè, the infinite, unknowable All, predating even the orisha and everything on Earth. Only Eji Ogbe, the sign of the Sun, was older than Eji Oko. In Eji Oko, my odu, a very different, primary principle ruled.

"My teachers call this odu Arrows between Brothers. I want you to feel the nature of it for yourself," Ernesto instructed, raising his arms and asking me to copy him. "Stretch out your left arm at shoulder height. Close your fist as if you're holding a bow. Now, lift your right arm and pretend to draw an arrow back. Pull the bow tauter and tauter. Now, let the arrow fly as fast and high as you can. Imagine shooting it out the door of this room, down the hallway, and out of the house."

I felt very silly. At first, I only did as he instructed in a half-hearted way. When I saw his serious expression, I tried harder. I pulled through my shoulder muscles stretching the bow. At its maximum, I let go my mind's arrow, seeing it winging out the door of the house on an arc up into that cerulean sky, no target, just flying.

Moments after this imaginary arrow zinged out the door I wondered what unknown target it would strike. It dawned on me that this was the point of the self-conscious exercise. I could not see outside the house or even outside the divination room, yet my arrow flew through the air, and it was falling somewhere.

"This," Ernesto repeated, shaking his head from side to side, "is the Arrow between Brothers. Judith, there's something wrong at home. It's time to fix it."

"I don't know what you mean," I replied truthfully, and somewhat stunned. "There's nothing happening at home."

"This odu is about your relationship with your husband. It's not in fortune. There is something coming between you. However, it is up to you what to do about it. There is no ritual, no cleansing and no herbs. I can't give you anything to reverse this. You must decide what to do."

I felt edgy when he uttered these words, but I brushed the feeling aside, convinced that everything was all right. At the same time, I knew I wasn't satisfied with my marriage, but I didn't have time to consider it or put it into words for myself. Now, very unexpectedly, the odu, Eji Oko, compelled me to think about it.

"Ernesto," I stressed, "I really don't know what the odu can be talking about. I'll remember it, but I don't know what to do about it."

I noticed he looked away, bowed his head a little, and nodded. I felt like he wanted to say more, but he didn't.

When I looked back on this reading, I knew he had seen the truth. The arrow mentioned in Eji Oko shot to pieces life as I knew it. But as they say, philosophically, *from destruction comes creation*. Of course, people usually state this complacently, when they're safely past the destruction part of that homily.

I discovered that the arrows in Eji Oko belonged to the orisha Ochosi, a wily, silent hunter. Ernesto said that Eji Oko was primal darkness, the void, and the West. It sat opposite Eji Ogbe in the East. Eji Ogbe was about self-love and oneness; by contrast, Eji Oko was about duality, the conflict between close relations, the splitting into two from what was once one.

Ochosi, god of arrows, was patron of the hunt, a transiting spirit who disappeared after he released his arrow, which would strike a destiny target, unstoppable, incurable and inevitable, with necessary collateral damage. Ochosi's metal bow and arrows are important Lucumí symbols found on many altars. Ochosi is a handsome hunter whose arrows penetrate right to the soul, yet no one sees his projectiles coming. They launch themselves at the perfect moment in time to the exact spot. If Ochosi shoots, the arrow won't miss: there will be a rending. I was close to my husband and his family, who felt like my own. However, Ochosi's arrow was in flight.

Although the reading made no rational sense at the time, a part of me recognized its relevance. I was surprised that young Ernesto could lead such a mature and serious discussion, digging deeply into my personal life. I thought the reading would be about my career or my life in a superficial and general way. I guess I was expecting the daily horoscope where the invisible sage forecasts something that can apply to every situation. I hadn't thought my first divination would be so direct and important, or so convincingly private, telling me my marriage was in trouble. It was so unexpected I put it away inside and didn't tell anyone.

Later that week I returned to see Ernesto one evening about nine. A group of us, including Carmen and Fernando, sitting in chairs around the long dining table where we'd eaten not long before, talked well past midnight. The Pichardos were nonplussed by vegetarians, never having met one before, and had provided a large plate of canned peas and carrots for me while they dined on yucca, chicken and red rice. What a lovely thing to do, I thought, and I ate them all, trying not to stare with hunger at the yucca and red rice.

Unexpectedly, the room grew quieter. Everyone was somehow more contained. In looking back, I think the messenger of the gods, Hermes, had arrived, but in his Yoruba and more ancient form of Elegba. Messages needed delivering, but a boundary had been reached. We had all become more introspective, waiting for what must come next, but without knowing what that might involve.

Carmen sat quietly for a while, then attracted my attention by rocking rapidly back and forth in her chair. I noticed her arms rested on the antique rocker's armrests, made of polished dark wood, her hands folded around the rounded ends. Her eyes were closed.

Suddenly, she began speaking in a high-pitched, falsetto voice, something in Spanish I didn't understand. Ernesto translated.

"My mother says you and your husband will have children in a very short time," Ernesto said, looking at me so I would know she was talking about me.

The large, blonde woman continued rocking, her eyes closed. In the next moment, she spoke again, but this time addressed her niece. Apparently, that was all she had to say to me.

My husband and I would soon have children. I remember wondering how could this be possible? I wasn't pregnant, and we weren't planning children. We were both working hard at our respective careers and not thinking about starting a family. Further, the odu, Eji Oko, only that week had forecast Arrows between Brothers. With my first divination and communiqué from the spirit world, I learned how comfortable Lucumí is with paradox. In the time it took for its transit of space (and no one knows the timing of the orisha), Ochosi's arrow became profound and certain.

Yet, paradoxically, Carmen was right too. Soon (within three months), my husband and I separated after a tumultuous soap drama filled with poor decisions, acrimonious sundering, vindictive wives, and eventually remorse. Life during that time was a thick fiery soup that I swam in daily.

Lucky for me, I was a lot younger than I am now. As part of the tumult, and without warning, I fell in love with my present husband, John, who had two children. I could never have predicted how that would change my life completely, yet push me in the direction of my destiny. My ex-husband remarried a year later and had twins. So we both soon had children, as Caridad, Carmen's spirit guide, predicted.

A few days after Carmen's guide spoke to me, I visited Ernesto again. That evening, he told me the name of his mother's spirit guide, Caridad, and described her history with his family.

When his mother Carmen was growing up in Cuba Catholicism was the status quo, and so was anti-African prejudice. Antolin and Maria Elena Pla, Ernesto's grandfather and grandmother, lived with their daughter Carmen outside Havana. Antolin was an atheist and anti-African, a common attitude among white Hispanics. He had no belief in God, let alone in spirit mediumship, and he adamantly proclaimed the magical techniques of Lucumí and other African religions in Cuba to be false. His wife, Maria Elena, was a medium who understood possession, but she suppressed her gifts because she was Catholic and because of her relationship with Antolin. Then a startling event changed the course of their lives. Their daughter Carmen began to exhibit what appeared to be epileptic fits.

Carmen's convulsions began when Antolin took over farmland he had acquired outside Havana. Many years after the 1886 abolition of slavery in Cuba, cruelty to Africans was still the norm. This bigotry impelled Ernesto's grandfather to unceremoniously evict the Paleros, Cuban people of African heritage, who were living on and farming his newly purchased land. This left them without food, let alone any means of support. Paleros practiced Palo Mayombe, a religion that came to Cuba with Kongo people sold as slaves. They were known for their ability to lay curses delivered by disembodied spirits. Working with cauldrons, which they used to conjure their ethereal helpers, they laid a curse on Antolin and Maria Elena.

After the Paleros vacated the land, illness stalked Carmen's family. Antolin and Maria Elena both became seriously ill, and their fortunes declined. Soon they were almost as poor as the people Antolin had evicted. Maria Elena had always understood the spiritual consequences of being cruel to less fortunate people. She believed that a Palero curse had destroyed their lives, and there was nothing they could do due to Antolin's cruel behaviour. He remained obstinately racist and cynical.

During this time of family decline, young Carmen began to exhibit the characteristics of spirit possession, falling onto the floor, her limbs out of control, and speaking in a foreign language that the family's servant, Felix, recognized as the Yoruba language from his homeland in Nigeria.

This was a remarkable development, and a great surprise to Carmen's parents. Felix's father had been born in Nigeria. He was a Yoruba man and Shangó priest, who had been kidnapped from his home in West Africa. He survived the slave ship. When he arrived in Cuba he was sold into slavery. Felix had been spiritually trained by his father, and so understood possession. Consequently, when Felix witnessed Carmen's fitful turns, he was certain she housed a soul who wished to speak.

Maria Elena had faith in Felix and pleaded with him to do whatever in his tradition would be right for Carmen. Felix used a simple ritual guided by the shells, which consisted of an offering for the spirit, welcoming her presence. With Felix' help, the spirit, now known to be Caridad, was eventually able to speak calmly through Carmen, without causing the young girl any discomfort. Felix also solicited advice from Cachirulu, his own spirit guide. Because who would know better what to do?

Maria Elena believed Caridad was a spirit come to help them, but Antolin was much slower to believe. Consequently, through the years, their fortunes continued to crumble. At the last moment help came through the intercession of Ernesto's paternal grandfather. Fortuitously, Ramon Pichardo operated a spiritualist temple in Havana, where Carmen attended spirit masses to develop her channelling abilities. Many Havana mediums during that era trained themselves during séances at spiritualist temples like Ramon's.

One night during a séance, when the spirit Caridad mounted Carmen, Caridad announced that Carmen's parents' only solution was to return the land Antolin had taken from the Afro-Cubans.

This was not an easy decision because they had little else left. However, persuaded by Caridad's spiritual insight (she had already proven her worth addressing other problems), and with Maria Elena's and Ramon Pichardo's encouragement, Antolin finally gave the land back to the people he had evicted. Soon after, the discord, illness and loss in their family ceased. Ernesto says his grandparents had to make amends to those they had wronged.

Caridad's full name was Encarnation de la Caridad y Rodrigues. According to Ernesto, Caridad had described a past life as a priest of Oshún, when she had lived in Cuba over two centuries earlier. During this life Caridad lived in a sugar plantation. She was an indoor slave whose work was not as hard as that of the unlucky field slaves. Caridad's owner's wife could not have children, so Caridad was conscripted to bear children for the family and care for them. Today, Caridad takes part in the Pichardo's family life through Carmen. It's Caridad who rocked Carmen in her chair when she had something to say, like she did when she talked to me that night about children. I've got to say Caridad could really sum things up in a few words.

Later, both spirits, Cachirulu and Caridad, were helpful in training Carmen's considerable psychic gifts. They were also instrumental in the discovery of Ernesto's destiny.

"The first Lucumí work done for me," he explained, "was in my mom's womb. Felix was guided by Cachirulu who, when he was alive, worshipped Shangó. His father was also a Shango priest." Cachirulu's name derived from *cachirulu*, a traditional Spanish head scarf, part of a farmer's outfit in Aragon, not unlike some head ties worn by Yoruba people.

Carmen didn't see Felix again for a long time. She was occupied with school and with growing up in elegant Havana. Then one day, years later, when Carmen was married and eight months pregnant, Felix happened to be in Havana, where he passed Carmen in the street and recognized her. Felix also spotted the infant Ernesto in Carmen's womb. Cachirulu manifested at once and spoke to the young bride, reminding her of the past, when she was so young and Felix came into her life.

Felix told Carmen that Cachirulu had stopped him because he needed to speak to her unborn baby. Cachirulu addressed her belly, swollen with the as yet unborn Ernesto. He said he would be seeing Ernesto again soon.

A month later, not long after Ernesto's birth, while Carmen was out for a stroll, the infant Ernesto in her arms, she heard an orisha drumming party at Felix's house. She was drawn by the magnetic power of the drum. When Felix saw the new mother and her baby at the door, Cachirulu mounted Felix instantly. Felix, in this state of possession, greeted Carmen and took little Ernesto in his arms. Felix/Cachirulu danced and jumped around the room joyfully, showing the babe to everyone.

"This is a child of Shangó," Cachirulu prophesised. "This is the one who will free our religion in a new land."

Many years later, when Felix was elderly, the good news arrived in Cuba that Ernesto Pichardo had fulfilled Felix/Cachirulu's predictions by winning a landmark victory for Lucumí in the United States Supreme Court. Now that Felix has passed on, Ernesto says he is one of the guiding spirits he calls upon, one who always responds, because his life-long connection with Felix can never be broken. Ernesto has Felix's birth name, his secret orisha name, and his photograph; with these he calls Felix home to him.

CHAPTER 3

Synchronicity

> In what is probably the most serious inquiry of my life,
> I have begun to look past reason,
> past the provable, in other directions.
> — Mary Oliver

WHEN I WAS STUDYING in graduate school there was a prevailing attitude that "they", those who believed in spirits and ancestor communication, lived far away, in jungles, deserts, or on high mountain peaks. These were places anthropologists went to study exotic peoples, fieldwork sites where they gathered research data for an article or to progress a degree. When academics returned to the university fold they once again became part of the rational crowd of educated westerners, the "us", for whom the beliefs of the fieldwork community were translated into academic prose.

After completing my research in Nigeria, when I was back home and teaching, I became very conscious of how much anthropologists received from their fieldwork peoples, and how little was returned to them. Anthropologists regularly referred to "my" people, from whom they gained expertise, faculty positions, salaries, publications, ranking and status. "Their" people usually stayed anonymous and unnamed, continuing their normal lives, with no increase in salary, and no promotion or fame.

Yoruba diaspora religions are practiced by over a hundred million people, making them influential throughout the world. When the slave ships arrived in the Americas and the Caribbean islands, the peoples they carried brought hundreds of African cultures and religions with them.

The most pronounced culture of the African diasporas remains that of the Yoruba speaking peoples. Santería in Cuba, Umbanda and Candomblé in Brazil, the Orisha religion in Trinidad, and Haiti's religion of Vodou, bear many commonalities with Yoruba religion.

With the onset of the Atlantic slave trade, Yoruba people from Nigeria and Benin were forcibly transported to America as slaves. Their religion expanded across many borders, to Trinidad, Cuba, Saint Lucia, Benin, Togo, Brazil, Guyana, Haiti, Jamaica, to name a few. Now there is no need to go to Nigeria, currently undergoing a revival of traditional religion destroyed by colonization, to understand Yoruba traditions. In fact, some anthropologists have become initiates and practitioners of traditional faiths like Yoruba religion.

Immigration and exile have brought Yoruba descendants to cities like Miami and New York, where it is possible to find diviners and ritual guides like Ernesto who have suburban houses or city apartments, who dress in western attire, yet practice an indigenous tradition. Over the many decades since my first divination with Ernesto I have continued to be involved as a participant. Frankly, the tradition of divination is inspiring and personal. There is an attraction for Anglos who enjoy Native American or other tradition forms of spirituality, and who respect indigenous faiths. I asked Ernesto what he thought about this.

"Why is it," he said, "I can sit down with Native Americans and find the overlapping commonalities in our spiritual beliefs in ten minutes, even in different languages? Most tribes connect to the creator, standing before the Sun. They call it the spirit of enlightenment, of purity. It's not different from Lucumí. The difference is only what we call the Sun."

To find a Lucumí priest is usually a story of luck, especially for an Anglo. There is no place to find one, no listings, no means of identification. Lucumí do not advertise or proselytize, there are no codified beliefs, no imposing buildings, no definitive book, no posters, no neighborhood missionary visits. Lucumí culture and religion survive because they give help to people with practical issues, and they connect people to divinity in a personal way.

Lucumí is a collection of healing practices, mastered through initiations in divination and ceremony, practices which are ancient in Africa.

The Yoruba have a long timeline, a four-thousand-year history in the lands that today constitute Nigeria.² Lucumí has adapted to new environments like Miami, and changed appropriately. New initiates at the lowest level are the godchildren of a priest. He becomes the neophyte's padrino and his wife the neophyte's madrina. An ile (house) is a group of people gathered around the godparents, who know one another well through meeting for various celebrations at the padrino and madrina's home. There are no church or regular meetings, and no requirements. Also, you can practice anything you want outside of Lucumí.

The subject matter of Lucumí is the soul, its purpose, destiny, and position in fortune or misfortune. Every practice is aimed towards the embodied soul, discovering its true identity, purpose and well-being. The major practices of Lucumí in Miami are communication with Orisha, holy beings with natural and cosmic powers. The Orisha include ocean dwelling interspecies, Yemayá and Olokun, who have fish tails. Other important Orisha are Shango, Oshun, Obatala, Oya, Elegguá and Ogun. Many of these names are frequently heard in salsa music from the Caribbean and Miami, where Orisha identities are familiar to many people. Other practices include reverence for ancestor spirits, divination, mediumship, altar building, dancing, prayer, spirit possession, feasting and sacrifice.

Divination is the most frequently used service of Lucumí priests, because it is the center of everything else in the religion. Divination translates divine wisdom to the human mind using a system of signs, whose patterns signify a complex compendium of ancient wisdoms. The Lucumí diviner uses sixteen cowrie shells to determine a person's sign. Cowrie shells convey spiritual and symbolic meanings. They talk to the ancient Orisha Elegguá, who translates a message to a diviner's client via the shells.

I can remember my nervousness the first time I sat in front of Ernesto for a reading. When I lived in Nigeria, I could only understand a little Yoruba. Since then I had read a lot about Yoruba divination, but I was a long way from comprehending anything. So my first divination reading in English with Ernesto caught my attention. His words to me were true and personal, and clearly not anything the young diviner could possibly have known about me.

After that I was caught in the net of attraction. I wanted to know the principle behind divination that could make it so significant for thousands of years. I had received a copy of Richard Wilheim's *I Ching* from a university colleague, Stanley, while I was living in Ibadan. He had written the words *Flying in the Night* inside the cover while he was in a plane over the Sahara coming to visit me in Ibadan. His major mission there, besides catching up with me, was to find a babaláwo, a diviner who uses the Ifá divination system.* Stanley's words went deep: *flying in the night*. That was what I needed, definitely. Advice for the night, the unknown, the confusing life we all navigate blindly. The night of the subconscious, dreams, intuitions, taboos and dark spaces. Stanley already understood this, because he was a psychologist. It took me a much longer to begin comprehending it, even with the book in my hands. How do I fly in the night?

A few days after my first reading with Ernesto I read Carl Jung's introduction to Wilheim's *I Ching* in the classic edition Stanley had sent me: "A certain curious principle that I have termed synchronicity, a concept that formulates a point of view diametrically opposed to that of causality. Since the latter is a merely statistical truth and not absolute, it is a sort of working hypothesis of how events evolve one out of another, whereas synchronicity takes the coincidence of events in space and time as meaning something more than mere chance."[3]

This was the first time that I contemplated synchronicity. The attribution of meaning to a coincidence is what makes it a synchronicity. If it's not meaningful, it's a coincidence, which is still interesting, but is probably not a path marker. Synchronicity is when you recognize a relationship between something on the inside and something on the outside of self, sort of an alchemy of mind and matter brought together through the principle of attraction, or what the Lucumí call, ashé. This summarizes how magic works, and yields a very good definition of how destiny moves forward, if you are awake to what we usually call coincidence.

I cast the I Ching and determine hexagrams for myself each day. I find its wisdom remarkable and worth contemplating. Ernesto has studied the

---

* In recognition of its outstanding brilliance and importance, Ifá divination was inscribed in 2008 on the Representative List of the Intangible Cultural Heritage of Humanity (originally proclaimed in 2005) by the United Nations

correspondences between the I Ching and the Dilogún and respects the I Ching as an oracle of wisdom similar to the Dilogún. I cast an I Ching hexagram as I was writing this chapter. My question was: What will be the importance of this book to its readers. The oracle's reply was hexagram 59, Dispersing, which originally had the idea of ice breaking up and vanishing. It portends good fortune. My casting had three changing lines which transformed Dispersing to hexagram 1, Vitality, Creative Force.

All three lines speak of good fortune, of the King arriving at his temple after crossing great rivers. One line speaks of a deteriorating situation, but which can be rescued if you use strong intention. The second line speaks of dispersing selfishness. The third line speaks of dispersing through refusing a selfish bond in favor of serving the just King. The just King symbolises the highest moral virtues. It signifies acknowledging and separating good from evil in your heart, and supporting right projects that can help others. Using these principles will lead to a renewal of life energy. This reading makes me hope that the oracle refers to ice breaking up in the hearts of readers with respect to indigenous cultures. It hints that those who open themselves to other knowledge will be reignited with life energy.

A good diviner has at least a decade of experience fielding questions about health, relationships, work and support networks, the virtue or not of a proposed enterprise, the energy alignments of a new work place, and many other realted issues. The divination system that Ernesto uses is the Dilogún, derived in Cuba from Ifá Divination. The word *Ifá* refers to the mystical figure Ifá, also known as Orúnmìlà, regarded by the Yoruba as the deity of wisdom and intellectual development.

In Nigeria, the city associated with Ifá is Ilé-If, the spiritual heart of Yoruba ancestral culture. In contrast to other forms of divination that employ spirit mediumship, Ifá divination does not rely on a person having oracular powers, but rather on the diviner being able to interpret a system of signs. Among the Yoruba people, the Ifá divination system was utilised whenever an important individual or collective decision had to be made.

The Ifá and Dilogún literary corpus, called Odu Ifá, consists of 256 parts, subdivided into verses called ese (Dilogún uses fewer of these than Ifá). These ese contain Yoruba history, language, beliefs, cosmovision and contemporary social issues. Diviners like Ernesto use the ese metaphorically, finding their universal meaning applicable to a place like Miami. The diviner combines knowledge and training with a client's destiny on the day the person seeks a reading, which will be personal and predictive and contain remedies and cures for the particular situation. My own reactions to a reading usually include some trepidation and anxiety. When I am out of balance with my own life, the oracle will not just see the surface of what's going on for me.

I have resisted writing about the reading I am about to discuss because it is the only one I've had which foretold a path of misfortune without offering any real guidance, and which doesn't point the way toward harmony and a good outcome. It also reminds me of a very painful time in my life when I was confused and hurt, and beginning to get sick.

The reading occurred when I visited Ernesto on September 20, 1994, just seven months after my mother died. Ernesto was at home that day. He delivered the information to me as objectively as any other reading. But my immediate reaction was to discount it. I suggested to myself that I was way beyond divination, that I could do as I wanted, and so the reading did not apply to me. I was wrong.

The odu that came up showed the cause to be World's Wickedness. It involved the ancestors reversing the wickedness of the world. However, the only advice Ernesto had for me was to do whatever I thought made sense to me that could cause a reversal. The odu had to do with the depths of the dark sea, but Ernesto's reading did not allow him to look at what the ancestors thought was necessary. Ernesto said it was about the struggles and misfortunes of life, and lessons to be learned. Even though the ancestors were primary, the whole scope was within Eshu, a flash of illumination in the depths of the dark sea.

"At the center we are dealing with a path your ancestors don't agree with," Ernesto expanded, "the continuation of which will cause more misfortune. Whatever you've been doing is a bad idea and if continued could lead to losses in a further state. The wickedness that exists now could move to entanglement," he reiterated, "then move further to losses. The odu also gives the idea of entrapment or being caged in. Keep it broad," he concluded. "Think about the struggles of life. It cuts across the board."

That described it exactly. My troubles were not just physical or spiritual or emotional or mental. They cut across the board and penetrated every aspect of my existence. I couldn't be without them for a second while awake, and they followed me into sleep. They were all bound up in family. It was the first time I had visited my father and his new wife, and I had stayed for only a day. I hated being with them, and felt every minute I was betraying my mother. I also had a tooth that was infected and affecting all my health. I still grieved for my mother without being able to talk about it. I was depressed, my face hurt, and I had no enthusiasm for life. It was the lowest ebb I could remember. My work seemed to have dissolved. I felt isolated and alone. My mother had died in agony knowing my father and her husband of 52 years had betrayed her. The knowledge had devastated every molecule of trust I had for my father. But the situation helped me see myself in the context of my parents.

Three weeks earlier, while I was in Santa Cruz practicing yoga at a Zen monastery, I felt the transition to another state: a state of misfortune. Up until that time I felt I was walking in the light, a light which began to be harsh and cold, but it was still light. Maybe it was the depth of the darkness in the Redwoods, but one afternoon at the monastery I understood my fate had changed to darkness and descent. I had no idea how to stop it. Like the ancient Mesopotamian goddess Inanna, I was lost to myself, all potential gone, talents stolen. I was tender, fragile, afraid and sinking. I had a bad case of flu and canceled a trip with the Florida woman's caucus to China that I had anticipated for months, missing an address given by one of my heroes, Hillary Clinton. I felt at odds with life, and without will of my own. In short, my soul suffered from loss, immobility and grief.

But that moment of transition was dramatic and different. I knew that I had crossed the line walking in the redwoods near Santa Cruz. Their beauty did not touch me. My inner self was paralyzed. Nature didn't help me feel peaceful any longer. The prayer workshop I had hoped would heal me had proved to be boring. I ached. I began to feel weaker and weaker. I knew something was wrong with me, but I had no idea what to do.

When I approached Ernesto for a reading, I asked about my career in art, specifically whether I should go to graduate school. Because I had started painting late in life, I always felt I should be studying and aligning myself with the art world. At the same time, I knew my path was an individual one, which could not be helped by more academia. I had already tried the university path when I did a PhD in anthropology, and it shut down my creative juices for two decades. I was just beginning to be able to write sentences that were clear and not deliberately obfuscated. Yet I still needed academic confirmation. I saw a friend enrolling for an MFA in writing who also had a PhD and I thought she really knew the way. I began to wonder if it was the thing to do to legitimate myself. Graduate schools are full of people who have thought like that. Ernesto's interpretation of the oracle sign was that I did need to make changes in my career, but not in that direction, either that year or the next one.

"This may be a wake-up call to take advantage of other opportunities around now. The response is totally negative," Ernesto said. "There is no path in that direction at this time from the point of view of the Gods. You will be too vulnerable and will miss other opportunities."

I asked if should I go back in my studio and do my own work?

The response was, "Yes! That is the answer. Return to your own path." But Ernesto also conveyed a warning: "Pay attention to contracts or agreements. Make sure your travel arrangements are in order."

How I wish now I had taken the oracle's advice. I went ahead and applied to graduate schools, knowing I did not want to go and, of course, was rejected at all three. Although I did not apply to many, it took lots of energy and time and made me feel vulnerable. Whatever other opportunities existed went by me. I felt miserable and sick. I began to have headaches every day. My stepson came to live with us for a year, and suddenly an alien boy who hated me invaded my safe world. My mental state was restricted and frightened. I still grieved my mother and was full of tears. It was definitely the path of misfortune.

After the oracle spoke to me, Ernesto suggested a ritual of remembrance for my mother, to whom I still felt deep connected. He asked me to put a picture, white flowers and a glass of water on my altar, and to light a white candle every day for nine days, let each burn out completely. While each candle was burning, I was to think of my mother and draw her toward me in whatever state she was in, and then move her out of my world and into hers.

"Light one candle for nine days," Ernesto said, "and do whatever comes to mind."

We were living in an apartment in Key Biscayne that was dark and cool with air-conditioning. Outside the day was blazing hot, the sidewalks and white sand beach shimmering with heat. I bought white candles and flowers at the local market, and returned to my darkened bedroom. I sat in front of the simple altar I had arranged in a corner facing the East, as a place of illumination and insight. I honour the ancestors in the West in my own practice. Accordingly, I set the picture of my mother, the candle, water and flowers in the room's west corner, facing East.

I began to think of my mother, to imagine her present, and to feel her state of being. I remember I could feel her anger, which made me want to wake up and do something. But remembering her surgeries, strokes and suffering, reliving the grotesque and frightening scenes of her in hospital, all I could do was cry.

I could sense she wanted to stop hurting, after the pain of her illnesses, not to speak of the pain of knowing her husband had betrayed her. She was hurting after a lifetime of marriage charade in which she had to feign perfect love beyond all ceremony.

On the day after her funeral, my father told me they had run away to get married in 1942, because my mother was pregnant. After that, for their whole lives, they had to be better than good. They had to make reparation to their conservative, patriarchal Republican parents, who damned them for being in love and having sex without being married. They had to pretend that what they did was what they really wanted to do. When they returned from the wedding trip over the state border, they had just $2 to last them the week.

Then, after all that drama, when they were settled in an apartment at my grandparents' home, Mom had a miscarriage, making moot the timing of the pregnancy for grandmother's church friends. My father said the fetus was a girl, my older sister who was never born.

Nonetheless, they had to stay married and make it work for life, as people thought and did in those days. But the shame remained. The fact my mother had never mentioned any of this during her life showed how much she didn't want to talk about it. My father was bursting after mother died. He had to tell someone and that was me, his fifty-year-old daughter, who could still feel abandoned.

To my eyes their marriage had always been far from perfect. Mother was irritated by my father's curious habits and mental deficiencies, but had to keep pretending she wasn't. This made her short tempered, and ultimately turned her into an alcoholic. As a child I grew up believing my parents represented true love, because they said so all the time, and they never shouted at one another. When my father was already seventy-seven and my mother dead three days, my father told me no that wasn't true. They had no volition, no joy. I was glad I hadn't known as a child. But now, as a fifty year old adult, I wished I hadn't been told. I wished my father had died with his secrets intact.

While the white candles burned, I contemplated my mother and her life, and my life with her. The preceding years had been wonderful, with exhibitions, workshops, work, friends and travel. Now I felt stranded on a lonely beach, unable to reach anyone. I was so anxious and afraid I couldn't stop the cascade of alienation. My life felt out of control, unhappy, and, suddenly, without hope. I had no idea how to right the balance and restore light in my world.

Nevertheless, I lied about my condition. Whenever anyone asked, I always said I felt fine. No one knew, so no one could help me. The oracle was right. I was well down the path of misfortune. It would be three more years until with, Ernesto's help, I found the means to reverse it. So much depended on my relationship with my friend, Laura, and on Miami. Laura and I found ways to go deeply into our lives and our Lucumí destinies together. Laura understood me.

CHAPTER 4

We Met in Miami

> It's the soul that stands the body up
> and gets it moving forward.
> Everybody's soul is on a journey.
> — Obatunde Ijimere

MIAMI IS A TROPICAL Latino city, where deco hotels on Miami Beach get big bucks offering crumbling plaster facades and tourist salsa. My Lucumí god-sister, Laura Cerwinske, whose head was ruled by the sensual Afro-Cuban Lucumí goddess, Oshun, contributed to this lucrative buzz on South Beach. She wrote and produced three books celebrating Miami style, *Tropical Deco*, *Miami Hot and Cool* and *South Beach Style*, all published by big houses, as my friends in publishing say. Easy to pick up and scan for their gorgeous Miami photographs, her books were on front shelves of Barnes and Noble and every other big book chain.

One of her books showed Laura in the jungle with her outstretched arms holding five large green and red parrots. Probably everyone who looked through these books made a plan to vacation in Miami, if not actually move there. In just a few decades, Laura and the Cuban exile community of over a million people had created a great transformation, from a retirement community to a Spanish-speaking international city. Laura learned a new Spanish word every day and conducted her business in Spanish. Lucumí priests showed their icons in her book, *Art in a Spiritual Style*. My art was there, too, part of the family.

Laura lived at the fever edge of commitment to her passions. I can still see her after dark, silhouetted by yellow light, her back ramrod straight in front of her computer, windows open to the night air. She was working on her Great Work, as well as many other lesser works. When she was in the bliss of creation she would cancel anyone or anything to stay there. She had written and produced nineteen books, but was still strapped for money. Recognition was imminent. Her less productive friends, who considered themselves serious writers, smugly referred to her work as coffee table books, having no serious aim, no angst, no fear, no bad news. They were correct. Beauty was Laura's sole aim and motivation. Her books were gorgeous, filled with original photography and essays that flowed and informed; they did belong on coffee tables. In addition, Laura's commentaries on architecture, interior design, garden design and fine art appeared regularly in numerous publications.

Our gay friends named Laura *Born to be Naked*. The name stuck and spread. Her breasts were legendary. I created the photographs and paintings that prove it. She needed a backdrop of arcane red roses on velvet covered tables, deep shadows. She had gypsy black hair and eyes. Her scarlet nails, fingers and toes matched her lips. Her pursuit of baroque beauty was absolute. Laura often garbed in a red flamenco dress, burning with a nearly visible flame, and green tap shoes. Or in cut-off jeans, a t-shirt and sandals. She was equally at home in Miami, New York, Israel or Italy. As a result of that, or at least in part, Laura had a lot of self-confidence. Behind her she left a trail of adventures.

The photographer for one of her books contacted me a few weeks after he'd worked with Laura, wanting to explain why he was no longer speaking to her. Laura and M had driven together to New Mexico, and Laura reserved a room for them to share, because, she said, her budget to produce the book was very slim. The room had two beds. The trip was going well. This was until they were both in their own bed, settling down to sleep, and Laura asked M if he wanted to fool around. He demurred. Laura left her bed, pulled down M's covers, and lay beside him. He lay still, surprised and confused. Then Laura kissed and touched him, but he turned away. Laura wasn't happy, said M, and he wasn't either.

A new book's cover assignment is the most coveted credit for a professional photographer, because it's harder to get noticed on the inside pages, compared to an elegant cover displayed across a bookshop shelf.

After the trip, Laura assigned the cover job to another photographer she often worked with. M was only paid for the inside photographs and barely made his expenses. Laura liked much younger men, or already taken men (like M), or any man who was Italian. She also liked women. She never mentioned M to me again, although she did summarize the awkward bed scene as "M is a tease." With all her faults, exuberance and charm, that was my friend Laura. As for M, I remember him as a young man who would phone me after many years, from whichever country he was in, and begin the conversation in a soft, sweet voice, using that old saw: "What are you wearing?" I don't think Laura tarnished his innocence.

After being away for a long time, I would speed to Laura's home when I reached Miami to enjoy the feel and smell her tropical garden. After jumping up and down, and clinging to one another screaming with happiness, we would walk around her neighborhood. She decried the rise of the mini mansions that were destroying our precious hammocks, live oaks, banyans and birds. Once, when I accompanied her on her morning walking circuit, Laura stopped in front of a small, concrete block house that was weedy and run down. She took a long look, turned to me, and smiled.

"Academic or redneck?" she queried, inclining her head to the house in question.

Academics were the stressed and overworked people with no money or time for property and garden upkeep. Rednecks were the stressed working-class people, who maybe needed two jobs. Despite their very different views, it all boiled down to something similar: foot high grass and peeling paint. The unspoken ironies made us laugh. There was no mark of beauty, no attempt to decorate or make lovely this place. No one who lived there seemed to love it. Laura was very wry: in her world the divine and the natural should intertwine perfectly to create harmony and inspiration.

Laura knew how to make friends feel good in their skins, while still wielding a detachment that could be maddening. She was allergic to bad news and preferred a fantasy view of the world, especially in relation to her financial affairs. She had spent a lot of money on her difficult son while he was growing up and had never caught up, running on debt and borrowed money, always full of plans to make more. Maybe her new blog would take off; maybe her online course would be oversubscribed; maybe reviews of her books could revive sales; maybe the perfect project would knock on her door. She stayed busy waiting for the next big job by writing magazine articles and art reviews, organising Radical Writing workshops, and offering online mentoring. And she loved to entertain.

Occasionally, on balmy winter nights, I dined with her and other friends under the full moon in her verdant garden. Night-blooming jasmine sweetened and softened us, our faces relaxed in candle and moon light, while crickets sang within our canopy of banyans and pines. Dining al fresco in Laura's back garden, where big trees still dominated the streets, we were far away from the ubiquitous traffic noise of the city. We were Cuban, Peruvian, Puerto Rican and Anglo, enjoying an excellent meal. Ernesto was there too, of course, talking non-stop, and his wife Nydia, whose beans and pumkin I especially loved. We were a smiling, laughing family.

Laura and I were both god-daughters (ahijadas) of Ernesto. Laura consulted him regularly for guidance with her family and her business, especially the latter. She had no interest in learning mystical Lucumí practice; she wanted Ernesto to tell her what was going on in her life and what she should do about it, especially financially and romantically. She needed comfort and guidance that she could understand and respect.

Laura first met Ernesto at an opening of my paintings at Cape Cod College in 1992. The exhibition's name was *Lifting the Curse*, a double entendre referring both to the curse of inferiority laid on women by patriarchy, and to the curse of silence over the longest holocaust in human history: the witch-hunts, trials and executions of early modern Europe.

I remember that exhibition because it was missing my painting *Patriarchal Oppression*, which depicted a seated priest holding a hanging rope around the neck of a naked woman, who lay at his feet. The painting was about the torture meted out to women by the patriarchal Christian religion, torture and repression that included the witch holocausts in Europe and women's continued relegation to second-rate status in every element of the religion.

My painting had been locked in the basement of the college on the President's orders. They had too many Catholic patrons, the President said, to even consider placing a painting like mine in the college's gallery.

I felt like energy from it was leaking out around the basement door, a tabooed bright light in the Christian darkness.

Serendipitously, Ernesto and Nydia were already in Boston, lecturing to anthropology classes at Harvard University. This happy synchronicity not only enabled Ernesto and Nydia to be with me for the opening, but it also facilitated an introduction between Ernesto and Laura, who travelled by train to the Cape from New York City. At this time I had known Ernesto for almost fifteen years.

From their first meeting, Ernesto and Laura bonded. Although she then knew nothing about African spirtituality, Lucumí or divination, she recognized his wisdom and insight. The day after my exhibition opened Laura had her first Dilogún reading with Ernesto. He always said when speaking of divination that we don't know what we know. Deeper problems may remain unspoken, but there was no hiding from the wisdom of the Dilogún. Laura's first reading turned out to be about her son.

"Laura," Ernesto said, after casting her Odu. "Your son can either be King of the Mountain or King of the Garbage Heap. Right now, he is King of the Garbage Heap."

His metaphor was compelling. Her son was in a boarding school for kids with conduct disorder. Ernesto had never met him and knew nothing about Laura's life as a single parent. Six months later, acting in part on his advice, she moved back to Miami from New York. What could she do with an impossible teenager? Seek comfort, guidance. From that time on, Laura saw Ernesto frequently.

Laura and I became part of a creative, intuitive and comforting group, called an ile, which gathered around Ernesto, our padrino, and his wife Nydia, our madrina. We liked to call them Momma and Pappa Bear. Their home was a repository of good art and superb altars, and a garden filled with trees and plants sacred to Lucumí.

In Lucumí, ancestral spirits help people walk positive destiny paths by sharing information they see from the spirit perspective. They are individual spirits with their own histories, personalities and families, who have a commitment to help their human charges. They are also ancestors of the land, to whom Ernesto frequently refers. "They are the owners of the land," he says of these spirits. "And you are the visitor." However, if by spiritual investigation he finds that the spiritual core contains an egun from an indigenous culture, it's a closer connection.

"The reason you live in a place is because an egun in your ancestral core, who lived on your land in the past, brings you there in this lifetime."

People who take part in Lucumí have an altar for their ancestors, which contains photos, glasses of water, candles and other personal mementos. It is a place where one talks with one's spirits and receives comfort. Some say pouring a cup of coffee for an egun who enjoyed caffeine in life helps communication.

One day, Laura recounted an amusing story about her ancestral altar. Ernesto had done a reading for her and uncovered that her ancestors were demanding attention. He advised her to communicate with them so she could tune her fortune to firm blessings. Her ancestral core, especially a particular aunt who was critical, mean and hard to please, needed positive activation. This aunt's spirit wanted attention, and if Laura could sincerely give her own awareness and offerings to her aunt's spirit, the two women, one in spirit, one embodied, might form a new spiritual friendship. Ernesto said that once the principle members of Laura's ancestral core were in motion through the energy of her offerings, it could help bring what Laura needed.

Ernesto gave Laura detailed instructions on how to prepare and make the appropriate food offerings for her aunt. At this point in their consultation, Laura froze and said nothing more, because Laura didn't cook. Ever. When she lived on the Upper West Side in New York City, when I visited, at dinnertime we would browse through the many delivery options in the take-away menus on her coffee table. Laura even drank her morning coffee at Starbucks or a Cuban restaurant.

In fact, there were no means to make food in her kitchen. I once made the mistake of opening her oven in Miami: stacks of books, stuffed tightly inside, tumbled out. For some reason, Laura once invited me to dinner and prepared brown rice and vegetables in her one pan on the working burner. They were odd and inedible with an unhealthy sheen. I didn't ask where the vegetables had come from.

On another occasion, she made an effort to eat at home, buying a small box of After Eight Mints and a jar of peanut butter, forgetting everything else. She carefully placed her purchases on the middle metal shelf of her old refrigerator. It was fine with me because I loved After Eights and absorbed quite a few. Still, everywhere I looked, there was proof of her culinary insufficiencies.

For all these reasons and more, she left her padrino's house realizing that she couldn't imagine cooking all the foods that her ancestors had loved the most. Her recipe list was long and tedious. Even simple Jewish foods like matzoh ball soup and potato latkes were way beyond her cooking ken. The cooking would take ages of time, far more than she had, not to speak of requiring an adequate kitchen.

She paced her hallway searching for a practical solution. Suddenly, she had an inspirational thought. Laura wrote for many magazines on subjects from cuisine to art history, architecture and landscape gardening. She gathered a stack of them and searched until she found excellent shots of tempting foods and convivial dinner scenes in elegant settings. She carefully cut them out. When she had a pile of pictures of delectable gourmet dishes, plated to perfection, she prepared a framed selection of them, making the food appear delicious and tempting, an occasion for fete and celebration.

Laura invited me to see her display, a mini exhibition around her altar. I was impressed with her ingenuity. She hadn't cooked a thing, yet it was a strong statement. She said she hoped that her efforts would open a subtle dialogue with her difficult aunt, helping to heal their mutual lineage wounds.

One day soon after that, Ernesto was in Laura's neighborhood and stopped by. He walked in her front door, pausing by her ancestral altar, located not far from the entrance. He looked at Laura's altar, arced by her food exhibition, for a long time. Laura said he peered closely at every photo, returning to several for more scrutiny. She was certain he was admiring them. Finally, he spoke.

"This is nice looking," he smiled. "The photos are great of the food and of your family. However, do you want your ancestors to give you a picture of a blessing? Or do you want them to give you the real thing? If you're serious about it, then you've got to give them real food."

"I thought it was a great idea because the food in the pictures was always there. It was my version of ancestral fast food," Laura complained laughing. "After all, my long-gone ancestors weren't *really* going to show up and dine with me. In my mind, it was my gesture that counted, and the image that held the power."

Finally, grasping the extent of the problem, Ernesto suggested she buy foods from a Jewish deli nearby. Laura's offerings from then on came from Miami delis, wholefood stores and restaurants.

Laura lived a New York life in Miami. Every month or so, she would visit Manhattan, stay with friends, and return highly charged by art and publishing. One close friend there, ironically, was an Asian chef with a popular wok cook book. Her book was on Laura's office shelf, a long way from her defunct kitchen.

One of the first ceremonies Laura organized with Ernesto and Nydia was an elaborate meal for the spirit of Sunny Storm, a celebrated artist who lived in Coconut Grove, a popular Miami village, for decades. She died at 97, still camping in New Mexico during holidays. Sunny was a star whose work defined Grove art movements in the 1970s. She was exhibited in the Corcoran, in galleries throughout Miami, and taught at the University. She created a famed tropical garden at her home in the Grove. And she was also a singer at festivals and churches. When Storm died, she instructed her friends to have a "wing-ding." She wanted no funeral or fuss.

It was easy to see how Sunny and Laura could be friends. Sunny's will bequeathed Laura several personal mementos, including her beloved paint brushes. When Laura told me, I realized they must have been very good friends for Sunny to think of Laura as the Miami artist who could carry on the work of her brushes.

After receiving Sunny's brushes, Laura always had them on her painting table, chunky bristle squares and rounds for making big statements, alongside several medium and smaller ones. All looked well used. Some of Sunny's brushes had been around a long time, but they were well cared for, still flexible, the ferules clean, with no visible paint. A painter may make thousands of brush strokes in one painting, adding, subtracting, transforming, covering, scraping, on and on. Brushes grow to be part of an artist, being relied on to make a line or a mark just as wanted, or to keep a point, an edge, delivering just the right amount of paint.

However, soon after receiving Sunny's legacy, Laura said she noticed unusual mechanical breakdowns around her home. Her washing machine stopped working, then the lawn mower. Not pleased, she called repair people. The next day, her blender would not turn on, and neither would her stereo. Only her small television remained untouched. So she took action. She called Ernesto. He said to come right over.

She drove to his home, about a half hour away, ran into his office, sat in front of his divination desk, and waited. Laura was impatient, always. The rest of us would take some time with Ernesto, pleasantries, you know, but Laura always said what she wanted directly and could not wait. So, Ernesto was ready and smiling. A big hug was enough before he joined her at his desk.

Ernesto identified a female spirit in Laura's home that was causing disruption. The spirit was lost and unaware she had died. Then, Ernesto asked Laura if she had recently brought something into her home that was owned by another person. Laura said she had inherited Sunny Storm's brushes, and when they were delivered she had unpacked them in her painting studio, planning to use them.

Ernesto studied the problem a bit longer, asking yes and no questions of the oracle. Finally, he said, "Yes, it is Sunny disrupting your house. This artist can't break the attachment to her most beloved working tools. She doesn't understand why they are here." Ernesto explained to Laura that she needed to throw a dinner in Sunny's honor and invite him and Nydia. Nydia was a medium and her skills could be needed.

The next day, Laura purchased her friend's favorite foods and arranged them on white plates on a table in her living room. For a finishing touch, she lit candles on the table and moved the flower arrangement to the center. Soon Ernesto, Nydia and Laura were casually relaxing on her sofa. Laura later told me she was thinking, *Ernesto's talking so much. Isn't something else supposed to happen?*

Suddenly Nydia, who had never met Sunny Storm, interrupted Ernesto. She described a female apparition who she said was standing in front of Laura's perfectly selected foods. From Nydia's description, Laura recognized her deceased friend immediately. Ernesto proceeded to tell Sunny what was happening. He praised her and helped her recognize that she had died. He chanted and called on Oya and other Orisha. Sunny's ghost stayed around the food about a half hour and then disappeared.

That day the mechanical failures stopped and Laura's routines returned to normal. Sunny's spirit was elevated by the praise and offering. Accepting that she was deceased, she left Laura's home. Not just Lucumí, but most spiritual traditions in Native America, Asia and Africa use food offerings to communicate with and call spirits. It is an unsurprising conclusion that both the living and the dead gravitate to—and are in much better temper because of—excellent meals.

Laura worked a debilitating schedule and seldom had enough money. The royalties from her books were eaten up by private schools for her son. He had been diagnosed as having a personality disorder. The two of them were constantly at war. When he was at her home I remember being stunned by the volume of his haranguing voice, his accusations and blame. He was overactive and hard-edged.

She worried about him a lot, as much as about her own career. But she drew comfort, as she often told me, from her divination readings. Sometimes her reading prescribed one of the many Yoruba ceremonies used in Lucumí healing. One evening, Laura invited me to accompany her to Ernesto's for a ceremony. She had scheduled a head rogation* at his place the next day.

I met Laura at Ernesto's on a luscious, balmy, blue Miami morning. She arrived ten minutes after I did, in her very old Mercedes, dressed in sandals and shorts. Ernesto saw us through the window and met us at the door. Natalia, Nydia and Ernesto's cocker spaniel, barked and jumped, needing petting before we went inside.

---

* Catholic churches celebrated Rogation Days long ago, when solemn processions invoked God's mercy. Yoruba slaves in Cuba were forced to be baptised by a Catholic priest and give up their own religion and language. To save their religion and culture, most Lucumí/Yoruba people (Lucumí means, My Friend) adopted Catholic names and stories to conceal their own true beliefs and practices. Rogation is a borrowing from the Catholic rite in name only. The ritual is based on Yoruba belief and practice in which the head, the orí, must be harmonized and cooled so one's destiny is not spoiled.

Ernesto looked at Laura's empty arms and said, "Where's the fruit you were supposed to bring?"

"What fruit?" Laura sounded truly puzzled. If food were involved, Laura would not remember.

"The fruit for the cleansing. I told you." Ernesto stood his ground with his arms folded in front of him. He knew Laura very well.

"Did you? I forgot. What should we do? Do you have some?" Laura wanted him to solve it for her, but he wasn't budging.

"I don't have everything I need. You have to go to the supermarket and buy an apple and an orange."

"All the way back out US-1 to the supermarket just to get a couple of pieces of fruit?" complained Laura.

"That's right."

Bowing to the inevitable, she turned quickly around, disappeared out the door, and didn't return for forty minutes, about the time it takes to traverse the crowded highway through long red lights, find a parking place at the vast shopping center, and enter the icy cold supermarket in search of the living red and orange fruits needed for her ceremony.

When Laura re-entered through the door, Natalia gave a little woof then went back to sleep. My friend was carrying a white plastic shopping bag with a couple of round objects in the bottom. As Ernesto walked to the front door to greet Laura, she smiled and swung her white bag to him in a long arc. He caught it, reached in for the apple and orange, each with a little supermarket sticker on it, turned around, and with the fruit in his hands, walked into the kitchen.

When it was time for her ceremony, Ernesto beckoned us into the Orisha room, the Pichardo's renovated former garage. I had seen it during its various stages of remodeling. It was now a quiet chapel with a serene altar bathed in light. As we slowly walked into the room, Laura and I fell silent. Laura knew what to do. She sat on the wooden chair in front of the altar. The room contained no other furniture, so I sat cross-legged on the floor, my back to the wall, facing Laura's right side. Laura planted her feet strongly on the Earth, sitting straight-backed on the simple wooden chair, a regal posture. She laid her forearms on her thighs, turning her palms upward to open her fingers in a gesture of receiving.

I could see the white crown of Obatalá on the highest place in the middle of the altar, and a bird's nest filled with filmy white cloth. Light shone down from the window at the top of the wall behind the altar, giving the illusion that it was glowing. Red and white cloth for Shangó, and blue and white cloth for Yemayá, draped the wall behind the altar.

After a few minutes Ernesto entered the room carrying a round wooden tray, laughing and joking about something. He abruptly changed to silence as he approached the altar, turning his attention inward. His tray held neatly stacked mounds of grated orange, apple, grapes, coconut and a large pad of cotton wool. A coconut shell filled with coconut water set on the salver surrounded by the fruit. He carefully placed the tray on the altar.

Then, standing in front of Laura, the radiant altar behind him, he turned to face her. After a pause, he walked closer until he stood in front of her chair. He studied her body pensively from head to toe. Ernesto was a very patient, slow moving man when he was in ceremony. He appraised Laura carefully, then knelt on one knee in front of her.

Taking a piece of white chalk from his pocket, Ernesto made a cross on the top of Laura's right foot. He did the same on her left, her summer-brown feet contrasting in a lovely way with the white chalk marks. He stood and bent over her, lifting her hands, one by one, and drawing an identical cross on her upturned palms. I could imagine how soft this felt on her sensitive skin, as the chalk stroked vertical and horizontal lines. Then he walked around to the back of her chair. He raised his hand with the chalk and drew a white cross on the top of his godchild's head, the place we call the crown chakra in yoga, which the Lucumí call the orí.

After completing this fifth cross, Ernesto walked around Laura's chair and returned to the altar. He took the wooden tray in his left hand, while with his right hand he mixed the separate fruits together, a little at a time, adding drops of coconut water to the mélange. This went on for five or six minutes, while Laura and I watched silently. The movement of his hand mixing the coconut water into individual mounds of mixed fruit reminded me of a Japanese tea master's patience, interminably whisking the bamboo around the green tea powder, until a perfect, frothing ceremonial tea was ready. A long, slow preparation, like Ernesto's mixing of the fruit, was calming and brought client and healer into the present together.

At last, Ernesto was ready. He took a small quantity of the fruit and coconut water mixture in his right hand and stooped down to Laura's feet once again. Shaking the fruit gently over the plate in his left hand, he allowed drops of juice to fall. When the drips had stopped, he shaped a mound of the sweet substance on top of the white cross on Laura's right foot. He repeated this technique, carefully shaping another mound of fruit on top of the cross on her left foot. Then he stood and treated the palms of Laura's hands. On them, just as on her feet, he fashioned rounded heaps of fresh fruit applied carefully on top of the crossed lines.

I watched how calmly Laura sat with her palms turned up to receive the poultices. Ernesto walked around to the back of Laura's chair and laid a neat bundle of the mixture squarely on the crown of her head. While Ernesto shaped the fruit on her head, Laura's body extended upward along her spine, her head leveled in order to keep the fruit from falling, creating a perfect posture for meditation. Now Laura really had to slow down, breathe deeply, and maintain her posture in order not to drop the chopped fruit that lay on her hands, head and feet. Laura was forced to be patient, very uncharacteristic of her as she lived her usually hectic life.

Ernesto returned to the altar and set down the tray. He picked up the cotton wool pad and tore off two large pieces. He kneaded one, then the other. He then walked to Laura and squatted on the floor. He stretched a piece of the cotton wool into a bandage and placed a square of it over the fruit on Laura's right foot, carefully covering the whole mound. He then turned to her left foot and did the same, covering the little pile of chopped fruit with cotton wool, until finally I could only see fuzzy wool on top of Laura's feet. He repeated the same procedure with the palms of her hands. After that, he walked around and stood at the back of her chair, and stretched and smoothed the cotton wool again, placing the fuzzy square on top of the fruit on her head.

Still silent, Ernesto returned to the altar, placing the remainder of the cotton on the tray. Then he turned and again walked behind Laura's chair. He placed his hands over the cotton wool on her head and rested them there. As he did this, Laura's face relaxed. I watched peace descend on Laura's countenance. I felt quite calm, too. Ernesto kept his hands on her head for several minutes while we were silent, our breathing soft and rhythmic.

During those minutes, when his hands were on her head, I thought of nothing in particular. I relaxed all over, went inside and listened to my breathing.

After about five minutes, he lifted his hands from Laura's head and walked to the altar. He removed the tray with the remaining fruit and set it in front of Laura's feet. He lit two candles on either side of the platter. Then he slowly stood up. In a quiet voice, he briefly instructed us to stay in silence. After that, he left the Orisha room.

I was sitting in lotus on Laura's right side in front of the altar. I decided that if the ritual's objective was to cool Laura's head I couldn't imagine a better way than with these fresh, sweet fruits I smelt around me. Our life in Miami during the summer included fruits and juices, sweet, divine, fragrant. At open air markets there were beautiful displays of mangos, watermelons, papayas, pineapples, sugar cane, mamey sapote and cherimoya. Coconut water, of course, and avocados everywhere. Every small Cuban café had fresh orange juice made in a constantly turning machine.

With her chakras covered in ritually prepared fruit, Laura touched the beauty and fragrance of this Edenic otherworld. The cotton wool sealed the fruit remedy, allowing its healing, calming energies to soothe the overheated energy centers or chakras on Laura's feet, hands, and the crown of her head. I liked the way Luc Sala puts it: "We have exchange centers allowing us to communicate with the extra-dimensional otherworld where truth, beauty, intuition and other ideals reside, and from where we can also perceive and influence the future."[4] If this wasn't so, we couldn't heal ourselves.

I listened to my breath. But obsessive thinking, day dreaming, speculation and memories now interrupted me. I felt inside for the channel of my breath and allowed myself to relax all over again. To my frail extent, I meditated, and although my deep periods of active concentration were limited, nevertheless, my mind slowed down. And when we left, about an hour later, I felt much calmer and happier.

Laura agreed. "Before the ceremony my thoughts were chaotic and my mind was filled with worries about my financial situation and my home. Now I feel calmed and able to go on with what I have to do."

We reminisced through the late afternoon. Suddenly, the full Moon quelled our talk. It had risen above the tall trees in the garden. Silver light sparkled on the pool and on the circle of palms around us, like it had done since the time we had met. Our history, Laura's and mine, went back to a tropical city where magic interleaved our lives, when giant trees lined the Miami boulevards, blooming in rhythm, dropping their flowers, enchanting us every year.

As the Moon rose higher, the temptation grew too strong. We doffed our clothes and walked to the side of the pool, which Laura had painted black just for nights like this. The Moon on the surface of the pool shone as brightly as the Moon in the sky. Magic at Ernesto's, and a night like tonight, helped us survive the disenchantment of the world.

.

CHAPTER 5

A Family Secret

*Eshu throws a stone today
And kills a bird of yesterday.*
— Traditional Yoruba Proverb

WE ARRIVED IN MIAMI mid-July from Australia, after traveling through Japan and being delayed for five hours in Las Vegas. It was midnight. We were exhausted and jet lagged. But we expected we would soon to be resting and spending several quiet weeks seeing our family and friends, working, and enjoying the waters of Key Biscayne. We had traded our house in Australia for one belonging to Alfred and Tina, friends on Key Biscayne. They were traveling to Australia to stay in our home for six weeks, while we stayed in theirs on the Key.

Unexpectedly, a few days before our departure we received a strange request from Tina, asking if she and someone named Harry Barry could stay in a spare room in the house after we arrived.

The house was small and we didn't want to share it; our own family was coming to stay with us. We asked when she would vacate the house, but received an ambiguous reply. I wrote Alfred, who was in California. We got an email and a phone call from him, both of which unequivocally stated: "No problem. Tina will move from the house before you arrive."

But the closer we got to Key Biscayne, the worse I felt. Something was wrong. We turned into the driveway and paid the cab driver. While we were picking up our suitcases, the front door opened and Crystal, Alfred's sixteen-year-old daughter, ran out.

"I thought you were coming tomorrow," she said. "Mom said you wouldn't be here until tomorrow night."

I had sent our schedule to Tina several times, explaining the exact date we would arrive in Miami. I tried to persuade myself they would be gone tomorrow.

As we walked through the door we discovered all the lights were on, as if a movie were being filmed there. The lights illumined jumbled paper over every level surface: magazines, books, boxes, newspapers, unopened envelopes. There were piles everywhere. I leafed through the paper on the table next to the door. Old bills, including some that looked important, like the power, others nonsensical notes made in Tina's scraggly writing, pictures of people I didn't know, ads from magazines.

A huge U Haul wardrobe stood on the living room floor, and next to it a bicycle with a basket and a flat tire. There was barely a clear place to put down my handbag, let alone the luggage. The bedroom was through a door on the side of the living room. The room was large, but swelled with gym equipment, mounds of clothes, boxes with photos and more paper. The wrinkled bed sheets suggested a hotel for the destitute. We were a day early by Crystal's reckoning, but I clearly saw that one more day would not be enough to prepare this home for a house trade.

I looked through the sliding glass door and there, lying soaking wet on the pool deck, was the bedspread. I looked through the dressers and closet, all packed with clothes. Only a small chest of drawers was empty. I noticed the tilted headboard and a lamp put together with rubber bands, its switch hanging alarmingly, wires exposed.

Suddenly, I remembered Crystal. She was on the floor in her room. Unable to look at me, she knelt over a backpack with clothes streaming out. Her room was vintage teenager, dark and dodgy, drawers pulled out, clothes strewn everywhere.

Crystal, still looking down, said, "I don't know why I'm not with my mother, or why my mother isn't with me."

It turned out her mother was in a hotel across the bridge, which she was sharing with Crystal's cousin, Harry. Tina was Harry's aunt. She was schizophrenic and had been hospitalized for a time. Crystal said her mother went to California and convinced Harry's father, her sister ex-husband, to let Harry come to Florida with her on the train. Crystal explained they were going to join her Dad in Australia, but not for a couple of weeks. Her Mom had unclear plans until then. This was, according to Crystal, the most disturbed she'd seen her mother since her childhood, when Tina's peculiar behaviour had led to her being diagnosed a schizophrenic.

Crystal said her Mom had placed her in charge of house cleaning for our arrival. She wasn't happy about it. The cleaner, Maria, had come that afternoon, but Crystal was unclear what to tell her. Tina stayed at the hotel while Crystal and the cleaner decided what to do. They didn't think of much because a few hours later when we arrived, the stove, the kitchen floor and the backsplash of the sink still needed a good thrashing. Trash filled the wastebasket and the recycle bin, food crowded the refrigerator shelves and doors, old papers, bags, pipes, tools, shoes, fertilizers half used and hundreds of cans of food crammed the pantry, whose folding doors could not close on this extraordinary hoarding. In the kitchen's present state we would have to leave our groceries outside.

I longed to go to a hotel. We had prepared our home in Australia carefully, buying new futons for the family's children and cleaning out all our closets and drawers. We employed a professional cleaner. We'd left new sheets on our king size bed and helpful, local information for the family.

I stepped into the back yard for some night air to clear my head of the vision of our home for the next six weeks. There I confronted the blue quilted bedspread lying topsy-turvy on the ground amid pools of dark water. A large Styrofoam cup with a globular plastic cover stood in the water next to the spread. The cup, extolling a sports hero, brimmed with fluffy orange liquid. The scene suggested someone had pulled the bedspread out to the backyard, returned inside for her enormous 32-ounce beverage, then deluged the bedspread and drink with a hose, which was lying beside the spread, before departing.

After a few hours of sleepless turning, we got up at eight the next morning. Crystal was up already. I cleared a small area on the dining table and we had coffee, tea and toast together, as if we had planned to be a family. When she finished, Crystal went into her bedroom.

Soon after, Tina, her mother, opened the front door and entered. She acted as if we weren't there. She was wearing a see-through chiffon jacket, tied with a gold ribbon at the neck, on top of a frayed, round-collared greenish blouse and old gray striped petal pushers. Her face was pale, carved with deep lines of suffering. Her thin, brown hair was uncombed. It was impossible not to feel sorry for her. But impossible to deal with her.

John and I phoned Alfred, explained the situation, and told him Tina needed his help. Instead of instantly flying back to Florida (my idea), he gave me the number for Tina's shrink.

While Tina was in a back bedroom "sorting" her things, I cleared the bedroom dressers, the kitchen counters, the dining room table and the floors. I pulled off the notes taped to the walls. Everything went into envelopes marked for one of the family members. Sheer junk went into a garbage bag.

While I worked, we received a call from a telephone carrier canceling the phone service for non-payment. When I asked Tina about it, she told us that Maria, her house cleaner, had the checkbook because she paid all the bills.

In the bedroom, where Tina was packing for her trip away, I watched her mysteriously and laboriously wrap framed pictures showing her family visiting Kenya and a picture of herself as a child with her mother. Tina did elicit our sympathy. Her condition had appeared years before, which meant Alfred bore responsibility for the state of the house and for Tina and his daughter, Crystal. Inexplicably, he had left her alone to oversee an important transaction with friends.

The situation was deteriorating. I badly needed rest. Before leaving Australia I had come down with a bad infection, for which I was still taking antibiotics. Now, John and I were strained and tense, while Alfred slept in our peaceful home in Australia.

We had no choice but to phone the number Alfred gave us for Tina's shrink. We described Tina and her house.

"The defining quality of Tina's mental illness is no self-knowledge," replied Ms. Shrink. "Tina has no idea how her behaviour appears to others, no insight into herself. In her mind she is living a normal life and all of us are wrong." Having defined Tina's condition for us, her shrink quickly rang off. We were on our own.

Crystal stayed with us for a few days. I spent a lot of the time with her. A gorgeous young girl, tall, thin and easy to get on with, she and I snorkeled, walked, rode bikes and ate together. She told me about her mom. She was worried that her illness was getting worse, because she had noticed Tina was cutting down on her medication. Every time Crystal talked about her mother, her face became mask-like, her eyes larger.

We also met Harry. We drove to Tina's hotel, found her room, and there saw a small, dark haired, twelve-year old boy lying in the far bed, watching television and playing a video game. He didn't look up or acknowledge us.

While there Tina handed me her car keys, declaring she didn't want to drive anymore. She couldn't see clearly, she said. The keychain had a dozen or more keys on it. I weighed the heavy metal in my hand and wondered what to do with it.

The next morning we drove Crystal to an appointment with her therapist (different from the shrink). When we returned to pick her up, Tina was with her. She had taken a cab. Harry, Tina said, was back at the hotel. She confirmed he had eaten no breakfast or lunch.

We drove Tina and Crystal back to the hotel, where we found Harry in a darkened room with the drapes closed and television on. It was just after noon. He had eaten nothing nor gone out of the room since the night before. He wouldn't speak to us. He was probably frightened from being in a foreign place and far from home.

He ran around the room like a caged puppy, but became calmer once Crystal talked to him. Harry said he wanted to go home to his family right away. We left him there with Tina and drove back to the house to phone Harry's family.

Felling increasingly frantic myself, I called Laura, whose son was also schizophrenic, and caught her up on what had happened since our crazy arrival. I needed to explain why I hadn't already shown up at her place. When she heard what was going on she was adamant that we leave.

"Get going now," she said in a commanding voice. "They have no right to push this on you. You will lose against this insane woman. Don't let them make you responsible. You can't handle it, and you have no idea what Tina is capable of, including pretending that's she's normal. Go now."

Later that day our cell rang. It was Harry.

"We're in a park," he said. "I want to go home."

Tina must have grabbed the phone from him because we heard her say, "No, you don't. We're looking at the sailboats, just having fun."

Harry yelled, "No, I'm not having fun. I'm not happy. I'm not!"

We found them just after sunset. They were in a small park on the bay, not far from Tina's hotel, where thick tropical foliage ran down to the seawall. We were near downtown Miami, and despite its beauty neither this park nor the surrounding area felt safe. Police cars cruised by.

The park's gates were closed, so we shouted Harry's name through the iron bars. We watched a guard trying to escort Tina away from the sea wall, up toward the road. Harry yelled to us. He ran from a coppice of trees below and started to sprint across the grass. Tina slowly walked up the drive with the guard, who opened the gate. When she reached us, Tina emptied her large leather bag on the grass. Her cell phone was missing.

Back at the hotel we told Tina we had organized for Harry to fly home the next day and that we wanted him to spend the night with us. Hearing this, Harry raced up the stairs to his room to pack. Crystal followed him.

Tina was furious that we had made the arrangements without consulting her. We asked her if we could talk in her room, but she yelled at us to get away and leave her alone.

"You are going behind my back, taking away my power," she screamed, flaming and frenzied.

At that moment the phone rang in the hotel lobby, near where we were standing.

Miraculously, Tina accepted the call and answered in a voice completely different from the agitated, bellowing voice she had just used with us. We heard a calm, collected voice say, "Oh, Janet, how nice of you to phone. No, there are no problems with Harry," she chirped. "Everything has gone fine. We went to the park and now we're all going out to dinner."

It was Ms. Shrink, calling to take the lay of the land, headed off by Tina's selective lucidity. Temporarily stunned by the timing of the call, we gaped at the lobby desk where Tina held the phone.

As Tina hung up, Harry and Crystal stepped from the elevator with his suitcase. Tina saw the suitcase and remembered we were sending Harry home. Her calm therapist voice gone. Rage returned. Her exact, bellowing words are hard to remember because they attracted the private security men at once, who asked us if everything was okay.

Crystal rushed to her mother, took her arm, pulled her outside, and spoke to her with a little, pleading voice. "Please calm down, Mom. You are yelling too loud."

I put Harry, who looked scared, in our car, while John went to find Tina and Crystal. They waited by the pool until Tina calmed down.

The next morning, at five o'clock, the phone rang. Whoever was on the line didn't speak. It rang again at five-thirty. At six, when the phone rang a third time, we let the machine answer. We heard Tina's voice telling us she was in a taxi on her way to the train station, where she would board a train to San Diego. She would meet Harry there.

We were jubilant. It was her habit, we found out later, to frequent trains as a way of living in the world, stopping here and there, staying in hotels. As we celebrated her departure, the phone rang yet again. I answered.

Tina said, "I'm at the train station and I want to say goodbye again. Do you want to come down and see me off?"

I replied, "There won't be enough time to do that and to take the kids to the airport. Goodbye. Have a great journey."

A couple of hours later, John took Harry to the airport. Inside, someone paged Harry, and the check-in employee handed him a note, naming a restaurant where Tina was waiting for him, not at all far from the departure gate. The page voice called Harry's name and said his aunt was looking for him. Before John took Harry to his plane, he found Tina in the restaurant and reasoned with her to let Harry go peacefully.

She finally left for the station to catch a train scheduled for later in the morning. Before taking a cab to the station John helped her go through her large cloth bag, but they couldn't find her tickets. Apparently, she did find them, because beginning that afternoon and for a couple of weeks after, we received phone calls from her aboard trains somewhere in America.

It had been a week of intense drama and anxiety. We felt more exhausted than when we'd arrived, the house was still filthy and congested, and we feared that Tina was a loose cannon on the rail and could pop up back at the front door any time.

John and I corresponded with Alfred. In lieu of a real solution, he asked us to suggest compensation for our losses. I was angry. I didn't see how anything could make up for this wholly unexpected and tormented arrival week. Nor did I see how we could go on living in the house.

Upset over how to respond to Alfred, who I felt was patronizing and mean, I went to Ernesto. I was furious that the only help Alfred had offered was the phone number of Tina's therapist. I sat with Ernesto and tried to put my feelings away, to empty my thoughts, and allow the oracle to penetrate me. I was sure that ultimately what was happening with our house exchange wasn't important. I relaxed as Ernesto touched the shells to my head and shoulders.

The shells chattered on Ernesto's desk. He stirred them around, then picked them up. As I waited for my current life situation to manifest through Odu I looked at a newspaper photo of Ernesto on the wall, dressed in African shirt and cap, on the cover of *New Times*. It was from the early 1990s, when the sacrifice case he initiated in the Supreme Court was big news in Miami. (I'll get to it later.)

Ernesto concluded the initial cast of shells and handed me the stone and the shell for questioning. I shook the shell and stone in my hands behind my back. I randomly chose the left or the right hand, holding the stone in one, the shell in the other.

He asked first for my right hand, then my left hand, querying yes and no from the shell and stone. I didn't know what questions he had asked, or which hand he would choose next. I hadn't told Ernesto much about the situation with Tina and Alfred. Although I was still obsessed about our disappointing house exchange, I nonetheless hoped that my reading would be about something else.

"Have you moved out of that house yet?" Ernesto finally asked.

I described the scene greeting us a few days earlier: grieving daughter, house filled with detritus, indecipherable notes taped to walls and fridge, stained tablecloth on dirty table, rotting food in the fridge, and wet, out-of-doors bedspread. Why did the simple act of exchanging our house with distant friends become such a nightmare? What we had thought would be background to our visit in Miami, a house to stay in, a car to drive, was now in the foreground.

I was relieved that Odu was going to illuminate my dilemma, although something in me always hesitated to speak my real concern when I asked for a reading, as if it were too petty, or something I should keep inside because it was too embarrassing to let out. I always wanted Odu to say that I was living a fortunate life, well balanced and healthy. I noticed that I never wanted it to talk about the sticky things, the things I didn't like. I wanted the oracle to deny the same things I denied. Instead, it ignored my wish and highlighted them.

"You are getting misfortune as a path due to malice and wickedness," Ernesto began. "It's coming from mankind in general. However, by extension the Odu also refers to you. This predicament is in your file. These are the things that naturally come up for you in life, the things you agreed to face. This is one of those for you: the possibility of encountering maliciousness or wickedness from others because it is part of your destiny. Not that you've provoked it or that it is something you did or didn't do. It is simply something you must face in life. The question now is how do you handle it? How do you divert it?"

"Is this something that has already happened or is it coming up for me in the future?" I asked.

"You're in the cycle for it now. You have to figure with an Odu like this, it will go on another 90 days. What's interesting to ask is, what reverses it? Because it's also saying you are the agent that reverses it. You are what will bring you back to fortune. We are dealing with an Odu, which zooms in on the human capacity to manage behavior. An evil spiritual nature is not causing this misfortune. Your destiny is causing the misfortune and its impact. There are evil human beings working against you as part of your destiny. The message for you is it's all about you. It's how you manage in the situation to escape the worst of it."

Ernesto explained further. "I can tell you that Araye, the evil divined, translates to humanity's wickedness, envy and ill will. However, it is in a category of neutral misfortune, where the cycle is just swinging from fortune into misfortune, at the start of everything, the breaking point, the first level of negativity. From here it grows and expands until it transforms into other levels of negativity and misfortune. It is just like a springboard. Here's where everything gets started. Right now the influence is at an early stage. It's not at a medium or upscale level yet in terms of the impact in your life. But the conception is there. The cycle has already given birth to it."

"The story that accompanies this Odu is about Eshu. The colours white and black represent Eshu."

Before he could finish, I interrupted. "Don't you remember? I wrote an article about Eshu years ago, and used the story of *Eshu and the Two Farmers* in it. I put you down as my co-author because I got so much information from you. I learned the story in grad school."

"I do remember now," Ernesto said. "I forgot we did that work together. Well, here it is again for you. You've had it come up for you many times before this. It must be time to think about it!"

The problem of *truth* vexed ancient Yoruba philosophers, who devised an entertaining way of teaching humility, tolerance and respect for other people. They used appealing stories, like the one that came with my Odu that day, to illustrate important things that we all need to know to get along in life. Divination sessions with Ernesto in Miami today, or with a babaláwo in Nigeria four hundred years ago, could both utilize this story of Eshu and the two farmers.

The story's point is that all people are subject to the law of relative truth, where differences in perspective between two people, although small, may be responsible for conflict that grows from a simple debate into a fight. What Ernesto was saying to me, using this allegorical story, was that I was involved in a conflict with a friend, still at a very early stage of development. However, if I did not learn the lesson offered by the story of Eshu and the two farmers, I would soon be involved in a war.

The story is straightforward. Two Yoruba farmers lived on adjoining pieces of land, separated by a road. Each morning they saw each other across the road, working in their respective fields.

"Good morning," said one farmer to the other. "Good weather we have today."

"Yes, but we need more rain," replied the second farmer.

"I hope the rains don't come yet," the first farmer answered, "my yams are ready to be harvested and they will rot underground if it's too wet."

While the two farmers conversed, a tall stranger, never previously seen in their village, walked down the road between them. When the stranger passed and was finally out of sight, the two farmers walked toward one another and met on the road that divided their fields.

"Did you see that tall, handsome man dressed in red?" asked the first farmer.

"Yes, I did. But he wasn't dressed in red, he was dressed in black. Why do you think he was dressed in red?"

"I think he was dressed in red, because he was dressed in red."

"Well, maybe you're right," conceded the second with a grumble. The farmers put their heads down and returned to work.

The next morning, the astonishing event happened again. The tall, handsome stranger walked down the lane, between the two farmers in their fields. As soon as he passed, the farmers rushed together in the middle of the road.

"Oh," said the first farmer. "I'm sorry. You were right. He was dressed in black."

"What," screamed the second farmer, "Are you trying to mock me? He wasn't dressed in black. He was dressed in red, just like you thought yesterday."

"Red," shouted the first farmer, "Are you insane? Yesterday, you also disagreed with me. What are you trying to do?"

"What am I trying to do," screamed the first farmer, "what am I trying to do? All because I'm trying to tell you what the stranger who walked down our road looks like, now I'm trying to do something to you?"

"You probably want my land and are trying to make me crazy," said one or the other of the farmers. It doesn't matter which one, because from that moment on they were enemies.

A few weeks later the farmers' heads were down, steadfastly ignoring one other while they worked their farms. The tall, handsome stranger abruptly appeared again. This time he walked quickly down the lane between them. Then, instead of rushing on out of sight as he had done before, he turned and walked back down the road from where he had come.

On his way down the lane, the first farmer had noted that the stranger was dressed in red. On the stranger's way back up the lane, the farmer now saw that the stranger was dressed in black. "What am I seeing?" wondered the first farmer. Suddenly, the farmer realized that the stranger was not dressed in red *or* black. The stranger was dressed in both colours.

At the exact moment of the first farmer's realization, the second farmer recognized the truth, too. They had both been right about the stranger's colour, but neither had the whole picture.

The stranger turned around and strolled to the farmers who now stood together on the road between their farms.

"Hello farmers," he said standing face to face with them. "I am Eshu, and I am looking for some land to buy around here. You two appear to be arguing and not enjoying this fine day in your gardens. Why not sell to me?"

Standing close to Eshu, the farmers clearly saw he was half red, half black, the two colours neatly divided neatly divided down the midline of his body. He was also handsome and charming, so they could not stay angry with him. They laughed together and soon the three of them were staggering down the road, first giggling, then shaking with laughter. The stranger between them was Eshu the Trickster God, entertaining himself at the expense of ignorant humans.

Trickster gods like Eshu are associated with synchronicities, events that happen at the same time that are linked in a deeper level of meaning. It is a synchronicity that the two farmers were working across from one another at the same time, in the same place, watching the same stranger, and simultaneously receiving the same, fundamental lesson in the law of relative truth. The trickster Eshu is a breaker of boundaries, bringing luck or misfortune and turning the best to the worst, or the worst to the best.

This is why Christian missionaries equated Eshu with the devil. But Eshu has nothing to do with evil, or the Devil. Eshu has to do with evolution. Eshu may break the peace between the farmers and stretch their reality, but it is for their own good. No one can have a happy life living in the illusion that he is right all the time. Now and then it is healing to see how right others can be. Eshu ties together previously unconnected people and events revealing what is really inside them.

For this reason Eshu is significant to Odu divination. He can go and collect the real story of a person's life, right in the moment it is happening.

When Eshu reveals the whole picture of the red and the black to the farmers, they stand abashed. Yet this humbling means they can be friends again. Eshu is the laughter in their universe, the tall stranger grinning at the end of their lane who says, "Hey, don't make yourself so important."

Eshu is in the middle of our mutually arising conflicts with others. We want to stick to our stories, which to us are obviously only red, and we want all others to be convinced of the way we see things too. We don't want to consider that the other person sees black. We too easily fall for illusions of our own creation, tempting Eshu to visit and wake us up to the truth. More than anything else, this is the role of Yoruba divination and of Eshu's role in it: to reveal the "whole truth" of our lives, which is sometimes a surprising truth, quite different from the "truth" we carry inside our conscious minds.

A Yoruba proverb about the trickster Orisha poetically states this principle. The proverb says, Eshu throws a stone today, yet hits a bird in yesterday. Every time Eshu moves, he moves unpredictably. That's why, when they go out and come back in, Lucumí priests remember Eshu's existence by placing his sacred icon in their doorways.

After we had discussed the story, Ernesto continued to explain how this reading applied to my and my husband's current situation.

"This Odu also deals with paranoia, schizophrenia and all kinds of mental disorders. It's where people become totally irrational and lose it. This is what you are going through with your friend, but without being prepared for it. As you can tell, the basic principle of the Odu is that things are normal when the story begins. Two friends are trying to exchange friendship, then a third element is introduced into the story. The two friends represent two points of view, and the third element is a divergent force that triggers conflict between them. Eshu, the third party, has the duality within his nature, which can become psychotic. In that context it describes what you found when you got to Miami," Enersto concluded.

"You were sitting in a foreign country coordinating this exchange with your friend over the phone. Everything was kind, fine and wonderful, so you got on the plane. Then when you got here, expecting to find what was normal, what you found was certainly not that. What did you find?

You found a third party who was psychotic, and that nothing was the way you thought it would be. Well, guess what, Judith? This was meant to be. You're always going to run into this kind of situation. However, it depends on you. It depends on how well you handle the situation so it doesn't take a toll on you."

"So in this case," I said, "the best thing I can to do is to acknowledge all points of view somehow?"

"Yes, you have to," replied Ernesto.

"So, I have to get on the email right away and say everything's okay, we're enjoying the house?"

"Yes, right away, so the psychotic woman is neutralized within the rationality of her irrationality."

I loved Ernesto's phrase, *neutralized within the rationality of her irrationality*. I had to find a way to defuse Tina and Alfred, to accept that perhaps the way I had found their home and family was normal for them. Tina, from her own perspective, was right.

"The one that's sitting in your home in Australia needs to be contacted," advised Ernesto, "and dealt with in a way that says, I'm going to be rational within your scope of view. Why? Because what happens when Eshu's suddenly thrusting two different elements at you is you react without thinking straight or looking carefully. Then, not knowing the other's point of view, you accelerate the conflict with your friend."

"Yes, that's right!" I exclaimed. "That's exactly what happened. We took a trip for one reason and, suddenly, unexpected circumstances confronted us, and we reacted to what we thought to be true. We feared for the children, and for what might happen to them left alone with a psychotic parent. However, we had no knowledge of their past with Tina, or of how capable they were of dealing with the situation alone. We acted in the only way that we thought right. And now, you're right, we're very much in conflict with the family. We've seen their secret life. Alfred told us that they'd hidden Tina's illness in their family for years. I wrote an email to Alfred saying as honestly as possible what we'd seen in his family, and now, of course, I'm afraid that Tina will see it and take some crazy action against us when she returns from her train odyssey."

"Yeah," agreed Ernesto. "This woman is capable of calling the police department and filing charges against you. She is demented. She can accuse you of anything. This Odu is also about thievery and lawsuits. It depicts the antisocial person, the criminal mind, at work. Both poles are equally present in your situation, and could simultaneously impact you with a degree of either one. You know she can be either rational or irrational. That makes it worse. She can sit in front of the police and be rational if she wants to. And in that moment the police might say, that woman appears to be a little nutty, but maybe these people are trying to extort money out of her."

"Boy, did we see that happen," I interjected, "at the hotel when her shrink phoned her. She was a completely different person, in control, quiet and rational. And Alfred is also backpedaling from his promise to provide a home for us in exchange for ours."

"You must already be seeing what this story of Eshu is about," laughed Ernesto. "Here are two friends saying, 'No, you didn't,' 'Yes, you did.'"

"I still feel the strong emotions of the past days," I said. "And the fatigue. What will Tina's next move be? I don't know. You're saying that this could escalate into something much bigger. You're saying that I need to write a conciliatory letter to Alfred and say something like, we were jet lagged when we got here, probably it wasn't as bad as we thought, we hoped we helped and didn't hurt. I need to eat a little crow so that this fight doesn't escalate. Is that what you think I should do?"

"Yes. Think about the friends in the story. If one of them had backed down, they wouldn't have ended up in so much conflict."

"So, I should say that we are getting the house in shape and it won't be too bad for the rest of our stay. And since the kids are safe, we can say that we know Tina is a good mother, just having a little problem, or something?"

"Yes, otherwise this can become very nasty. You know how I do readings and I don't get into the theatrics. But this one is a big thing. The potential is very nasty. You can get caught up in being accused for whatever reason, in litigation big time. But it's at its point of inception, the initiating point. It hasn't gone that far yet. It is up to you. It doesn't require candles or rituals or anything to reverse it."

"It's only me, then, my behaviour?"

"Exactly," said Ernesto. "It's how you handle it. That's the ritual Judith. How do you handle it? Everyone always thinks that everything in Lucumí is taken care of with a candle or an herbal bath, but here's a case that doesn't require that. The ritual is behavior. How you understand a scenario, how you observe it and manage it. I would move on it as fast as possible. Why wait on something like this? It is at its early stage. Don't allow it to escalate to become something larger than it is already. Do it in an email where you have tangible things in writing. Think paranoid. Think the worst about these people. It's not there now, but it does have this potential."

"Do you think we should just vacate that house?"

"If you vacate it sounds great cause you're out of that environment. But if you vacate, what proof do you have of how you've left the place. In order to do that, cover your tail and video everything. *Think this way* is what the odu is saying. Just remember the two friends and the story of Eshu. He came in and turned things upside down."

"Why does this have to be my destiny?" I asked. "Why couldn't I be enjoying our stay in Miami, working with you, not worrying about this entirely ridiculous situation?"

"Remember what we said," asked Ernesto. "Before we reincarnate we stand before God. 'Okay, here's what you're coming down with,' he tells you. 'You're going to have these kinds of challenges.' One thing is clear. This is not some unexpected, bizarre situation. It is Eshu at his finest waking you up to a part of yourself that needs changing."

"I wrote about this story, but I never really grasped its meaning. This is finally hitting me in the face. I need to tell myself, 'It's time to stop Judith and acknowledge the other. Even though you did not create it, even though you may be right from your point of view, this is what is going to happen when you stick to your own truth.'"

"That's right," Ernesto concurred. "It's always going to be the same monkey dressed differently until you get it. Just remember to deal with these people as if expecting the worst. Don't try to feel sorry for the mother because she is mentally ill. Why would that justify her evil actions? Plenty of mentally ill people do no evil to other people. Why isn't her madness capable of impacting others with kindness? Instead, she impacts others with evil, and that's what you need to guard yourself from here. Try to remember that what you do is insane to the insane person. That person will never appreciate what you do. Your actions—even your need to clean her house and arrange things less chaotically and take all the taped messages down from the walls—that's insane to her, because she needs her world arranged like that. Cover your back on the exit and reduce this conflict so there is no possibility of them coming up with any allegations."

"You're saying that no matter what craziness is created around me, I should not take the bait and say, 'Wait, hold on there, I am the voice of truth'! I feel like I always take that role, trying to straighten people out, fixing everything to my standard. There is always a fine line between helping and hurting. I've also not been clear enough in my expectations of people. Because I think my standards are universal, I think all people will simply act as I do. But to many people, my standards are wrong, insane, unworkable. Isn't it interesting to be talking about this in the context of what we are doing? Isn't it appropriate that this story, out of so many hundreds of possible stories, should appear today, and that my life should unfold this way while we are working together? In fact, it's more than 'interesting.'"

"That's right," Ernesto agreed. "The Orisha are saying, 'Hey you still don't get it!' It's amazing, I agree. I forgot you wrote that story. Well, it's the story of this Odu, 11.8 numerical value in our system. Your patron Eshu has never changed over the years. There's a lot of Eshu in you, Judith. If you don't manage yourself at present you are going to get burnt. The Orisha are saying, 'We're trying to embarrass you, so that you can save yourself.' This is happening to you, but you can change it."

"This is blowing my mind," I said, still cringing at the thought of the apologetic email I would soon write. "This is my biggest challenge in life."

"So start managing it! The cycle of this Odu is about 90 days. That is how long this energy will last for you."

Just as Ernesto predicted, almost 90 days after the initial Odu reading, the story of our friends and the house exchange was resolved amicably between us, because each of us worked to see the other's point of view. There was no final breakdown or fight, although our negotiations over compensation lasted several more months. I think that if I hadn't taken Ernesto's advice, I might still have repercussions from this summer.

CHAPTER 6

I Meet Elegguá

> The unique function of Eshu within the realm of
> Orisha Awo (Mysteries of Nature) is to translate the language
> of humans into the language of Nature and to translate
> the language of Nature into the language of humans.
> — Awo Fá'lokun Fatunmbi

AURA AND I WERE GOING to have our head Orisha determined at the home of Nydia's godfather, Juan Carlos. The two of us sat on a sofa in the living room, talking softly with our other godsisters, Diane and Alda. I was called first.

This is a ceremony one's padrino does not carry out to avoid bias. However, Juan Carlos would be working with Ernesto's divination shells. Everyone has a special Orisha guide whose archetypal qualities are deeply spiritual and philosophical. We each have a personal Orisha with whom we resonate, and who resonates with us. There are many stories, myths, songs, dances and colours typical of each Orisha. They vary around the Yoruba diaspora. Shango is one of the names heard in popular Cuban music like salsa. He was an esteemed dancer, the inventor of the batá drum, and a warrior king who died and resurrected to become a powerful deity in his city of Oyo, in present day Nigeria. Shango is known as Obá Koso, the King Does Not Die.

After a gesture of invitation from Juan Carlos I sat on the low bench in front of him. He was an oríaté (reader of the shells) and one of Nydia's godparents. I would have preferred to sit on the floor, because I found the low bench uncomfortable. I thought perhaps the bench was a compromise for Norteamericanos, because Juan Carlos was in a comfortably cross-legged posture, sitting on the mat on the floor in front of me. But Ernesto and Nydia sat behind me on chairs in the corner of the small divination sanctuary, so they weren't on the floor either. We had gathered to discover my head Orisha, the divinity who had selected me before birth. It felt like a definitive identity moment.

Nonetheless, it felt odd not sitting in front of Ernesto. Juan Carlos spoke little English. He proceeded to divine, throwing the sixteen shells down on the mat between us, kneading them with his hand, then picking up the shells and casting them on the mat again. He considered their pattern carefully, then handed me the stone and cone shell, which began the long process of enquiry. Finally, Juan Carlos nodded and looked up at Ernesto and Nydia.

"Elegguá is her guardian orisha," Juan Carlos stated firmly, without hesitation.

"We always thought so," Nydia said. "She is an Elegguá for sure!"

It was one of those "Mmmmmm," replies from me.

Ernesto and Nydia smiled, feeling validated in their assessment of my character and path. For years, they had both believed I was a child of Elegguá. They never said why, but considering Elegguá's trickster reputation, I don't think the reasons can have been all good. Now it was confirmed: I was Elegguá's spiritual progeny.

This Orisha had always drawn me, his stories, icons, drums, connection to nature and his ever-present role in divination. I had lived the story of Elegguá (also known as Eshu), the two farmers, and the common road which divided them, and I appreciated Yoruba storytellers who had described the human condition in this single Elegguá tale. I was twenty-three when I first heard it, firmly situated at the center of my own world. When I thought about this pataki (story) I understood the concept of relativity. I could never know what another person is experiencing without asking them. Each person is part of a greater whole, and there is no Truth without including everyone's point of view. For me, this realization is profound. I'm still grappling with it as a fundamental quality of our conditioned existence. (I believe this recognition, that there is no Truth without everyone's point of view, is the reason for multiple viewpoints in modernist literature, Cubism and Einstein's Theory of Relativity.)

Two weeks later, once again at Juan Carlos' house, I was fortunate to learn more about myself and Elegguá. It was on the second day of an Orisha ordination, when a new initiate is presented to guests. The new initiate had already gone through an extensive ritual process that had enthroned the Orisha in his head. Guests were invited the day after that to take part in the fortune of the blessings the newly-made priest of Elegguá would bestow.

Nydia arrived looking her best: bright red lipstick and her thick black hair brushed back from her face. She had come from work, so she was wearing a lavender suit, feminine and authoritative at the same time. She escorted us into the next room where we saw a fanciful jungle hut, two wooden pillars supporting a palm thatched roof and woven wall panels. Nydia said this was the preserve of Elegguá, whose domain was the tropical forest, and everywhere else in nature. Multicoloured candies and little plastic toys were tied at eye-level in the palm leaf thatching.

When I turned my attention to the initiate I was surprised to see that he was attired as a dashing gentleman from a Spanish court. He had pinkish bronze skin and flushed cheeks, and he introduced himself as Steve. He was dressed in knee-length breeches, with a close-fitting jacket called a doublet, clothing Spanish noblemen wore in the late fifteenth to seventeenth centuries. Steve's doublet and breaches were made of velvet displaying the Elegguá colours of red and black. He also wore a velvet beret with long variegated feathers pointing backwards. This handsome headwear sat on top of his newly shaved, pink bald head.

The costume contained a history lesson of an encounter between Yoruba and Spanish. The new olosha was an Anglo man, initiated in a Miami suburb into a Cuban Lucumí sect of the West African Yoruba religion, a culture first disrupted by British colonialists in Nigeria, then dominated by Spanish Catholics in Cuba. The imperial court, domination and royalty combined in the costume worn by Elegguá, at once elegant and, to me, humorous. Elegguá was laughing at his human children, appropriating their symbols of power and wealth. He could walk between the conquerors without exposing himself. But our Elegguá initiate did not have the same powers, unfortunately.

Steve told me he had walked around the neighbourhood with his madrina and padrino first thing in the morning, dispensing some of Elegguá's small wrapped candies to the neighbors.

"Get away from my house," he had heard from an opened door on the opposite side of the street. "I don't want your filthy candy!" An older woman stepped out with a mobile phone and loudly demonstrated she was calling the police.

"We walked back home waiting for them to arrive," said Steve. "When the officer showed up, guess what? He was a crowned (initiated) Elegguá priest, so he knew we were just spreading blessings from Elegguá who loves these hard candies."

No wonder Ernesto was now talking with a police officer, the two of them sitting on lawn chairs in the shade. He didn't want a repeat of the morning, in case the next cop wasn't a Lucumí priest.

Later, in the middle of the afternoon, four drummers appeared with Yoruba conga and batá drums, along with a gautaca (cow bell with striker) and achere (small gourd rattle). They set up their instruments in the back room. Before they began playing I was surprised to see a video photographer and two reporters from the Miami Herald arrive to record the musicians' demonstration performance.

The three reporters showed no reaction to the drumming when it started. They sat expressionless, not moving a muscle. I wondered if they had been given paralyzing drugs, because no one could sit in front of these professional drummers and not move something to the rhythm. How they could stop their feet from keeping the beat indicated their level of detachment. They continued to sit as if dead. As well as the police, Ernesto had invited these Herald reporters to counter the barrage of negative publicity the religion had accrued.

When the stiff journalists departed, the music started again for real. The very talented drummers, recent exiles from Havana, performed the rhythms of each Orisha, starting with Elegguá, who is first in every ceremony. Olosha danced the moves of Elegguá, the more experienced ones dancing closer to the drums. Within about ten minutes the percussion rhythms had woven a crescendo of beats, becoming a burning, white-hot vortex that could be felt inside and out.

The Lucumí believe that certain sacred rhythms, like those being played here, speak to spiritual forces in nature. They empower the music to call a spirit, who may then possess a follower—in a positive way. This is a fortunate and prized occurrence. A gifted possessed person may offer prophecies to certain members of the community who are present.

The musical passion increased exponentially. So did the dancing. The room was hot. Everyone was moving with the drums, which were having their way with us. Nothing could slow them down. Neither would anything stop the other world from connecting.

I saw it happen. I was at the back of the room. The heads of two people just in front of me began rolling forward and back in response to the music, discernible waves of energy traveling up and down their spines. The energy flowed in undulations, fluidly upward and along the dancers' backs like a fast-moving water dragon under their clothes and skin.

Over others' heads I watched a tall, heavy-set man in a vermillion T-shirt. His arm shot repeatedly into the air, then down again, while he yipped and barked like a dog. His name was Luis. He was a priest of Elegguá and his god had taken over his body and voice. Luis hadn't been in Miami very long. Most of his Lucumí life had been lived in Cuba. The golden-skinned, black-haired, slender Teresa was also possessed by Elegguá. I had been told that Teresa had an ashé, a talent, for possession.

The anthropologist Michael Mason, a priest of Oshún, was there. Michael worked at the Smithsonian in Washington. He was in Miami carrying out research and taking part in the Elegguá initiation. He'd been near me since the drumming began. Now he whispered in my ear:

"The ceremony organizers paid the two possessed dancers to attend because their psychic gifts are so special."

Unexpectedly, the dark-haired Teresa, shining in the heat, dancing like the wind, stopped just to my right. I turned and was surprised to see Laura. Teresa stood in front of her. They flung their arms wide, as if they were long lost friends. They then hugged each other tightly. Laura, her eyes closed, had an expression of peace and fulfilment on her face. The possessed Teresa stepped back to hold Laura at arm's length. She gazed deeply into Laura's eyes, then embraced her passionately again as the drums continued to enchant everyone.

The space around my heart tingled. I leaned forwards and whispered to Diana, my god sister, standing near me: "There's a lot of heart energy around right now."

"Isn't that love?" she whispered back.

"I think it's something like love, but it feels unattached and all-enfolding." I felt exactly that. But I still had a moment of Laura envy. She had been hugged by the spirits. She was always cooler than me—a stupid thought I quickly pushed away.

In front of me the Eleggúa-possessed Luis surrounded a woman with his arms. I could hear his strange voice transmitting messages. Ernesto had given a strict set of rules about what we four women, his and Nydia's godchildren, could do. We must stay well back of the drums and initiated priests. We were not carry on conversations or go anywhere in the house we were not invited.

I kept my eyes down as much as possible, not wanting to draw attention to myself. I had transgressed on both those fronts at a ceremony not long before. For that reason I was hiding behind two olosha when the robust, hugely sweating Luis, possessed by Eleggúa, glided past me, surrounded and followed by a densely packed group. They passed so quickly I hardly noticed them. Diana whispered to me when they'd gone:

"I've heard complaints that too many people are chasing the orisha around."

Orisha groupies, I thought to myself, determined to stand my ground and not join them. But then, despite my determination, our cluster moved slowly into the next room and to a hallway entrance. We were so tightly packed together it was not possible not to go where everyone went. It was as if an invisible string had attached us to the red T-shirted Eleggúa possessed Luis. I became aware he had disappeared into a shrine room at the end of the hallway. I heard chanting and banging sounds. Then the door opened and eager people poured out and down the hall, pushing past us, again with no regard for our presence. They were making way for the god in their midst.

Then, in an instant, the Eleggúa's large persona filled the hall. In the shrine room, Luis' changed clothes. He was now dressed as Eleggúa, in an elegant red and black satin shirt that strained to hold his heft, and short knee pants. At the time I hardly noticed this change of vestment because the level of excitement was running so high: the charged atmosphere seemed occluded by mist. The man possessed by a god flowed down the hall toward me, in the middle of a knot of followers.

Although I lowered my eyes and turned away from Elegguá, he moved sideways out of the bunch, pushed through the crowd, and opened his arms to embrace me. Foolishly, I was unaware and thinking, rather than feeling. I worried that I'd made a mistake standing in the way of the possessed dancer. However, in an instant Elegguá had me, doubts and all, in a mighty clutch. His face bent to mine, staring powerfully into my eyes. He hadn't waited for me to make up my mind; I was caught in his net. I felt touched and honoured, like a little cloth doll moved by the god. Time stopped and people disappeared.

I only came up to Luis' chin, so I had to tilt my head to look into his face. One of his eyes rolled back so only the white showed; the other squinted into my left and right eye alternately. I don't know why, but it felt like he saw me with his whole being, not with his physical eyes at all. Rather, what saw me was a spiritual presence that stood apart from Luis's body. Perspiration beaded on the possessed dancer's forehead, running down his face. His satin shirt was streaked with sweat and the buttons were near to popping off. I could feel his big belly pushing into mine while I held him tight.

Still holding my gaze, Elegguá spoke to me in a mixture of Yoruba and Spanish. I heard Nydia next to me (I hadn't realized she was there) translating his words:

"Elegguá wants you to go to the forest and find seven sticks for Ogún. He says these sticks will help you win the conflicts in your life. You just go from conflict to conflict and you need to win them!"

Before turning away from me, the possessed Elegguá struck my right shoulder sharply with the palm of his hand, as if to say, "Wake up!"

I was slow to react because I was temporarily dumbfounded. But when I eventually did, I realized his great embrace had ceased and he was already moving into the crowd that had closed around him.

Elegguá had spoken to me personally. I was shaken and very grateful for his acknowledgement. It was like divination. The possessed man had revealed what was inside me, what I most wanted to hide. I was getting tired of conflicted and sticky situations in my life that I felt too weak to successfully resolve. I needed help. And here it was. But what did it mean?

A few minutes later, Michael separated me from the crowd.

"I saw him speaking to you. What did he say?"

I probably wouldn't have told anyone, but since he'd asked, I repeated what Elegguá had imparted to me.

"He talked to me too," Michael said. "Elegguá says he brought me the new apartment I've just rented in Washington. In fact, I did ask Elegguá to help me find a new apartment. I always base the truth of the possessions on how accurate the information is they pass on to me. That was pretty good."

I saw Luis again several times that year, but he never noticed me or signalled that we'd met before, even though he had held me in his arms, looked inside me, and spoken as a god to the depths of my soul.

When I returned home I felt a curious agitation. Seven sticks for Ogun! He said I should gather them to win my conflicts. I thought of calling Ernesto about a reading (which he later said I should have done), but I longed to gather these sticks. Ernesto's remedies had sent me on nature journeys before, so I looked forward to trees and sweet branches, smelling the wild river, and being alone. I decided to find my sticks, immediately. I had no idea where they were. But I was undeterred.

At that time I had been living for a short while north west of Miami, near Myakka State Park. The parkland extended across both sides of the Myakka River. It contained many old growth oaks in the palm forest. Several times I had kayaked over thirty miles of the river, including floating rapidly through the forest itself when the river was in flood after a torrential summer rain. My sticks would be somewhere there, I decided.

I visited the park early in the morning. Three fishermen were casting lines into the sparkling, fast-flowing river from the low bridge. I left my car in the space at the end of the bridge, where a trailhead opened. The shady path stretched into the distance. It wove around mammoth live oak trees, whose branches held grey sphagnum moss growing to the ground like a wizard's hair. When the path turned toward the river, blue ripples appeared through the forest leaves. I left the path to walk to the water's swampy edge.

To my left, a few meters off the trail, grew a tall sable palm, Florida's only native palm, which was only found here and in the Fakahatchee Swamp near Naples. This palm sings of old Florida, a time when, as a child, I adored swimming in the ocean, rivers and the jewel-like Florida springs. The beaches were almost all undeveloped, and there were huge stretches of swamp like the Myakka or Fakahatchee filled with old trees.

I had decided to take an adimú (food offering) to the forest. My offering would be my gift to the spirits of this place. I opened my backpack on the ground in front of the sable palm and emptied its contents. At the base of the tall, thick tree, I arranged a pineapple, bananas, a coconut and some oranges in a colourful pyramid that looked quite striking. I removed a sage stick from my pocket and lit it. The fragrant herb was quite dry; a plume of grey smoke tangled in the palm fronds above my head. After I had waited a while it started to rain, a healing, gentle rain that thankfully cooled me and kept away the mosquitoes and no-see-ums.*

As the rain began, I felt it was time to start searching for my sticks. I turned off the path and immediately stepped deep into leaf litter. I had to jump over palmetto palms while avoiding the low hung thick arms of the giant oaks. I was up to my knees in twisted, fallen branches as I climbed through vines, binding myself in their tendrils, taking what seemed like hours to free myself.

I stopped and looked around me. I was standing next to a gnarly old tree, its trunk covered with pieces of bark the size of my hand. Laden by moss and bromeliads, this tree had dead-fall three feet high beneath the lowest branches. I tugged on a long hefty branch to separate it from the others in the pile. I laid my full weight against it, watching as large limbs and twigs broke away while it dissolved in my hands into chunks of honeycombed, rotten wood and leaves. It was soaking wet, the wood pitted inside and out, and the bark came away in mottled sheets.

The moist wood was weak, easily crumbled, and snapped under very little pressure. I could almost hear the forest grinding the fallen branches

---

* North American slang for the tiny biting midges common around the world.

into new soil like parrotfish grinding a coral reef into sand. The piles of wood around me would be gone in a few months. It was already almost compost, not suitable for the sticks of the orisha Ogún. But it was beautiful, sweet smelling; breaking down, yet full of life.

Ogún is the god of fire. His sticks need to be dry so they will easily ignite. I hoped he would help me win my battles! For that I needed dry wood. An image of a pile of branches I had seen earlier came to mind. They were way back toward the road, in an open place exposed to more sunlight.

When I found the large pile of fallen limbs, I circled them and, as before, laboriously pulled out several. Soon I had four large branches lying by the sides of the pile. I began to break them apart, stepping on them and hitting them against the ground, searching for pieces that were tough, until I had a collection of seven sticks. Each was about two feet long, a wand of live oak two inches or so in diameter. I chose the sturdiest seven, the ones I couldn't break or bend, carefully laying aside each one as I found it. I returned the rest of the wood to the heap, knowing it would be gone by the end of the rainy season.

My face, hands and clothes were covered in leaves and mud. I was soaking wet and my hair matted, so I returned to the river where I washed my arms and face in the warm dark water and ran my fingers through my hair. I had to resist the urge to fall into the water and float away.

Herons and egrets rose gracefully from the riverbank. Part of my spirit rose with them as I remembered the story of Oshún and the river where she had attained enlightenment. Lucumí healing cures often send people into the forest, or at least into contact with trees, to facilitate healing.

Part of me wanted to phone Ernesto and discuss my journey with him. But another part wanted to follow my own image and likeness, as the Irish say. I was in touch with something. I was in the "other world", searching for answers. Answers to my deepest needs and desires. Elegba had seen me and spoken to me. He had recommended the seven sticks of Ogun, which were the seven powers of the African gods. To pick them up was to acknowledge the presence of Ogun, Shango, Oshun, Yemayá, Obatala, Elegba and Oya. I knew that. But I kept pushing the truth away.

The other world communicates via thought and in divination. The "other world" doesn't speak English. Rather, it speaks all languages, using codes developed thousands of years ago. In the case of the I Ching, the world's most ancient divination system, solid and broken lines arranged in hexagrams symbolized complex personal, social and political states that ranged from *Pure Force* through to *After the End*. The Yoruba Ifá divination system is not possible to date precisely, but it predates Christianity and Islam in West Africa. It is also a means of communication with the other world through a system of single and double lines arranged in two columns. These lines, as in the I Ching, symbolize complex personal, social and political conditions.

I believed my sticks were a sign that I needed to integrate the seven African powers, the powers of nature and culture, represented by seven major Orisha. Justice, Death and Rebirth, Creativity, Abundance, Truth and many other virtues were represented by these seven Yoruba Orisha. They also represented wild nature, thunder, lightning, rivers, oceans, forests and the various forces that guide consciousness. That is a lot for seven sticks to carry.

My sticks' peeling bark and their lingering oak smell placed them in the forest I remembered from my childhood. My seeking something in nature that can be freely given, and returning something of equal value, is a transaction between myself and the other world. Only we know the balance; only we are responsible.

Somewhere in the overlapping spheres of consciousness, between myself and other, as my hands touched my sticks, they arranged themselves into the seven powers. The sticks grouped together naturally with the one on the left of the piece, dog-legging around the other six, a strong Ogun with protection for all. In the middle, the long green-ribboned pointed stick reminded me of the ashé/kundalini that dragon-raced up and down the spine of the man possessed by Elegguá, who had delivered the god's message to me.

I could remember Nydia, just arrived from work in her lavender business suit and black heels, her black hair and eyes shining, translating the god's words to me, while a knot of people pushed against us. I felt excitement and trepidation. Elegguá really had caught me and told me something I needed to hear. Win your battles! If you engage in conflict, win!

CHAPTER 7

Move a Mountain with a Toothpick

> Energetically, you feel it. And this point ritual is so important because it helps you to have the external indication that something's taking place, and this is very grounding. So these three things—the energetic/visceral experience, the sensory recognition, and the ritual—help your conventional self, your emotional self, to "get it."
> — Theodore Tsaousidis

MAGIC AND RITUAL are languages that speak to the subconscious, reaching deeper and deeper into the layers of the energetic construct, myself. Despite the world and its pandemics, over-consumption, habitat and species destruction, wars and inequality, magic has survived the world's embitterment. In essence, Laura and I agreed that magic is the beauty of the world seen with soft eyes, soft face. It is the beauty behind the tough guy with the whip and iron glove. He will be gone forever when beauty is still young.

Magic is a word often used in the promotion of products and experiences: the magic effect of anti-aging cosmetics, the magic touch of a ball player, a lover, a beloved dog. But practicing magic is different. To practice magic means to awaken that part of yourself which remembers enchantment, the golden light, the first glass of champagne on the way to a brightly lit future.

The process of magic begins with a plan for taking focused action to create a change, using a system of correspondences between worlds, the other world and the world of physical reality. One guiding premise is what you effect in the other world will be reflected in the world of your reality. Although it is playful, magic isn't play. It requires a total suspension of disbelief, as well as complete commitment. It is deadly serious—but only as serious as the fruit on Laura's head.

When the economic waterfall of broken dreams cascaded in 2008, my husband John and I were part of the carnage. We lost a lot of money to a corrupt Ponzi scheme manager in Australia, who had the temerity to go into forced liquidation in October without telling us, then became hostile. In a monumental role reversal, he described himself, the criminal, as the victim. After that, over-medicating himself with drugs, he pretended to be insane until he found a doctor who would certify this cowardly diagnosis.

Later, when I read about sociopaths, I found the key take-away: if a sociopath tells a lie and it isn't believed, he simply tells a larger lie, or multiple new lies. Sociopaths get away with this because you and I do not expect people to lie to us.

John and I had been very naïve, like so many investors, even those who had careers in money management. In Florida many people lost money, jobs, homes, careers, businesses and, indirectly, families—losses that continued over the next saturnine years.

In 2001, Ernesto had warned me in a divination reading to avoid investments that were too far away and out of our control. I didn't take that advice. Instead, we continued to invest far away, in Australia, in a fund over which we had no authority. After we received the sobering news about the liquidation, I phoned Ernesto to schedule a reading.

We drove to Ernesto's house the next day, traveling silently down the turnpike to his home. He was waiting at the door when we arrived. His face was as glum as mine. We greeted one another warmly, but it was a cheerless gathering. It felt remote and cold, like it was happening to someone else. Without his usual delay, he ushered us into his divination consulting office. Ernesto took his time with the shells, but when the divination sign in misfortune appeared, he quickly read the situation, not keeping us waiting with any other talk.

"Your friend has betrayed you and lied to you," he stated firmly. "Don't repeat this mistake. You will be okay down the track. **But your money is gone.**"

A few times in the past Ernesto's words had transformed into bold typeface in my mind. This was one of those. I had lived in the false expectation that Ernesto would say we had a temporary financial problem that would right itself. Nothing like that. In fact, he had no further words to add to his prognosis, which was very unusual for Ernesto. He did give us calming baths made with herbs and goat's milk, and a protective charm for our doorway. These things were very comforting, and I was glad to have them, but Ernesto never said he could get our money back or control the actions of the Australian swindler.

Of course, that was exactly what I had wanted him to say. Perhaps he was going on the principle of "misery loves company" when he added that his clients in Hialeah, Miami, had lost millions in the 2008 financial crash. They had beaten us to Ernesto's consultation room with their own tales of woe. *Darn them,* I thought, *they used up Ernesto's sympathy before we even got here!* They, like us, had sought reversals, periapts and conjurations, but to our disappointment, Ernesto was not assuming any of the responsibility for getting our lives back on track minus our vanished fortunes.

"You've lost money in a bad business and nothing can restore it," he said flatly. "The baths and charms will help to heal and stabilize your financial situation as time passes."

A part of me believed Ernesto. I wasn't deaf and dumb to the economic blood bath taking place in America. Bernie Madoff was in the news, and every headline showed another financial villain juxtaposed with photos of his weeping victims. The plummeting (as the news described it) of the Dow Jones index was mirrored in home prices; no one knew where the bottom might be. Our Australian investment had always had warning signs; now I knew what they were. I had never heard of a Ponzi scheme before Madoff, whose name is now as linked to Ponzi as Heinz is to ketchup. Still, despite all this, part of me was numb to the truth. That Neptunian, foggy part of my brain believed there had to be a way to restore our money.

Soon after we returned from Ernesto's, John flew to Australia. He had contacted Roger, the fund miscreant, who assured John he would meet with him when he arrived in Brisbane. However, a day after John arrived Roger failed to return his messages. I spoke with other people who also lost money in the collapsed investment firm, but they couldn't run the Australian to ground either. Obviously, Roger was avoiding his investors.

I had to do something, but the crook was a hemisphere away, and so were the Australian Securities and Investment Commission, the liquidator, and most of the other shareholders. My stress level was doing the opposite of plummeting. I needed to step back, calm down, and reverse the negative flow.

I decided to contact Jesus Suarez, who had magical understanding flowing in his blood, a mind to which symbols were transparent, and a Cuban charm that could turn to scary outrage in an instant, resulting in long raves. Yet he saw the world in a connected, magical way that was compassionate and empathetic. We talked about my situation and what the deepest power was that we could affect with a ritual or spell. Jesus believed Lucumí came down to understanding the principles of ashé.

"Ashé is the life force by which everything in the entire universe is both held together and kept separate," Jesus said.

Ashé is the basic energy signature on our planet. Its outward sign is the moving spiral, a mysterious momentum that creates synchronicities in the development of personal destiny. Jesus believed it might be possible, through the principles of attraction and repulsion, to affect the momentum of energy in my situation.

Jesus listened carefully to my description of the situation, asking numerous questions about our fund manager, Roger.

"Look," he said, "getting that fucking creep to meet John won't be hard. Judith, you must know how to make a lamp of attraction."

"What?" I replied incredulously. "I have no idea what you're talking about."

Jesus shook his head at my ignorance. I pressed him to reveal every detail of this lamp's construction. I wrote his directions carefully in my notebook.

A few minutes later, the notebook beside me, I was in my car on my way to a small local shopping area. First, I visited an organic market, where I selected the largest, juiciest and most attractive orange I could find, as Jesus had instructed. I concentrated on each individual orange, turning it around, feeling it gently, then smelling its deep fragrance.

When I reached home, I carried my bag inside and went back to the kitchen where I set it on the bench. The large orange I had selected rested next to my other purchases. I unpacked the orange with care and turned it in my hands for a few minutes, until it felt warm. I then washed it carefully with filtered water, rubbing it while visualizing within it a positive result. For the first time since we'd lost our money, my stomach was settled enough to eat something. Taking practical action felt wonderful. The orange lay on the table next to me while I dined alone. After that, I set it on my altar to await nightfall.

When the shadows were long and the sky darkening, I showered and rubbed sweet smelling oil over my body, then dressed in a yellow sundress. The out of doors exhaled the blue day, leaving behind sunset colors and crickets stirring. I lined the short path leading to the front door with white candles in cups, then walked back up the path, lighting the candles as I went. When I was finished, I remembered childhood Halloweens in Pennsylvania, when pumpkin-lantern faces, grinning with yellow light, were glamorously alive in windows and doorways, when autumn leaves burned in crackling piles, and groups of costumed kids ran in packs through the shadows.

I carried the anticipation of the night within me like going to meet a new lover. The atmosphere was balmy, velvety and serene. Walking directly to my altar, I cleared a space for a small cutting board. I placed the orange in the center of the board. With my sharpest knife I cut the plump, sweet orange in half. Then, with a smaller, sharper and pointed knife, I carefully removed the juicy fruit and white pips without piercing the skin or pith between the segments. This took much longer than I had imagined, because it is very hard to do this without puncturing the pithy spokes of the inner orange.

Next, I plated the orange wheel, minus seeds and flesh, on a blue plate the colour of cornflowers. I stepped back to look carefully at my creation. My orange wheel had a little navel in the middle. That's where I poured a few drops of sunflower oil. I next placed a short wick in the center of the fruit, which still smelled like a blue Florida morning.

Whenever I spend time close to a fresh orange I begin to notice the large number of juicy cells that make up the flesh, the colour and smell of the fruit's skin. In these moments our world becomes a baroque fantasy, which it would do more frequently if we more closely examined the elements of the natural world that make up our ordinary day.

I struck a match and held it to the wick. To my surprise it caught immediately, flamed up, then burned steadily. The radiance spread around the room, illuminating my altar's icons with transparent orange light, causing amber shadows to dance on the wall. I saw my Seven Sticks for Ogun, the head of Queen Idia of Benin, a dancing Devi come to life. Frankly, I had thought my little half orange would sputter out or not even light; I certainly didn't expect it to emanate such an enchanted light show.

Sighing with pleasure, I gently moved the lamp to the floor, where I sat in a crossed legged posture, gazing at the tip of its flame. In a series of deep inhalations and exhalations, I absorbed the light. After that I held a vision of the rendezvous between my husband and our former friend, whom Ernesto said had betrayed us.

John still hadn't heard from him and didn't know how to contact him. There was a little Oz coffee shop with large windows on the highway south of Brisbane that runs along the Gold Coast. I had a clear image of my husband and the thief sitting opposite him. Roger loved espresso and John cappuccino, so I envisaged them in the cafe, sitting across from one another with their white cups and saucers.

Sometime after midnight I went to bed feeling elevated and excited. My windows and doors were open to the soft night air, allowing a cool breeze to waft through the house, a sensual feeling, a light touch of heaven on the skin, and causing the orange flame to flicker. Long, willowy silhouettes quivered on the ceiling.

I awoke about three o'clock in the morning to find an eerie orange incandescence still twinkling near my altar. Returning to bed, I fell back into a deep sleep until dawn. By then, the now inanimate orange had burned out, every bit of fire sacrificed to the charm of the night.

As soon as I could, I rang Jesus, whose very drowsy voice answered. He took a minute to light a cigarette and run some water, then returned to the phone. He was astounded by the length of time the oil lamp had burned. Usually, he said, they went out after 15 minutes.

This fact seemed to contain a recondite message, but we didn't try to define it. Instead, he announced I had one more thing to do: take my lamp to the nearest fresh water river and set it adrift. I knew immediately what this meant. I had to drive to the wild Florida river about fifty minutes away.

After hanging up the phone, I carefully packed the empty orange lamp on the car seat next to me, and then, still filled with the sense of purpose and mission I'd had the night before, I drove to the river.

The final ten minutes of the drive was through the oak forest, where moss hung from branches arced over the river park's entrance road. I parked my car by a bridge and strode the short walk to the river.

I squatted on the river bank and watched the tannin-red waters, their level high from recent rains, flow past me on their journey to the inland sea. I leaned over the water and could see my face swimming on the surface. I placed my ritual orange on the river's body. Then I gently pushed the orange away from the bank. It was soon caught in a small, side eddy. The eddy circled the half orange around and around, only two meters from shore.

Will it ever be carried away? I wondered. But the eddy suddenly and decisively delivered my orange lamp to the fast current in the middle of the river. It looked a slight orange object bobbing up and down in the wide darkened water, then was rapidly swept downstream.

Sighing, I turned around, stepped back onto the path, and noticed my mood change. When the ceremonial orange left my sight, melancholy filled the void caused by its absence. I felt flat and tired. While creating the lamp of attraction, I had suspended time and belief within myself. I almost felt the very bad thing about our money hadn't happened, that when the veils of the illusion parted I would find things back to the way they had been before.

But now that the spell was complete. I had to wait for results. No sign in the sky lit up with an answer. Feeling sad and spent, I stood listlessly on the river bank, watching the foamy, madder water flow around a bend, after which the orange finally disappeared from me forever. It was carrying the vision I'd had during the ceremonial night to divinities of river and sea.

When I arrived home the day hadn't yet started in Australia. I paced and worried, which caused the hours to pass even more slowly. Finally, in the late afternoon, the phone rang. John sounded weary, but a little hopeful.

The coward had texted him at the last minute, as John was changing his ticket, and they had arranged to meet at a coffee shop in the morning.

Could my lamp of attraction have helped draw Roger to my husband? Through it, I had participated in their meeting. However, their encounter yielded no good news. The fraudster blamed my husband for asking to see his financial records (wow, we did that way too late!), raving on and on while revealing nothing about our money. Although he did ominously suggest we sell our house.

It was sad news, but in any case it was part of the answer that I'd set out to find. Roger had continued to lie and tell us our money would be returned. This was a strong indication that it wasn't coming back. I walked across the street, to a neighbour who had offered to buy our house, and sold it to him on the spot.

Skeptics will say the Australian criminal would have kept his appointment with my husband without my magical work. However, my intention to bring John together with the Aussie was powerfully engaged by strong emotions and a ritual of creation. I was deeply concentrated in the beautiful spell that Jesus taught me, mesmerized by the golden, esoteric mystique of the orange fruit's light.

Orange and gold were connected to the Orisha Oshún, the divinity of beauty, riches, sweet waters and magnetic attraction. A magician, sorcerer, shaman or diviner used objects like the lamp of attraction, imbued with the emblems of sacred power—in this case the Goddess of the River, Oshun—to draw the attention of other world intelligences who might be persuaded to help. A point of concentration, like the magically prepared orange, was a gateway through which vitalizing images could travel through the energy field of ashé. Of course, I couldn't prove this was how it worked, but I operated as if I believed it fully. If I hadn't done so, there would not have been any results. The fact was, the criminal had contacted my husband and their meeting took place.

As soon as I got off the phone with my husband, I rang Jesus again with the news about the meeting.

"Not especially surprised," he said, "We call this using a toothpick to move a mountain."

I loved his phrase. Enraptured memories of the evening lived inside me. My ceremony was a blessing. On the energetic level, my lamp of attraction had been a success. I had temporarily moved the obese money crook in another hemisphere, as well as my own melancholy and fear, big mountains to move with only an orange, some oil, a match, and a friend to guide me.

Nonetheless, Ernesto's words, **your money is gone**, were a black obituary over our financial life, one I couldn't yet accept. Letting go was a slow process, not something we could come to terms with immediately. The memory of our money disappeared like a jet's thick condensation trail on a windless day, evaporating slowly, until there was nothing left to grasp. But until that inevitability occurred, I followed every lead and lit every lamp.

CHAPTER 8

A Healing Ceremony

> Ahora vengo Mama Chola Mama Chola
> Ahora vengo Mama Chola (north side)
> Ahora vengo Mama Chola mama chola
> Ahora vengo Mama Chola (south side)
> — Carlos Santana

A FEW DAYS AFTER John's return from Australia, Jesus invited us to visit him again. He thought there might be a chance to find our money with the ceremonial help of a friend of his who was visiting from Cuba. It was her first trip to the United States.

Inspired by the lamp of attraction ritual, I immediately accepted. I wanted to meet his friend, Xiomara, a medium from Havana and a priest of Lucumí and Palo. Palo has roots in the Congo from the Kikongo-speaking peoples who were brought to Cuba as slaves in the 16th and 17th centuries. Paleros work with spirits of the dead housed in cauldrons called nganga. Sticks, earth, bones and other earth-objects fill this caldera and feed the spirit.

I had not yet been to a Palero practitioner. Would the Palero agree with Ernesto, I wondered? It is hard to accept great loss as the final outcome of events. Maybe there was another version to these apparent facts.

Jesus' apartment inspired me the moment I walked through the front door. The walls were burnished gold, with paintings of avatars within ornate silver and gold frames. There were Orisha, multi-armed Hindu deities and Catholic saints with halos. Medicinal herbs grew in containers on the balcony, complex charms adorned the front door, and in a back room there was an altar with many icons of Yemayá. There were surprises, such as

Jesus' ten-inch Florida land turtle that crawled very slowly under his living room chairs, so slowly that, strangely, I tended to forget it was alive, as if it had turned to stone.

The summer before Jesus had stayed with us in the Florida Keys, where we rented a house for a few weeks. There he and his godson, Bruce, entertained us with their zany humor, female impersonations, and gay mannerisms and sensibilities. While Jesus was ready for anything that might happen in gnarly Key West nightclubs later that night, he was afraid to walk out on the dock in front of the house, particularly getting anywhere near the warm, shallow waters. He feared Yemayá, also known as the Mother of Mermaids and Fishes, might attempt to pull him under the water where he would drown, which would allow her to carry him to her home. Jesus was forbidden by his initiation vows to enter her waters. Finally, after a long discussion, I convinced Jesus to have dinner on the dock, where he would be assured not to touch the ocean waters of Yemayá. He agreed reluctantly, tempted by the lobsters John had caught.

After we finished eating I walked with Jesus back to the house. Quite suddenly, a small rogue wave washed over the wooden boards, tipping the walkway down on Jesus' side. The big man stumbled but caught himself, resisting Yemaja's attempt to upend him. "I told you so," he said smugly, after we met him on the sandy shore he had escaped to, where Yemayá couldn't touch him.

Now we waited in Jesus' apartment while he and Xiomara showered and dressed. We ate dinner in a Cuban restaurant near Calle Ocho. It was fascinating to dine with Xiomara, the Palera who had never previously left Cuba. Xiomara was close to my age, gray-haired and lively. She smacked her lips under saucer eyes when she saw the dishes at the Cuban restaurant we had invited her to. They were ordinary Cuban recipes served all over Miami, but when they arrived at the table Xiomara bent over them like a hungry dog. They were the same dishes Cubans in Cuba used to eat: rice, grilled fish, fried plantains and black beans, seasoned perfectly, with plenty of garlic and fresh Cuban bread. However, that was before Castro bled the country dry.

In Havana Xiomara and her neighbours worried about dinner each night, risking police attention if they bought or sold something on the black market, while facing the impossibility of buying food above-board on their pitiful wages. They often went hungry. During the early part of the month, when people still had some oil or sugar, rice or beans, they pooled their rations. Xiomara told us she often received food as payment for her mediumship abilities. Lucumí festivities in Cuba were very popular because, in addition to everyday rice and beans, people could share goat and chicken dishes at the communal feast after an initiation. Jesus pointed out the Cuban owner of the restaurant where we were dining. Xiomara was astounded that an ordinary man could own a restaurant filled with so many diners. In Cuba, the Castros owned everything, except the crumbs from the giants' table.

After we returned from the restaurant, we sat informally conversing in Jesus' small living room. Xiomara stared for a long time at John. She said that he had an egun (spirit): a skinny, old woman with long white hair. His mother, who had died a few months earlier, fit Xiomara's description.

Although I hadn't thought about it previously, there was no doubt in my mind that my mother-in-law might still be near my husband. John's mother hadn't lived a life of her own due to a little-known brain condition. She had wrapped herself around her only son for decades, as completely dependent on John as she had been on John's father. Xiomara said that in addition to the presence of John's mother, she could sense an obstacle hindering John and me. This obstacle needed removing. She agreed to work with her Palo spirits on our behalf. Jesus consented to assist her in the ceremony to remove our obstacle.

As instructed, John and I arrived at Jesus' apartment in the early morning. We anticipated the healing Palo ceremony with a combination of hope, fear, curiosity and uncertainty. A few minutes after we knocked, Jesus answered the door, still groggy. Xiomara was barely moving in the back bedroom. They'd stayed up until after 3 a.m.

Jesus had slept in the living room, so we helped him roll up the mattress on the floor. They both needed coffee, the house needed straightening, and they made no mention of our Palo ceremony. It was a lot like going to Ernesto for a reading. There was no schedule. Anytime from now something might happen—or not. The wind-up would take as long as needed, so relax! And that's what we did. We cleaned, helped make coffee, and washed the glasses on Jesus' ancestor altar.

There were phone calls, a Jamaican neighbor brought something to Jesus in a paper bag, a Haitian mambo (priest) of the Vodou Loa (spirit) Erzuli (a Loa divinity quite similar to Oshún) stopped by to speak with Jesus, and a Zambian man knocked on the door to inquire about the time of his upcoming spirit mass. Muted drum rhythms played in the background from one of Jesus' favorite albums. Morning transformed into afternoon without a word about our ceremony.

I felt like I was riding on the top of ocean swells on a warm summer day. After a late lunch of avocado, white cheese and bread, Jesus and Xiomara permitted John and me to clean the kitchen while they retired to the altar room to diagnose our problem. They spent many minutes in Jesus' altar room. From time to time we heard deep throated chanting.

When they reappeared, Jesus said they'd had confirmation of the obstacle. Xiomara had thrown the coconut shells. Called chanalongo, a simple "yes" or "no" divination (simple compared to the Dilogún) is performed by throwing four coconut shells onto the floor. The answer depends on how many fall with the white side up and the dark shell side down. Chanalongo had answered a long list of queries about ingredients needed to lift our obstacle and change our fortune.

On the list Jesus handed me, there were plants, stones, sticks, gunpowder, candles and several birds including a rooster, a hen and a guinea fowl. We needed to gather these things as quickly as we could so the ceremony could go forward in the evening. Jesus gave us the addresses of two botánicas that stocked these items and we prepared to depart. Botánicas are shops that sell religious supplies for many Miami religions, including Lucumí, Vodou, Palo, Catholicism and Wicca. They stock dried herbs, icons, charms, stones, shells, grimoires, reference books, clothing, Orisha beads and more.

When we visited the botánica called La Caridad, we found Andrea, Jesus' sister, behind the counter. Her big smile greeted us as she talked on the phone. The botánica was inside a small shopping center next to a Latin restaurant. When you walked through the door you were greeted by a life-size statue of a Native American man in chiefly regalia, alongside many other statues of Orisha and Catholic saints. The cases were full of incense, herbs and the large ceramic containers called soperas (soup tureens), which house otanes (sacred stones) and other Orisha emblems for when someone initiates. A large pile of yellowish stones (for Oshún) lay in front of a bookcase filled with paperbacks about magical spells, herbs and alternative spirituality.

We walked to the back of the shop and through a doorway, which led to a room filled with large, clean cages holding a small number of colourful and healthy-looking roosters, chickens, guinea fowl and doves. With Andrea's husband's help we selected the birds we needed. Our birds and some yellow stones also on the list cost around $25.

I was very disappointed in the quality of the dried plants at the well-known botánica we visited on the Tamiami Trail.* I was surprised by the lack of life force in nearly every plant: very old, too dried out, too expensive! I thought of Ernesto's words about how few present day Lucumí olosha grow their own plants or find them in the wild as he does, and as people once did in Cuba and Nigeria. Jesus cultivated what he could on the tiny balcony of his small apartment, but it was far from the long list of plants prescribed.

When we met up with him later, Jesus wasn't happy with the dusty, old botánica plants either. So we jumped in his truck and started driving slowly down the streets, where Jesus knew people. We were looking for particular trees in bloom and shrubs with fruits. In several places Jesus had Lucumí godchildren, whose gardens we visited. He pulled into one drive and entered the backyard, walking under the limbs of a giant jacaranda laden with bouquets of purple flowers. The Cuban-Spanish voices of Jesus and his godchild reached us as we sat in the truck. Jesus was asking permission to cut the flowers and plants that he needed for a healing. His godchild gave him permission to take what he needed. Then we waited.

When Jesus returned, his arms were full of long cuttings from two trees with yellow flowers, which he placed on my lap in the front seat.

---

* Also called 8th Street, or Calle Ocho. The Tamiami Trail (Tampa-Miami) runs from downtown Miami through the heart of Little Havana. It then continues, as US 41, across the Everglades to Naples and Tampa, before wending its way all the way to the Upper Peninsula of Michigan.

The air smelled of blooms, the blue sky was unexceled, and bald headed, handsome Jesus had his arms full of long-stemmed flowers. Big bundles of them which he handed to me. Magic could never be worked with the desolate plant material we saw in the Miami botánicas, not if this was an example of what was really needed.

We stopped a second time. Jesus returned with luscious plants, native and exotic, which he piled on John's lap. After a third stop more flowers and branches were piled onto mine. During the fourth and fifth stops even more foliage was stacked on the spare back seat of Jesus' small green truck.

Returning, we climbed the steep, high stairway to Jesus' apartment, our arms wrapped around thick, tall stacks of fresh green cuttings, some with fragrant flowers. Jesus returned to the truck and brought up the boxes with our rooster and guinea fowl. He instructed me to set the well-ventilated boxes in the hallway. The foliage disappeared into the altar room.

Presently, Jesus and Xiomara asked us to wait in the living room while they conferred once more in the altar room. This time we heard chanting and the pounding of wood against wood.

An hour later, the door opened and they entered the small back bedroom where Xiomara was staying. When they emerged, they had completed their transformation into Paleros, ready to perform our ceremony. Xiomara and Jesus had exchanged their Miami casual wear for white caps and colourful, beaded belts worn diagonally over white T-shirts. The belts stretched from shoulder to waist, above their knee length, white cotton pants. Jaunty red sashes held small machetes by their right sides. I felt touched by these costumes that evoked another, more rural time and place, dramatically resetting the scene from urban, twenty-first century Miami.

Jesus invited us into the altar room. We entered the room illuminated only by candles. Jesus' Yemayá birthday party had been held not long before, when forty people, many ordained Lucumí priests, were guests.* Then the altar room's back wall had been a reflective sea of elegant blue drapes streaked with silver. On the floor in front of the drapes candle light shadows flickered across shining mounds of perfect fruits and vegetables,

---

* The birthday is a celebration of the day Jesus was initiated into Yemayá mysteries. One of his godchildren was an iyawo, a new wife of the Orisha Oshún whom Jesus had initiated nine months earlier. She was an woman from Ft. Lauderdale, who graciously

a dream tropical market. Rich cakes and candies, plus a multitude of candles on beautiful cloths, evoked the presence of the great Orisha, Yemayá.

Today, however, Yemaja's altar was inactive. Jesus' large soperas—pottery vessels with Orisha-imbued stones—were draped with fabrics, leaving little else visible. Instead, the opposite side of the small room was animated. The door to a closet facing the altar stood wide open. Xiomara stood in front, just failing to conceal the closet's interior, which was matt black. Candles burned near a large nganga, a metal cauldron perhaps sixteen inches high set in the middle of the closet. The nganga was black and filled to overflowing with earth, sticks, bones and cobwebs, a dense tangling of natural materials. Not only did it look natural, it looked formidable.

Jesus took a place just behind Xiomara, who stood in front of her cauldron. John and I stood to one side of him, near the entrance door. Xiomara demanded answers from her Palo spirits, surprising me with her guttural voice. After sending pieces of coconut shell clattering onto the floor beside the cauldron, Xiomara spoke Spanish and some Kikongo words. Her chants and songs were all Kikongo.

Jesus translated, speaking quickly. Xiomara could see us surrounded by paper (account statements were piled high on John's desk and on our dining table). Our situation had gone far; things needed doing immediately. Mama Chola (the Palo god of abundance and sweet water, a counterpart to Lucumí's Oshún), was stepping up to defend us. Mama Chola would bless this!

Jesus went on translating as Xiomara talked in her strange, deep voice. The coconut shells crashed on the closet floor again and again. Then, flash! bang! Xiomara flung gunpowder on the candle flames, as if they were exclamation marks emphasizing the importance of her demands. She cajoled and excoriated in a tone of voice both loud and fierce, chasing the spirits and talking to Mama Chola. Xiomara and Jesus sang Palo songs, performed incantations and chanted with intricate complexity in a mixture of Kikongo and Spanish. Their ritual supplication was a moving performance, which opened the possibility of deliverance.

---

served me a glass of wine and a plate of beans, rice, and avocado salad. During the first year of priesthood, new priests must dress in immaculate white and do service for their godfather and godmother.

About thirty minutes into the ceremony Jesus disappeared from the room. He returned with the plant boughs we had collected earlier with him, masses of green that he divided between John and me.

Xiomara stood in front of us, took the branches from me, and tried to bend them in half and break them. She struggled to do it. When the boughs wouldn't break, I started to help her, but Jesus stopped me, saying she must do it herself. The boughs were freshly cut and green, hard to split, springing back when they were ineffectively bent.

When she finally had broken them, Xiomara rubbed them over our bodies, thick sponges of greenery massaging me everywhere. I turned around so that Xiomara could massage the leaves over me completely. When she had finished with me, she repeated the procedure with John. Finally, with this part of the ceremony complete, Jesus escorted us back to the living room. Once again, we paused.

It was now after dark, around 8 p.m. We had been waiting, driving around, thinking about, taking part in, and gathering things for the ritual for twelve hours, but I was far from tired or frustrated. Next to making the lamp of attraction, it was the most engaging day I'd had in a long time. I was filled with conviviality and good will.

Jesus and Xiomara had summoned a compelling presence to their Palo altar. They continued chanting, talking and praying, as they prepared the offerings we would take to the river.

The sounds of the birds in their boxes came through the walls. A clucking sound, not much more. Earlier, we gave them water and feed. To remove the obstacle hindering John and me the birds might be set free, but it was also possible they would have to be sacrificed. Jesus had told me that if that is necessary we must agree to their deaths in exchange for our lives, since our obstacle was a heavy one, long lasting and palpable. If this option was chosen, the birds would take the obstacle from us.

When Jesus and Xiomara finished, they took showers and changed their clothes. Back in the living room, they were again dressed as urban Miamians, in T-shirts and cotton slacks. They didn't mention what had gone on in the altar room. We simply carried the birds down the stairs to Jesus' truck. When we were all settled, we set off for the Miami River.

We traveled down dark streets, through neighborhoods of small bungalows with lighted windows. At the end of a short road, we parked beneath a flickering yellow streetlight. We set our birds in their boxes on the pavement and locked the doors of the truck.

Jesus asked us to stand at the edge of the road, by the footpath, where a small poinsettia tree grew and overhung the path. John and I stood next to one another, Xiomara stood in front of us, and Jesus stood off to one side. Then, one by one, he handed our birds to Xiomara. She accepted them, prudently restraining them by holding them around the legs, chest and neck. Her actions were practiced and professional.

First, she approached me with the large rooster, lifting him up to my shoulder height. She brought the bird against my chest and midriff, then rubbed its warm, soft breast over my arms, legs and back. The lovely rooster's downy feathers, his warm breast against mine, and his yielding body as she gently moved it over my arms and legs, was very sensual. The rooster was alive, a breathing being who weighed his life against ours. I had spoken extensively to the birds when they were at the apartment. Now I felt a real connection between us.

When she was finished cleansing John, Xiomara handed the bird to Jesus, who took him, almost hidden in his hand, and in less than an eye blink, broke the rooster's neck without a sound. The big bird hung limp in Jesus' hand. It was done! A bird had died for me and for John.

Unexpectedly, I felt tearfully grateful for his life, for his dark eyes, into which I had stared, for his beauty and for his destiny that was now intertwined with mine. I had felt the lifting of the obstacle enough to accept the death of the birds in return for my own well-being.

The whole procedure was repeated with our two remaining birds. Their bodies touched the humans over north, south, east and west, feathers strangely comforting, as they are in a duvet or pillow. After which the bronzed hierophant, Jesus, accepted the birds, and soundlessly broke their necks. The birds had absorbed our obstacle.

Finally, Jesus turned to walk toward the river with the lifeless birds in his hands. I followed, with John and Xiomara following me.

Suddenly, a tall, elderly black man jumped onto the pathway in front of Jesus. He was bone thin and dressed in a short-sleeved white shirt and pressed trousers. The elderly man teetered on the shadowy path in front of Jesus while they argued in English. The man, who was Afro-American, screamed, "What you're doing is not Christian! It's from the Devil! Stop!"

Jesus was furious and vehemently rebuked the elderly man for butting into our business. The man was so taken aback he said nothing more and quickly walked away.

What an irony! A golden-skinned American of Cuban descent (Jesus) and a nut-brown Cuban (Xiomara) were completing a Palo (African) ritual cleansing for two tanned Anglo Miamians (John and me). Meanwhile, the elderly man was Christian and of African descent.

Jesus turned and embraced me. He apologized for the disruption of our sacred ceremony.

"Not your fault," I told him.

Religious intolerance is ubiquitous. Many in each of the world's 10,000 religions believe their religion has exclusively revealed God's truth. The Afro-American man had proven that religion can separate people from one another more than skin colour.

Now we walked to the river, kneeling together on the bank. Jesus asked me to place the birds in the water until the current accepted them. The last I saw of our birds was when the flowing waters took them into the darkness. I can't say how it happened exactly, but from that night I did feel more empowered and less stressed than before the ceremony.

CHAPTER 9

Ma Rufina

> If we had never seen fishes,
> we should be at a loss to understand
> how any living beings could exist in the sea.
> — Allan Kardec

THE YOUNG GIRL with a skull flying through her room, retained into adolescence and adulthood a deep curiosity about spirit worlds and non-western beliefs like Lucumí and Palo. I was drawn to them because they felt real to me, offering a clue to my own inner truth.

When searching for blossoms and leaves with Jesus, I remembered the ecstasy and curiosity I had felt as a small child, when my dog and I roamed for miles and miles through the nearby forest, searching creeks for amphibians and water nymphs. The small pool in the creek I visited most days had salamanders, shiny and blue-black, living in dark holes on the banks. I also pretended to find roots with which I made drinks, using seeds and twigs to make food.

That was in Pennsylvania. The deciduous forest starkly contrasted to the Florida hammock and beach terrain where I spent my teenage years. But it was in Florida that I found my longing for the wild spirits sweetened by the Palo ritual with its use of vegetation magic for healing.

Xiomara had used fresh, sweet boughs of leaves, and the vitality of the trees and shrubs with their healing presences, to cleanse us spiritually. The foliage revitalized my soul in a way not possible to put in words. I understood that Xiomara was removing the aura of our blockage, neutralizing it. The long, thin branches Jesus had chosen were flexible and green, bending in Xiomara's hands, but refusing to break. The metaphor was undeniable. We had an accretion of bad fortune, cursed relationships, poor decisions, and events that were dense and heavy. I had not been following my own inner truth. I had departed that path some years before, and I knew it. I wanted to return, but the vines holding me in place were too entangling.

Xiomara's ceremony had helped me begin my return. Just traveling around the back streets of tropical Miami neighborhoods, looking for trees in bloom, was calming, bringing me into close contact with nature, with leaves, blooms and birds. It also introduced me to Jesus' community of godchildren and friends.

How did a man like Jesus come to be a priest of Lucumí and Palo? It is easier to understand if you have a background in a culture and religion which honors and supports mediumship and spirit divination. I had a little of that in my upbringing. I was raised in a Midwestern Christian extended family which thought itself the lost tribe of Israel. At least that's what my mother said, because her father had told her so.

At the same time, my mother secretly believed that spirits of the dead could communicate with the living. Her outward persona confessed the Apostle's Creed on Sunday, wearing formal attire: girdle, hose, big bra and slip under a gray suit, medium high heels and matching hat and purse. By contrast, at home her inward persona dressed in shorts and sandals while playing the Ouija board with her sister and me, addressing questions to her deceased father.

For many decades now I've been around people for whom spirit mediumship is, to use Ernesto's memorable words, "like drinking water". It's hard to grasp that phrase if you are a westerner with a typical westerner's education and life. Impossible, really. Making it harder still is the fact that for many mediumship is inherited.

Jesus was born with a natural potential to become a medium. His grandmother was a medium. His mother said that when Jesus was four years old he was already making cigar offerings, blowing smoke at the Catholic statues she kept on her home altar. His mother's statues were plaster, hand-painted figures of Catholic saints, who also held the spirit of the Orisha, because each saint was syncretized with a well-known Yoruba deity. For instance, Shango was identified with St. Barbara, Yemayá with the Virgin of Regla, and Oshun with La Caridad of Cobre, each saint selected for their similarity to the colors, temperament and dress of the Orisha. This enmeshing was the way Yoruba in Cuba (and in Brazil, the Carribean, and wherever else Yoruba lived) dealt with the colonial religion imposed on them, absorbing the saints' power into the power of the Orisha.

But for the young Jesus Suarez, his mother's altar represented the holy spirit of peace, not the artifacts of an intolerant colonial religion. Jesus says that he thought the representations of the saints were real because their shining glass eyes seemed alive. He looked deeply into them, he remembers, feeling the chill of spiritual presence. He would then make a honey or tobacco offering, according to customary Cuban-Creole practices. Everything in nature is reciprocal: the spirits returned a deep well of mystical understanding to the young boy.

One day in school, Jesus succumbed to a crying fit, shivering and shaking. The school called his mother to come and fetch him. She took him home, comforted him with hot tea, and together they prayed to St. Jude. She couldn't understand why he had reacted this way. It wasn't until four days later that it all made sense. A telegram arrived from Cuba explaining that her mother had died at the exact time Jesus was overtaken by the crying fit at school.

It was then his mother recognised Jesus would inherit the family spirits. It is widely understood that spirits stay in a family until their work is done. As the saying goes, the Devil is afraid of them, and God isn't ready to receive them.

Jesus was raised in a culture where mediumship and mysticism are accepted, and can be inherited. This rich ancestral background helped ensure powers were channeled to him. But he still had to acquire his culture's music, liturgy and healing skills, and to be consecrated into a complex priesthood, all of which requires unrelenting and never-ending study. Neither is it easy to then acquire clients who, like the people I know in Miami, judge the medium by the fruit of the spirit message.

Jesus' maternal grandmother had lived for a time in Matanzas, a Cuban city of artists, musicians and Afro-Cuban folklore, situated ninety kilometers southeast of Havana. Matanzas was founded in 1693 as San

Carlos y San Severino de Matanzas. This followed a real cédula (royal decree) issued on September 25, 1690, which ordered that the bay and port of Matanzas be settled by thirty families from the Canary Islands, off the coast of North Africa, which was overpopulated and where many were starving. Jesus' great grandmother was among those who migrated from the Canary Islands to Matanzas, bringing with them the cultural and spiritual energies of the Guanche, the Canary Islands' indigenous inhabitants, who believe their heritage derives from the North African Berber people and ancient Atlanteans.

During the eighteenth century the colonising British initially took advantage of a civil war in south-western Africa to purchase captives, shipping them to work as slaves in the Carribean and Central and South America. Later, Africans were captured and shipped to work in the cane fields of Cuba. As a result, in Matanzas the Africans' cultural and spiritual traditions became intertwined with the beliefs and practices of the indigenous Taino peoples, who prayed to all natural forces and presences, and asked permission or forgiveness before harvesting or taking bark and leaves for cocimientos (healing remedies).

Jesus' grandmother's spiritual practices were derived from the Tenerife Guanche witches' tradition, which were blended with Taino practices. She died giving birth to Jesus' mother's mother. When a mother with mediumistic abilities dies in childbirth, it is believed they are passed on to the new-born child. Those abilities were subsequently passed down to Jesus.

Jesus also has a longstanding connection with Ernesto through Ernesto's mother, Carmen Pla. Carmen's spirit, Caridad, brought the trance down on Jesus for the first time and taught him how to channel her. Caridad also taught Jesus prayers, songs and focused meditation. He said Caridad had a very kind face. She was a black woman, very round, heavy and strong. She wore a long dress and a shawl, had coral-colored wood beads hanging around her neck, and her head was wrapped in cloth and tied at the front. None of her clothing was from the twentieth century.

Years later, Jesus had a dream in which Caridad indicated that he should pick wildflowers from street gardens and put them in a small vase. As soon as he woke he began gathering wildflowers. Two weeks later, when he returned to Miami, he learned Carmen had died the day he had dreamed of Caridada, Carmen's spirit guide.

Not long after our Palo experience with Xiomara, Jesus phoned and invited John and I to a spirit mass at his apartment the next day. He said that after enjoying dinner together, he would hold a spirit gathering sponsored by one of his godchildren. Xiomara would be taking part, too. I felt excited about coming into contact with the divine sources that Jesus and Xiomara channeled, but held no expectations about the unfolding events.

The apartment door was open when we arrived, so we walked in. We found supermarket bags on the kitchen bench, but no Jesus. I called out and he shouted back from the shower. He said Xiomara was in the back bedroom talking on the phone to her son. We made ourselves at home on the sofa and chose some music for the player.

After a while Jesus and Xiomara appeared, greeting us with hugs and kisses. We unloaded the bags, found two chopping boards and knives, and soon, working under Xiomara's direction, we had Cuban rice and shrimp with red and green peppers, garlic, onions and achiote powder simmering in Jesus' large iron skillet. While Xiomara supervised the creole shrimp, I sliced avocadoes and tomatoes for a salad. Two large Cuban bread loaves were warming in the oven. I learned that the man who had paid for the mass and the food would join us for dinner.

About eight o'clock a young man with deep umber skin and short, ebony hair arrived dressed in Miami evening casual, a white guayabera (Cuban short sleeved shirt), white cotton slacks and leather sandals. His name was Mulenga. He greeted each of us quite formally, shaking hands around the room. He sat on the opposite small sofa where he sank into the cushions. It was clear he was avoiding conversation. I sympathized, knowing there were crisis times in life when any further interaction, however small, was too much.

Earlier, Jesus told us that Mulenga had many troubles, which was the reason he had sponsored this séance. Mulenga had lived in Miami for a few years, working as a manager at a large chain warehouse. He was married to a woman from his village in Zambia, where they'd both grown up. They had immigrated to Miami together. He had sought out Jesus when he learned at a drumming ceremony held at Jesus' madrina's (godmother's) house that Jesus was a spirit medium. Jesus was Mulenga's augur now. Mulenga had paid for the evening's mass to see if Ma Rufina, a spirit Jesus commonly channeled, could help him with his problems.

Ma Rafina was a family legacy guide he had inherited through his ancestral line. I had never heard of this spirit or group of spirits before. But after she manifested during the séance I decided I wanted to learn more about her. Her presence was a startling new part of my friend.

A few minutes after Mulenga arrived, Jesus' sister Kathy knocked on the door and joined us. The shrimp and rice were ready, so we filled our plates and ate with them on our laps. Mulenga was still quiet, saying little. But he enjoyed the dish, eating it with as much gusto as the rest of us.

The séance took place in the small alcove next to the kitchen, where we crowded around the altar table. Jesus sat on the left, Xiomara on his right, both of them with their backs to the wall. Mulenga, Kathy, John and I sat on chairs opposite the two mediums. Jesus ancestors' photos were on a shelf just higher than Xiomara and him, nine newly filled glasses of water beside them. I watched Jesus wash and polish these glasses very slowly and carefully before the séance. He then refilled them with fresh, cool water. The glasses of water enabled communication with the spirit world. A book of Spiritualist prayers written by Allan Kardec lay near the photos, illuminated by many white candles.

With everyone seated in front the altar table, Jesus led us in the reading and recitation of prayers and supplications to the spirits. After that, the others sang songs that John, Mulenga and I didn't know, so we sat quietly.

At some point in our service Jesus' bald head dropped forward. We all silently watched him. Without warning, his arms danced and his body shook. Ma Rufina was descending. Suddenly, he looked up with fierce round eyes and shouted in a loud and petulant falsetto voice:

"Someone had better bring Ma Rufina a malt liquor and a cigarette!" She squealed and pounded the table for emphasis.

Kathy jumped up to accommodate Ma Rufina's demands. She poured the malt liquor into a tin cup and gave her a lit cigarette. Ma Rufina drained the cup quickly, dragged on the cigarette, and exhaled blue smoke around

Jesus' shiny head. During the evening Ma Rufina drank maybe eight or nine malt liquors (I lost count) and smoked cigarettes non-stop.

With the smoke whirling around, Ma Rufina's voice became even higher and more staccato, all while gesturing dramatically at Mulenga with her hands and arms. She spoke frenetically. Kathy translated for Mulenga, but he didn't acknowledge her words. The young man was folded over in his chair with his arms wrapped around himself, as if he did not want Ma Rufina or anyone to notice him. However, Ma Rufina really did notice him! She didn't start with gentle and nice words. She chided, reproached and nagged Mulenga, challenging Kathy to keep up her translation.

"Your wife is an enemy who is making you ill. You must know this!" Ma Rufina shouted. "Why aren't you doing anything about it? You and your wife may have lived in the same Zambian village all your lives, but your families are not from that village. You married there but it doesn't matter. You are suspect. Your wife's clan wants to kill you now. You are too stupid, a real dick, not to see it all around you."

Kathy patiently interpreted Ma Rufina's messages, while the irritable spirit guide drank and smoked. Mulenga responded by shaking his head, no, no, no. Kathy, translating Ma Rufina, explained to Mulenga that his wife may have lived in his village when they grew up and married, but they were not from the same ethnic group. She told Mulenga that at the time of their marriage, a few years earlier, before they came to Miami, his wife's clan had wanted to murder Mulenga. However, his wife wouldn't agree. Subsequently, his wife was persuaded to became the willing instrument of her clan's revenge for a past wrong her extended family imagined Mulenga's family had committed. Kathy tried to remain impartial, but this was clearly difficult information to pass on. And it got harder.

"No, this isn't true. That's not correct," Mulenga stated flatly, still looking down at his trouser legs.

"What an idiot you are!" roared Ma Rufina at an ear-splitting volume. "What a fool! You must leave your house at once. TONIGHT! Because your wife is using black magic against you. She will kill you. You must have noticed some hair missing! Are you too much of an idiot to hear your wife on the phone speaking in whispers? This is how she will kill you, moron. Maybe you deserve to die because you're too stupid to live!"

I could tell when Ma Rufina asked her questions Mulenga was thinking hard. She then stated the situation was even worse.

"Your wife's relatives have sent her black magic stones to kill you. If you go home at once you will find these stones. You must look everywhere for them."

Mulenga, still looking down, said softly, "No, you are wrong. My wife doesn't have stones. She would not kill me."

"Okay idiot, now I tell you the truth. Your wife is fucking another man at work. You're a cuckold. Don't you notice anything?"

Mulenga, now personally involved and on the edge of his seat, replied in a strong voice, "My wife has not been with another man! I would know it! She could never do something like that without my knowledge!"

Finally, after that blow, Mulenga sat back and was silent for the rest of the evening.

During Ma Rufina's whole oration to him she continued to steep herself in his liquor, smoking his cigarettes non-stop while chair dancing, moving her arms and body to an unseen but dramatic music.

When Ma Rufina turned to me, I felt very uncomfortable, having seen her performance for poor Mulenga. Thankfully, she dealt with me quickly. She said my troubles would end if I used sweetness as a manipulative tool to handle the scoundrel who stole our money. Oshún had brought hypocrisy into the world for those circumstances when we can't be absolutely truthful, when we had to prevaricate and wiggle around someone who was powerful enough that he couldn't be approached directly. Ma Rufina reminded me of the lamp of attraction. That was the strategy I needed to continue to pursue our money.

At that moment I was sure our money wasn't coming back, and that the sweetness strategy wouldn't work, because it was clear we had been part of a Ponzi scheme. Nevertheless, I continued to enjoy Ma Rufina's unusual advice, happy she didn't see darkness in my personal life like she had in Mulenga's.

Xiomara spoke with her spirit guide for a while, but it was nothing like the drama of Ma Rufina. Soon, I looked at my watch because hours had passed on the hard chairs. I laughed silently, remembering our prayers to begin the séance, and the fact they had led to Ma Rufina's presence, a spirit guide unlike anything I expected. However, the entire evening would have appealed to Shakespeare, who wrote of warring families, betrayal, witchcraft, ghosts who warn of danger and the treachery of the world.

The séance ended at 4 a.m., when Jesus came out of trance. I was surprised that he wasn't drunk, despite the enormous quantity of alcohol his guide Ma Rufina had consumed, hour after hour. Not long before his trance ended Ma Rufina was hoarse with smoking and shouting, and reeling from drink. Then, abruptly, Jesus was back with us, cold sober, speaking in a normal voice.

I appreciated how different he was from his tempestuous spirit guide. I later checked about the malt liquor, because I was intrigued by Jesus' sobriety. I was surprised to find malt liquor is a high alcohol beer—in fact very high, an 8.5% malt liquor not being considered high. I watched a beer expert on YouTube say that if someone drank 40 ounces in an evening, they would be inebriated for two days. I reckoned Jesus had that much. Well, I concluded, Ma Rufina is a souse, but a wildly interesting one.

Jesus said Ma Rufina was known to be a tough spirit. But Mulenga must have deserved her hard treatment. But what was Ma Rufina? Who was she? What did being tough mean? And how did this spirit become common first in Cuba, then in Miami?

There is no Orisha named Rufina. I looked up the name and discovered Rufina is the feminine form of the Latin word *rufus*, which means redheaded. So why did Jesus' spirit have this name? Further searching online revealed the name Rufina was ubiquitous in the Latin world from the third century onward. After Jesus told me Rufina was not only his guide, but a guide for many others, I decided I needed to learn more.

In the third century a Spanish saint named Rufina became celebrated throughout the Christian world. She and her sister Justa were martyred during the imperial reign of the Roman Empire. Their story is apocryphal; there is no evidence to confirm it. Rufina and Justa are said to have been potters who refused to sell their wares to pagans on festival days. They supposedly smashed a statue of the pagan goddess Venus, which earned them instant arrest in the Roman city where they lived. The local prefect wanted them to recant their actions and their faith. They refused. They were tortured, and still refused, then put in a cell without food or water. Justa died, and Rufina was then forced into an amphitheater to face a lion. But the lion wouldn't attack her. Apparently, the prefect was outraged by all this and ordered that Rufina be strangled to death. This secured the status of Rufina and her sister Justa as saints and martyrs of the Catholic Church. They were given the feast day of July 19. The image of Rufina, with a lion licking her foot, subsequently became famous. In Goya's painting, *Saints Justa and Rufina*, installed in the Seville Cathedral, he shows the sisters looking toward the heavens beside a tamed lion.

I was surprised to further discover that in Christian martyrdom history there are several other Rufinas. They lived long after the original Rufina, but share many aspects of the Spanish sisters' story. Spirits and avatars who return in bodily form are common in many traditions, particularly in Africa and India, where very ancient practices persist. Hinduism and Buddhism speak of avatars as manifestations in bodily form of deities or realised souls. Some incarnate as divine teachers.

But why were there so many Christian Rufinas? My idea is that through the centuries an energy gathered around the Rufina archetype. An archetype is a universally understood symbol or pattern of behaviour. Archetypes are frequent in many cultures' folk stories and mythologies. These archetypical energies continue to resonate among worshippers practicing the religion for which they are figureheads.

However, the Ma Rufina who manifested through Jesus had African rather than Christian characteristics. Ma Rufina was a spirit that brooked no argument, was schooled in African tradition, spoke Spanish, and hailed from Matanzas. So I researched to see if any Rufinas stood out in Cuban history, who could have contributed to the contemporary spirit, Ma Rufina.

One Ma Rufina who lived in the nineteenth century captured my attention. She was brought to Uruguay as a slave, gained her freedom, then was recaptured by Brazilian slavers. Rufina referred to herself as Mina. Mina is associated with Africans coming from the Bight of Benin. In the eighteenth century, it usually referred to speakers of Gbe languages; in the nineteenth century, the term could also be used for those who spoke Yoruba.

Rufina was shipped from the West African coast, probably from Lagos, the region's main port for exporting Africans. This was likely some time after 1825. I can still remember standing in the former slave fort in the city of Elmina, on the central Ghanaian Coast, where millions of souls passed through the door of no return. They often spent months with hundreds of other women in dungeon cells, covered in excrement and menstrual blood, always wet with urine. Many died. But the fort contained worse horrors, such as the "dead cell", where the sick and feeble were thrown into total blackness, with no food or water, until they died.

It is awful to imagine teenagers and children, which is what Rufina was, in places like Elmina Castle. During the final period of the slave trade there were by far more child slaves than in any other period. The slave ship *Aguila I*, set sail in October 1833 carrying 141 Africans, of whom 124 were children aged eight or nine. On the *Delfina*, which arrived in Montevideo in 1835, 70% of the Africans were between eight and twelve years old. Not one of these children is remembered individually. All vanished into the void.

For those captured to feed the Atlantic slave trade, travel to the Americas was in the bottom of a ship, where the captives were stowed on their side, one in front and one in back, all spooning, all starving, all in pain. Rufina survived that hell and was sold into slavery in Uruguay.

In court testimony she gave years later, Rufina said she lived in the Uruguayan town of Passo Pereira, on the coast of Río Negro near Tacuarembó, close to the Brazilian border. She reported that she and Matheus, with whom she lived for many years, had six children together. They were the slaves of Lieutenant Colonel João José Cabral and his wife Francisca. When those two died, the Colonel's sons, who lived in Montevideo, wanted nothing to do with their parents' former slaves (slavery was illegal at that point in Uruguay). Rufina and her family considered themselves freed and went to live nearby.

The slave trade officially came to an end in Brazil in the 1850s. But a new form of trafficking then began, with Brazilian raiders crossing the borders of Brazil's neighboring countries to kidnap free people—mainly women and children living in small communities in Uruguay and Argentina—and selling them into slavery in Brazil. This happened to Rufina and several of her children, after the ranch where she worked was raided by

Brazilian slavers. Fifteen hundred years earlier, the Spanish Rufina and her sister were forced to walk barefoot and starving over Spain's highest mountain range. Now Rufina, the West African, was forced to walk barefoot with her children through rugged forest, sleeping each night on the ground. The kidnappers rode horses and used whips to force the march forward.

After Rufina and her children arrived in Brazil, they were sold to plantation masters who needed laborers for their rapidly multiplying coffee plantations. The Uruguayan authorities were informed of this new illegal form of slavery, leading to the plantations being raided by police. Rufina was among those who were freed.

Rufina then became the subject of intense correspondence between authorities in Uruguay, Brazil and England. As Keila Grinbergh, a Brazilian scholar, explains, Rufina was an African woman at the center of a series of international pressures that, if ignored, would have left Brazil in a very uncomfortable political and economic situation. There is no doubt, however, that for every attempt at enslavement that spurred action from the authorities and led to a trial, numerous people were taken to the border, sold as indentured servants, then were lost in Brazil, leaving no records.

But Rufina was different. She was freed by the court and the authorities took credit for their action. On November 18, 1854, Cipriano Gaetano, commander of the village of Artigas, sent a letter to Manuel Pereira Vargas, commander of the border and the Jaguarão garrison, saying he had received Rufina and her four children. He took the opportunity to "congratulate and thank the Government of that State for such philanthropic conduct." I try not to snigger at the term *philanthropic*.

So now I had discovered that Ma Rufina, in addition to being a famous Catholic martyr, was also a nineteenth century West African woman living in Uruguay who caused history to be rewritten. No slave had previously won their freedom in a Brazilian court. Brazil's sea trade with Cuba was a big part of both economies, which had been closely linked via European commodities trading as well as slavery. Rufina's case would have been argued and recounted many times over in the ports of Havana and Matanzas.

What about the spirit named Ma Rufina Jesus channeled? The Cuban city of Matanzas, where his grandmother had lived, had historically had huge numbers of slaves. In 1817, the city's slave population was over 10,000, comprising nearly 50% of the overall population. By 1841, the 53,331 slaves made up 62.7% of the population. Census figures for 1859 put the Matanzas slave population at 104,519. Could it be that Ma Rufina, perhaps from Rufina in Matanzas, is an embodiment of black anger, her predominant emotion as she manifests in Jesus?

A few months after the séance I asked Jesus if he had seen Mulenga again. He replied that he had seen him briefly.

"He was standing on the street corner in a cast from ankle to hip, looking very sad. I asked him if he'd had an accident, but he didn't want to tell me what had happened."

Jesus shrugged his shoulders. He said Ma Rufina was so tough with him because that was what was needed to make him listen. The couple divorced soon after. Their US student visas were running out, so Mulenga's wife had begun an affair with an American, hoping to obtain a residency visa by marrying him. Her ploy worked. Mulenga eventually returned to his home city in Zambia. Jesus helped him with protection after he started a business there selling computer parts.

CHAPTER 10

Set Fire to the Shrine

> You have just dined, and however scrupulously the slaughterhouse is concealed in the graceful distance of miles, there is complicity.
> — Ralph Waldo Emerson

WHEN I VISITED Nydia later that week I was still full of the energy of victory, but the energy was unformed and anticipatory, rather than defined and present. I was excited by my insights, yet aware there was a piece of Lucumí I hadn't thought about despite, in many people's view, it being the center of the religion.

Afro-Cuban practices of spirit mediumship, divination, herbal cleansing, ritual and ceremony, drumming, dancing and nature reverence appeal to people on different spiritual journeys and from many walks of life. Lucumí is a religion that addresses immediate and practical life situations. Most people want more guidance, and especially want to know they are on a destiny path leading to fortune. Laura and I believed ourselves lucky because we could access a deep soul level of guidance from ceremony and divination that gave our lives a deeper meaning.

However, the practice of sacred slaughter, whereby animals are made sacred for communal meals and offerings to the Orisha, is a far less understood, far more contentious Lucumí practice. During all the years Ernesto has been my godfather, I hadn't seen him kill an animal, although I had witnessed Jesus Suarez decapitate a chicken so quickly I hardly knew it had happened. However, mention Ernesto's name and anyone who has read or heard about Lucumí thinks immediately of animal sacrifice. I've seen people in Miami grimace at the simple mention of the word Santería (the colonial name of Lucumí) saying with their faces precisely what is on their minds.

From the mid-1980s until 1993, Ernesto was involved in a legal process to make Lucumí animal offerings legal. He began by challenging a Miami-Dade County city of Hialeah ordinance outlawing ritual animal slaughter. The ordinance had been passed to cripple Ernesto's newly established Church of the Lucumí Babalú-Ayé. In Dade County Circuit Court, he lost both the case and the appeal. After those losses, he rebounded against great odds to win an unlikely hearing and subsequent victory before the U.S. Supreme Court, which upheld Lucumí's first amendment rights.*

This well publicized case was the subject of a book by David M. O'Brien, a leading Supreme Court scholar and professor at the University of Virginia.[5] In it O'Brien detailed the spectacular odds against Ernesto. The Supreme Court grants less than 1% of all appeals of circuit court decisions, of which there are hundreds of thousands every year. Out of that 1%, the same year the Court selected the Lucumí case the judges heard oral arguments in only 112 cases out of 6,770 cases on their docket.

Justice Kennedy wrote the opinion for the Court. The bottom line was in his introduction: "Our review confirms that the laws in question were enacted by officials who did not understand, failed to perceive, or chose to ignore the fact that their official actions violated the Nation's essential commitment to religious freedom ... We invalidate the challenged enactments and reverse the judgment of the Court of Appeals."[6]

The Washington justices understood that Lucumí ritual sacrifice of goats and fowl was much like American Thanksgiving, and that, even more, there was ubiquitous animal killing in America outside slaughter houses, most of it not for religious reasons, and much of it very cruel.

"Can you boil a live lobster in Hialeah?" asked Justice Sandra Day O'Connor in the Supreme Court of the United States on November 4, 1992. She posed the question to the attorneys who had defended Hialeah's

---

* The First Amendment to the U.S. Constitution reads: Congress shall make no law respecting an establishment of religion, or prohibiting the free exercise thereof; or abridging the freedom of speech, or of the press; or the right of the people peaceably to assemble, and to petition the Government for a redress of grievances.

prohibition on Lucumí ritual slaughter. "Yes, you can boil a living lobster in Hialeah," agreed the Hialeah attorneys, who no doubt often selected live lobsters and other seafood in Hialeah restaurants, which would die miserably in boiling water or over a fire to satisfy their hunger.

Quite improbably, the victory of the day went to Lucumí.

Ernesto's remarkable Lucumí case is now included in *One Hundred Americans Making Constitutional History*, where he appears with people like Sherman Booth and Eugene Debs.[7] Although the First Amendment protects ritual animal slaughter, this ruling is under continuous dispute in Miami and elsewhere. However, the Supreme Court victory gave Ernesto an important voice in contemporary Lucumí's evolution in American society and made legal Lucumí's ceremonies where sacrifice is required.

When Ernesto went to the Supreme Court, his case was widely covered in newspapers and television, but not necessarily from a neutral point of view. Because of this, Ernesto gained street recognition in Miami as an animal killer in a cult from the Caribbean. One Hialeah counselor warned that a plague would spread over Miami from tainted, discarded meat, and a minister suggested that Ernesto was the Antichrist. Among the huge pile of hate mail that accumulated at his home, he even received an insulting and threatening letter with no address line other than Antichrist on the envelope. Apparently, the Miami post office knew who the Antichrist was and where he lived.

Over the seven years of the case, Ernesto lost his first wife to divorce, a victim of stress caused by threats and unpleasant media exposure. He also lost most of his clients, who did not want to identify with him. Most visibly, he lost a lot of his thick, black hair. However, on the positive side, he gained a new wife, Nydia, already a powerful Lucumí priest from Puerto Rico, and a new position in American Lucumí. Those who had denounced him in the Lucumí community were quick to reverse their opinions, calling him The Man on the winning day.

What is it that made this Santería/Lucumí case so unpopular that it nearly cost Ernesto his life? This occurred when an unidentified driver raced up over the curb on the sidewalk where he was walking and nearly, but not quite, struck him with his car. I think one of the biggest reasons for the hysteria over religious offerings was not that people objected to killing animals. After all, most objectors were meat eaters; not many were vegan activists. Rather, it was that ordained Lucumí priests sacrificed animals in closed ceremonies where there were no uninitiated people or cameras present. The Eleggúa initiate, Steve, would have had animals sacrificed for his initiation. The blood would have spiritually fed the Orisha, and we, Steve's guests, enjoyed the flesh the next night. However, with few eye witnesses, it was possible to imagine Hollywood inspired orgies of bloodletting where screaming sacrificial animals, their throats sawed with dull knives, held in the hands of bloodthirsty priests, died in agony.

Further, there was a common belief that more advanced religions, said to be Judaism and Christianity, evolved and abandoned the practice of sacrifice. Religions which hadn't abandoned it were backward. I've heard numerous people make this statement, as if it were something that everyone knows to be true. Probably many of us were taught to think that native/pagan polytheisms and animisms were replaced by more highly evolved European, Asian and North American monotheisms. I think this contention is a prejudice born with colonialists and their missionaries. For instance, Lucumí is from Africa, and most of the other religions in the world, which sacrifice animals, are also from the Third World. The deleterious and racist effects of Christianity and colonial administrations were similar everywhere; and these aren't over.

"We put Mother Hubbard dresses on all the naked women," bragged the missionaries in Polynesia. "We cut down the sacred groves," the pastors and the merchants who wanted the timber in Africa and Indonesia proudly claimed. And from the pulpits of Nigeria and Cuba, parsons and bishops declared, "Worshiping false idols with the blood of animals will send you to hell." Meanwhile, they collected—for their museums back home—these same idols of the pagan gods, while ordering their new flocks to destroy images of their old gods and stop sacrificing to them.

Most cultures in Africa still sacrifice their own animals, just as people in India, Bali, Muslim countries and many parts of China still offer animals to their gods. For instance, after the Bali bombings in 2002 and 2005, priests sacrificed bulls in Hindu ceremonies to return peace to the land.

"Animal sacrifice is what barbaric savages who have no compassion or ethics do," said a college professor to me at a party in Miami some years ago.

She spoke from her safe high ground while she dined on little pork hors-d'oeuvres, smoked turkey and seared steak. The moral high ground is often a place of glaring contradiction. I can't think of a time I tried to occupy it that I didn't tumble down quickly because of my blindness.

The Anglo party scene reminded me of Lucumí parties during initiation ceremonies where people sit around and enjoy holiday foods together. Both tropical parties were celebrating a holiday by dining together on a lovely evening. A big difference was that the faculty member's invitees didn't raise and kill the animals they feasted on, nor was the party a religious celebration, although it was a holiday Christmas party. The faculty member's guests had not killed the animals they were eating—the pig, cow and turkey—and they congratulated themselves for not sacrificing animals like Lucumí priests, whom they believed to be guilty of animal cruelty. That's such an ironic thing to say in the age of mass slaughterhouses, supermarkets, and a meat-sated public.

I've noticed that people object less strongly to religious sacrifice when they hear the Lucumí eat the animals they kill and are well trained in humane slaughtering techniques. Most sacrificial animals become main courses at luscious feasts held after important rituals. If there are leftovers, they go home to the freezer. However, in a certain number of cases, a healing or cleansing may require an animal offering to carry away illness. In that case, after the priest transfers the illness to the animal—usually a rooster, chicken, dove, quail or in extreme cases, a goat—he quickly kills the animal, after which he or the client may discard the carcass depending on instructions from the Dilogún.

As a consequence of Ernesto's successful outcome in Washington and the publicity around him and religious sacrifice, many people now believe that animal sacrifice is the central and most important ritual in Lucumí. In fact, the most important ritual is divination.

People are often surprised to find that many people, like me, for example, who take part in the religion, never come near a sacrificial animal at an initiation except at the celebratory dinner. Even full initiates may only sacrifice an animal once every few years, although a chicken or rooster offering is more common. Another misunderstanding is that ebó (sacrifices or offerings) are always animals. The most common offering in Lucumí that I've made is an adimú, a small portion of food placed in the out-of-doors at the right time and in the right frame of mind.

Jesus Suarez says that his Cuban elders consider a blood offering to be hot. They make sure with thorough divination that they are not offering an elephant when a calabash will do.

"When a priest sacrifices an animal," Jesus says, "it is like setting fire to the shrine and to the Orisha stones, and the fire must be put out with holy water and fruit to cool everything. Most people are running with overheated radiators anyway, so an animal sacrifice is something that is very carefully considered in divination by the elders before it is carried out on behalf of a sick person."

Otherwise, animal sacrifice is only called for at the highest initiations, where the priests pray to and sacrifice the animals for the communal feast. They offer animal blood in sacred vessels to the Orisha on their altars, where it infuses sacred objects, like initiation necklaces, with ashé.

Like my Christmas party hostess, I didn't grow up in a religion where a priest sacrificed the animals we were going to eat on holidays. While I was visiting Ernesto and Nydia at their home one day I asked why Lucumí holds it sacred to kill one's own festive animals.

"It's what the gods want people to do," Ernesto replied, looking up from the espresso pot he was loading with finely ground coffee. "And my experience tells me it works." Usually, he was quite long-winded. This was one of the most direct, concise statements I'd heard him utter.

Ernesto was making Cuban coffee, a loving procedure frequently repeated. I left him alone in the kitchen with his coffee preparations and returned to the living room to look out the window. Across the street I could see a new home development behind the green verge of Brazilian pepper and lantana. The sky was wide and clear, with only a few afternoon storm clouds languishing on the horizon. I could almost feel the intense heat baking my car outside the front gate.

When Ernesto returned to the living room, he had a little well-sugared espresso in his cup, which he whipped into foam, studying it carefully as the spoon went round. When he finished, he returned to the kitchen and added the rest of the strong brew to his small cup. Ah, the perfect black Cuban café with an icing of golden foam!

"Why do the Orisha want sacrificed animals," I repeated, hoping for something more than the simple statement he had already made, yet nervous about asking about this so closely held practice.

Finally, he drained his cup, placing it carefully on the table beside him.

"A priest slaughters an animal in the name of a person being ordained, because it's important that a new initiate's imprint (something like an energy vibration) reaches the Orisha. The animal's spirit willingly takes the imprint of the initiate to the gods, accepting its own death, in order to travel in spirit realms."

He explained that the initiate, often badly in need of healing, knows that his or her vibrational signature is on the way to the Orisha via the sacrificial animal, which has removed the negativity (curse or sin) from his or her life. This is an ancient idea—that a spirit animal can help relieve illness—found in the world's many variations of its oldest religion, shamanism.

Further, according to Ernesto, the animal's flesh is an important form of communion for the priests, just as Thanksgiving turkey is an important form of communion for American families. Most people don't realize that animals die humanely because priests learn an expert method of slaughtering in an initiation ceremony called Pinaldo.

"A trained professional priest slaughters animals by quickly severing the carotid artery of a goat, or rapidly decapitating a bird with his hands," Ernesto said.

Before the Supreme Court hearing, the Dade County Medical Examiner testified in Miami Federal Court and corroborated this statement. He said in sworn testimony that no one could kill an animal quicker or better than the Lucumí priests he had observed in many ceremonies in Miami.

"We can't go to Burger King or MacDonald's," Ernesto said with a big smile. "Food served at our initiations has to be ritually prepared, just as kosher Jews require kosher meat. It would be much easier to eliminate that part of our religion and the next day order take-out or have lasagna instead."

While Ernesto and I laughed over the thought of Olosha ordering take-out lasagna, Nydia joined us in the living room. She had finished up the flan she was making in the kitchen. Nydia smiled and waited for us to quiet down, then asked me if I knew what the Pinaldo ceremony was about. I knew that the Pinaldo was the highest order of priesthood in Lucumí, but admitted I had only superficial knowledge of it. Nydia said that if I understood what happened at a Pinaldo I would be a long way toward understanding ritual animal sacrifice.

According to Nydia, during the nineteenth century in Cuba, a Yoruba priest of Ochosi named Efunshe (also known as Ña Rosalía) created the Pinaldo ceremony. This was some time after her arrival in Havana. Efunshe was a free woman. She may have been a market trader in Nigeria, a profession dominated by hard headed, successful business women. After she arrived in Cuba, she recognized the need for religious restoration due to all that the Yoruba religion had lost during the slave trade. For that reason, she established the ritually complex Pinaldo ceremony. In the ceremony, an Orisha priest became a Balogun—high priest of Ogún, meaning "warrior chief" in Yoruba—able to carry out the many demands of each Orisha's preference for fowl and mammals. This included their treatment in ceremony, a knowledge of prayers and chants, and how the animals are slaughtered with a minimum of pain and quick efficiency. The Pinaldo in Cuba became a second initiation, comparable to ordination, one that did not exist in Nigeria.

Pinaldo constituted an affirmation of Efunshe's Yoruba religious expertise for Lucumí priests in Cuba. It was, in turn, a confirmation for her of the knowledge of the Cuban priests who underwent the ceremony, a sort of a cross-check on everyone's spiritual abilities. The priests who worked with Efunshe must have been impressed with her because strong memories of her survive to this day. Pinaldo is the penultimate initiation, with many Lucumí lineages tracing their origin to Efunshe. For instance, when you hear the Olosha doing the moyuba, the invocation of respect to the ancestors, you hear her name repeated frequently.

Efunshe was an important Obá Oríaté, diviner and master of ceremonies, who established fundamental Lucumí practices, like the Pinaldo, in Cuba. In nineteenth century Cuba many Obá Oríaté were women; in Miami today there are few. I suspect that the more patriarchal Hispanic peoples naturally supported more men in leadership roles in Lucumí, as well in Cuban society as a whole. Efunshe's descendants say she was from a royal family in Nigeria, and that during her leadership of the Cabildo San José 80 in Havana, she was the Queen, never allowed to walk on the streets, carried about in a sedan chair. Cabildos were mutual aid societies established by Africans in Cuba. Some became houses of Orisha worship, like the one that Efunshe led until her death in the late 1920s. Today, most Lucumí priests in Havana claim descent from her.[8] Nydia's own Lucumí ancestry stretches back to Efunshe through the priests who initiated her in her homeland of Puerto Rico.

During their Pinaldo ceremonies, Nydia and Ernesto received sacrificial knives. These knives held the ashé of Ogún, who rules metal. Ogún also inspires the sacrificial act. Nydia's knife was a sacred blade, which, if used correctly, could take the life of a sacred animal. Ancient religions like Lucumí depend on sacrifice to make an animal holy, after which the animal—or certain parts of its body and its blood—are offered to the immortals. Sacrifice attracts the numinous energy of ashé and transmits its effects onto a participant.

Ordinarily, Nydia explained to me, a priest did not undertake Pinaldo for many years after her or his ordination, because it was a culmination of sacred learning reserved for the experienced. Nydia was a priest for over twenty years before the Dilogún decreed she must take the Pinaldo training. During the week of Pinaldo, priests taught a neophyte how to approach, talk with, and sacrifice animals. Could Nydia, whom I knew adored her dog and the wild young cats living under her house, have killed an animal?

"I was up all night worrying about what would happen," she confessed. "I didn't want to kill an animal because I love them. It was the last thing in the world I wanted to do. I was shaking with nervousness when we began the ceremony, but by the time I had to perform the sacrifice, I was calm and relaxed."

Before the sacrifice of her first goat, Nydia prayed for its soul, addressing Orisha and Olódúmarè. At last, she got close to the animal and placed her head on its head, while she prayed sincerely for many different things. She especially thanked the being for sacrificing its life for her and the other priests. When she described these prayers, suddenly I could imagine the silky forehead of a goat pressing against Nydia's forehead, while she looked deeply into the golden slits of its Neolithic eyes, feeling its warm breath on her face. It was during this communion that the goat accepted her energy imprint, the signature unique to every human that helps the Orisha identify and communicate with their children on Earth.

When it was time to slaughter the goat, a priest who is expert at killing instructed her. This priest is similar to a Jewish rabbi, trained to slaughter in a kosher manner. The Balogun used his hand to cover Nydia's hand, in which she held the sacrificial knife. Their hands together, he directed the severing of the goat's carotid artery with the well-sharpened ritual blade. Then he showed her how to spiritually treat the sacrificed animal. After that, under his instruction, Nydia helped to slaughter the remaining animals. Other Olosha at the ceremony removed the carcasses from the sacred room in order to begin the long, laborious process of skinning and butchering for cooking.

The priests who assisted at the ceremony were her witnesses, people who would assert that they had been there and knew that Nydia had received her ceremonial knife to become a fully ordained high priest of Pinaldo. Later that night, they were her dinner guests.

"Keep in mind that on the second day the Pinaldo is celebrated like a grand party," she emphasized, surprising me with her smile and palpable happiness.

In the afternoon before her Pinaldo, Nydia and the other priests had prepared the dining tables with flowers and new glassware bought for the ceremony. They arranged separate glasses for water, champagne and four or five types of wine and liquor, before the new white dishware was set on the table. These plates would hold chicken, meats, seafood and different types of rice and beans. Then, professional priests, people with excellent taste and decorating skills, completed Nydia's tables with graceful, colorful themes representing her spiritual heritage. On behalf of Nydia's Shangó affiliation, they created a red and white table, and for her Yemayá connection, a blue and white one, these decorations evoking the ocean. However, none of these decorations had anything to do with Lucumí's requirements. Nydia did all this because she could afford it and wanted to do it.

And, for the pièce de résistance, she provided six or seven different desserts, one of them a red and white rum cake in the shape of a castle for Shangó. An Oshún priest who is a pastry artist in Miami created this edible castle. Delicious! There was always something on Nydia's stove top. Nydia knew the secret of perfect burnt sugar flan, and while she talked about her Pinaldo, I could smell the flan she'd made earlier wafting a delicious scent of sugar and cream.

"The entire banquet was an affirmation of me!" she passionately affirmed about her beautiful party, empowerment and confidence in her voice.

However, it wasn't only about herself, because she also bought gifts for everyone, bottles of wine, perfume for men and women, and some gift-wrapped pottery. She personally presented these gifts to her guests, offering special ones to her padrino and oríaté. Then, while everyone was talking quietly, each priest stopped by her seat at the head of the table to discuss her divination session and fine tune her understanding. Nydia said the in-depth divination reading during her Pinaldo, performed by her Obá Oríaté, was a coherent picture of her life, quite similar to the one (her itá) she'd received at her first ordination.

I could imagine how lavish Nydia's dining tables were from having seen altars and offerings created by talented Lucumí hands. The altars in the Pichardo home were themselves often works of art incorporating intricately designed cloths, natural elements, special lighting, candles and icons. When Ernesto taught his course at the university, he organized a Lucumí Art exhibition with paintings, dancers dressed in the exciting colors of the Orisha, and drumming by a fantastic Cuban drumming group. Art, singing, dancing, and artistic and ritual decoration are essential to the Lucumí culture and religion.

Who could imagine Nydia's Pinaldo ceremony, if all you heard about it was that "Priests learn the Lucumí way of slaughtering an animal"? I know I didn't picture a holiday atmosphere with gourmet feasting, wines and champagne, heartfelt gift exchange and spiritual inspiration. My family's North American holidays, like Thanksgiving, didn't begin with chanting, praying and long preparations for ritually killing the turkey. Nor did they involve plucking, bleeding or eviscerating our sacrificial fowl.

Rather, they conveniently began with the supermarket purchase of a frozen–by-the-pound turkey, a hardened carcass, folded in a tight egg shape, wrapped inside a thick plastic bag closed with metal clips. The deceased fowl reminded me of a pharaoh's mummy. A small cloth bag inside the turkey held its smooth internal organs; an anonymous factory worker, working from an unknown location and time, had stuffed this bag into the turkey's abdomen. There was not a hint of feathers or blood, seeing eyes or warm breath. Our turkey was dead long before we baked and consumed it. We sure as heck didn't thank the turkey for dying. The family would have laughed at that notion.

I asked myself, after hearing Nydia's story, why people think it is better to kill animals in unfeeling, corporate slaughterhouses devoid of spiritual content, rather than within sacred Lucumí initiation ceremonies? After all, the old roots of the word *sacrifice* mean to make *sacred*.* Doesn't the Lucumí religious belief that animals are so important to humans that they must be killed personally with trained precision, in an atmosphere of prayer, purity and song, protect them from cruelty? I know if I were an animal, I would choose to die by the hand of the Olosha (especially Nydia), rather than suffer death by an impersonal machine or uncaring worker at a highly mechanized slaughterhouse, where I'd find myself treated as an unfeeling unit in a profit-driven industry. The reader who doubts my choice could dip into factory farm exposés on the web. This makes some of the ghastliest reading one can imagine, even in this violence-soaked world.

---

* Sacrifice: from a Middle English verb meaning "to make sacred", from Old French and from Latin *sacrificium*: *sacr* "sacred" and *facere*, "to make").

CHAPTER 11

The Hillbilly Circus

> Our police force was not created to serve black Americans; it was created to police black Americans and serve white Americans.
> — Ijeoma Oluo

SOON AFTER I TALKED with Nydia, I wasn't surprised to find that in Miami intolerance of Lucumí was continuing. There had been a recent police crackdown on a Lucumí ceremony, and my non-Lucumí friends were talking about Miami's Afro-Cuban religions with disgust. They believed Lucumí to be a mixture of animal cruelty and perversion, and nearly snarled when they described recent television news stories, in which they had seen Lucumí priests dressed in white, huddling outside a house, barricaded from the street by yellow police tape.

Police cruisers and a paddy wagon flashed their lights continuously, while officers, some with helmets and high-powered rifles, a SWAT team*, came and went via the front door. A commentator had reported that the police were investigating animal cruelty in a Lucumí ceremony.

"How could I possibly continue to work with them?'" an anthropologist who had heard the story asked me.

Newspapers in Miami, and eventually media all around the country, reported that neighbors had complained of people killing crying animals inside a house in the "City Beautiful"—the marketing name for the neighborhood of wealthy Coral Gables. Apparently, locals had witnessed these

---

* In the United States, SWAT (special weapons and tactics) team is a generic term for a law enforcement unit that uses specialized or military equipment and tactics.

outrages and called 911. The reports suggested that children had observed the killings and that the extreme police presence was a justified response to alleged animal cruelty.

Wow! I said to myself as I read these stories. *What happened?*

I knew that initiation ceremonies employed trained priests to ritually slaughter animals. If protocol was followed, the animals' suffering was minimal, especially compared to their treatment in slaughter houses. I needed to learn more about what happened.

But first I needed advice on how to proceed in this delicate matter. So I consulted the I Ching, believing that its impartiality and inspiring ancient virtues would create a picture of the situation for me. I was not surprised to see the *Marrying Maiden*, hexagram number 54, appear when my cowrie shells fell to the mat for the sixth time. The Chinese symbol for this hexagram is a concubine who is a clear subordinate to the official wives of the husband. The marrying maiden is not able to lead, should not impose her will, or discipline people. She represents a situation that draws her in without her permission, and which is not under her control. At the same time, this situation contains hidden transformational potential.

I felt like the marrying maiden, pulled into the debate about Lucumí and animal cruelty without much experience. I needed to talk to Jesus about what had happened.

When I caught up with Jesus he told me that the Pinaldo ceremony in the Gables had taken place at the home of Noriel Batista, a pharmacist. Jesus gave me the address of Batista's house. I visited it the next day, walking the streets around it to get an impression of the setting where the police raid had taken place.

I found Mr. Batista's one-story home was on a corner, surrounded by dense tropical foliage perhaps ten feet high. The thick hedges and tall trees were well cared for, with the house set within them. The only thing I could see from his drive-way was an entrance porch covered by an overhanging roof, with a small lawn in front. I couldn't see the house; only part of the roof was visible. There was no trace of the infamous raid.

I asked Jesus to describe that day from his perspective. At about 1:45 or so in the afternoon, he recalled, he was in the garage. The priest in charge of the sacrifice finished offering three goats by rapidly severing the carotid arteries. The dark-skinned Eleggúa priest, Luis Aviles, carried the goats' carcasses from the garage into the side yard and placed them on a sturdy table, where he* and his 21-year-old son began butchering and skinning the animals for the communal meal that would complete the ceremony.

What those in the garage couldn't hear was that at that moment the police were knocking on the front door of the house. The cook in the kitchen yelled to Noriel, the pharmacist whose house this was, to answer the front door. When Noriel opened it a full-vested SWAT team member violently pulled him outside, threw him to his knees, and pointed a rifle his head. The team then entered the house. Some went quickly to the left, where the bedrooms were, checking each, and shouting "Clear!" when they saw the bedrooms were empty. Others went right, into the dining room and kitchen. They then swarmed through the kitchen, out the back door and down the stairs, towards the garage.

Jesus was in the garage with fifteen Olosha, the majority elderly women. Suddenly, without warning, they heard screaming: "Put your fucking hands up! Get your fucking hands up!" Another barked, "Freeze!" The orders were audible to everyone, including two of Luis' younger children, also initiated priests, who were standing near Jesus.

Jesus says that since he was the only English-speaking Balogun (High Priest) present, he quickly translated, while controlling his own feelings of dread. Hearing his translation, the others became dazed, unable to respond to the incomprehensible situation. Jesus took control and authoritatively issued commands in Spanish, which the others followed. Jesus pushed the kids behind him, saying firmly, "You can't go out!" While he shouted orders to the others in Spanish, the police repeatedly screamed for him to shut up.

He heard someone scream in English from the garden, "If anyone comes outside, we will shoot you. Don't come out!"

Jesus knew when he heard the police intimidation and threats that he had to bring order to the mayhem. Otherwise, the murderous threats of the police would become prophecies.

---

* Luis Alviles was the Eleggúa Olosha who delivered the "seven sticks" message to me from Ogún.

Not only was the incursion a violent circus of yelling, threats, crying, boot stomping, doors slamming, sirens and police radios, there was also a police helicopter circling and roaring above the house. More police rolled out of the chopper to assist those already there. It was a major police invasion of a private property in an upscale suburb.

Meanwhile, outside in the garden, Luis and his son hadn't raised their hands, so the officers continued shouting. They kept their hands down because the police commands were confusing them. Luis and his children were born and raised in the communist regime of Cuba where Lucumí activities weren't disturbed as long as they were licensed. In addition, Ernesto's successful Supreme Court ruling recognizing Lucumí's right to practice religious sacrifice was known throughout the USA and Cuba.

For these reasons Luis was confident that he was not violating any American laws. This was as helmeted, anonymous storm troopers, shouting in a language he didn't understand, threatened him with high powered rifles. The SWAT Team was employed by an elite city, Coral Gables, and was representative of the American militarized police forces.

Mounting evidence proves the police are strongly prejudiced in favor of white people, using violence much more frequently toward people of colour. Luis, whose skin was black, was seeing the American Empire in action for the first time. He had left Cuba only a few months earlier, but now could be in no doubt that the US police were as violent and dangerous as the Cuban military.

Simultaneously, Jesus had to stop Luis' two other kids, twelve and eighteen, from running out of the garage to be with their father. They had also just arrived in Miami, didn't speak English, and weren't familiar with the city or its culture. Jesus physically held them back, while their arms kept reaching around him, desperate to see their father in the garden was okay. The youngest was crying and asking for his father. Anyone can understand how scared this kid was. Jesus controlled the kids while translating for the rest of the priests, calming the situation as much as he could.

Suddenly, their terror ratcheted up another notch as they saw red laser dots squiggling up and down the garage walls and over the bodies of everyone. With a terrible, sinking feeling, Jesus realized that members of the SWAT team had their telescopic rifles trained on them all. When he looked down at his own body, he saw red lights crawling across his clothing. Jesus told me that at that moment his mind kept repeating: "This is really a stupid way to die."

The two kids beside Jesus kept crying out, "My father! My father!" But Jesus knew there was nothing he could do, so kept himself between the kids and the door.

No one had an opportunity to ask whether the officers had a search warrant, or why they were being threatened at gunpoint. Jesus was the only one who understood English, but the police refused to speak to him.

Soon the SWAT team, aiming their rifles at everyone, forced them out of the garage, up the stairs, into the kitchen, through the hallway, and out the front door onto the little concrete porch. There the officers ordered everyone to put their hands in the air. In Spanish Jesus told everyone to keep their hands down, then yelled back at the police, "These are elderly people. They're not going to put their hands up!" After yet more shouting and threats, the police finally relented and let them stand there.

Now they were outside the front of the house Jesus could see the police had cordoned off the street with yellow ribbon and barriers. He counted the police cars—twenty-two marked cruisers, a paddy wagon, a SWAT team van, three detective cars and a city car from code enforcement: twenty-eight law enforcement vehicles in total. He also watched television crews arriving, and saw the police parking them across the street while reporters started organising their broadcast equipment. A major media effort was accompanying the law enforcement army.

Jesus remembers it being intensely sunny, hot and humid on the small concrete veranda. Soon some of the elderly Olosha began to complain of their diabetes and heart pains. Frightened and confused, they leaned for support against the exterior wall of the house.

Although the temperature was in the high 80s, the police allowed none of their detainees to go to the bathroom, or even have a drink of water, for the entire three hours they stood there. Soon Jesus demanded the police call an ambulance because many of the elderly priests were feeling more and more ill.

By now the news media was transmitting live coverage. Vans from six local channels had satellite dishes erected, and their camera operators were filming. Jesus observed reporters speaking with the police officers and taking down their information. However, the officers wouldn't allow the media to talk to the priests on the porch.

While the Lucumí priests remained coralled there, several police officers went inside carrying cameras. Presumably they photographed everything in the house and garage. However, although Ernesto and Jesus were later able to obtain the police report and the 911 call, they didn't see any of the photographs the police and/or code enforcement officials took. Ernesto says that Lucumí does not allow photography of its sacred initiation room (the igbodu), its altars or practices. Therefore, practitioners consider photographs to be blasphemous.

An ambulance arrived. As medics checked the elderly, Jesus overheard the police radio carried by the officer in charge. Jesus told him the police were violating their rights. "Show me your badges! When this is over I'll have all your badges and put them on my wall as trophies!" He then demanded to speak to the District Attorney.

The police chief asked Jesus for his ID. Jesus showed it to him, along with his Church of the Lucumí Babalu Aiye card, identifying him as a member of the Lucumí church that had won the animal sacrifice case in the Supreme Court.

Now the police chief decided he needed to talk to his superiors. He made a call on his radio, but didn't like what he was told, because Jesus clearly heard him asking permission to use the Patriot Act* to remain at the house. Why did he want to use the Patriot Act to legitimize their actions? Because, Jesus learned as he listened, the SWAT team had entered the house *without a search warrant*. Everyone was being illegally detained!

It turned out the police chief was talking with the Miami Dade State Attorney, Katherine Fernandez Rundle. Jesus recognised her voice as she instructed the officer, "Get into your cars and leave right now!"

The chief shouted, "What do you mean, just leave!"

She yelled right back at the police chief, "GET THE HELL OUT OF THERE!" Her voice carried over the radio to everyone close by, including Jesus.

---

* Title I of the Patriot Act authorizes measures to enhance the ability of domestic security services to prevent terrorism.

The police chief then shouted at his men to leave. They do so quickly. Within a few minutes, without saying a word, they had all gone.

However, some of the media remained behind. Jesus gave an interview to one camera crew, describing everything that had happened, making clear that everything they were doing for their ceremony was legal, approved by the Supreme Court, and that the police had dangerously violated their rights.

Jesus then rejoined everyone in the house, where they were sitting down, exhausted. They were still looking toward him for direction, so he began to give instructions. They worked together well past midnight to complete the Pinaldo ceremony for Noriel.

While they were working, Jesus suggested to several of the old people that they go to the hospital as a medic had recommended, but they adamantly refused, certain the police would torture or even murder them on the way. They were familiar with the enforcement tactics of the military police in Cuba's totalitarian regime, where their torture and/or murder on the way to the hospital might be a plausible scenario. In fact, they knew murder by the police in the United States was a possibility.

I've condensed Jesus' story into a few paragraphs. When he related it to me the first time, he could hardly stop shouting in anger. After several attempts, he finally poured out a long, detailed version which made my own heart beat faster.

That night I dreamed of red laser lights flickering on my body as I tried to escape from riflemen. I woke up sweating. I really liked Jesus. I was stunned that the police had done this awful thing. I found the invasion a frightening incrimination of the direction the American Homeland Security organization was taking.

Soon after the SWAT raid, I met a woman my age at an aerobics class. Full of endorphins, we chatted afterwards. I talked about the invasion of the Lucumí ceremony and my anger. The other woman cut me off, shaking her head in sympathy and making *tsk tsk tsk* sounds. At first, I thought she was sympathetic to this story of police overreach and the trauma that Jesus and his friends would still be experiencing.

Ah nah, that wasn't it at all. She worked for Homeland Security. She believed the Act was there, more or less, to get rid of immigrants with disgusting practices like animal sacrifice. My chest tightened and I felt confused about her. It's so easy to get paranoid. I backpedaled and got away from the agent, but not until she had extracted my phone number.

I expected a call any time. She had wanted to know details, names, my connection. I warily answered the phone for a while, careful to check the caller's details. I had been depressed and sad for my Lucumí friends and I wanted others to know about this grave injustice. But now, suddenly, I could feel what the Lucumí regularly experienced myself. It wasn't anything like being in their shoes, but I experienced a moment of terror when the women said she was a Homeland Security agent and listened hyper-alert to my story.

How could this have happened, I wondered? A SWAT team with laser rifles does not investigate animal cruelty. I reasoned to myself that the neighbors' complaints registered on the 911 call must have been substantial.

Presently, I found out Jesus and Ernesto had obtained a recorded copy of the call. I listened to it with Jesus in his apartment. I then transcribed it verbatim. It was interesting to read the conversation between Mr. Batista's young, male neighbor, who made the call, and the 911 operator:

YOUNG MAN: I'm hearing, like, noises coming from my neighbors, like, hurting an animal or something, and like, we, me and my parents, have seen them before do something.

OPERATOR: (Repeats the address and the directions to reach the caller's house) Was it a dog yelping or something?

YOUNG MAN: It sounded more like a goat. Like, me and my parents think they do some kind of a religious thing, like, with animals, like, and every now and then, every month we get, like, a smell, like a dead like, coming from there.

OPERATOR: Do you know if they are in the front or back yard?

YOUNG MAN: I can't tell if they are in the front or back, but I think it is the front. It's near the street, like. Now they are going inside. It's, like, raining now. I'm going to like, walk my dog real quick.

OPERATOR: (Takes the young man's name.) Do you want contact from the police?

YOUNG MAN: No, like, I just want to make sure that stuff like that stops. It's just, like, "ugh."

When we finished listening to the tape I was so surprised I had to laugh out loud. I wasn't sure what I expected I would hear, but I know I thought it would be very hysterical, urgent, specific and serious, with eye-witness reports of animal cruelty. I hadn't expected the voice of a young person who hadn't seen anything and only heard the cry of a possible goat. I certainly hadn't expected a caller who repeated the word "like" several times in each sentence (not that grammar is an indication of sincerity), and who, in the middle of his complaint, decided that the matter was not as important as taking his dog for a walk. I absolutely hadn't expected this almost trivial 911 call, because the scale of the police response was tantamount to a serious terrorist threat.

However, this underwhelming complaint about a crying goat set off a firestorm response from the Coral Gables police. On the tape, after the young man hung up, we heard numerous many officers call in, recording their arrival at the scene, each giving his code number.

During the crackling dispatch, one voice says, "We have dismembered animals in the yard and two black males (this was Luis Aviles and his son) and knives."

Soon after the report of the "black males and knives" on the 911 tape there were loud, male voices, commanding people to put their "fucking hands up", then stomach-churning sounds of Olosha screaming in the background. It was very hard to listen to.

I decided to read the public statements I had missed, made about the incident in the days after it happened.

"Apparently, someone heard screaming," said Coral Gables Police Assistant Chief, Richard Naue. "They thought animals were being hurt. The person who opened the door was a blood-soaked individual with a knife. The officer saw several decapitated animals and about fifteen people in the house."

The Assistant Chief claimed there were numerous knives and a lot of blood.[9] In contrast, Jesus said Noriel Batista had no blood on his clothing nor was he holding a knife when he answered the door. He said there was no screaming, at least not until the police's sudden arrival. Ernesto wondered why, with all the television cameras, they did not catch Batista or Aviles, whom they also claimed were blood-soaked, on film with blood stains.

"I am appalled that there may be a case of animal cruelty in the Gables," asserted a politician, Coral Gables Mayor, Don Slesnick. He added that neighbors and children in the neighborhood could see animals being slaughtered.[10]

In contradiction to the Mayor's view, the young man who made the 911 call, by his own admission, did not see anything. Later, when I walked around the house, I couldn't see into any part of the garage or side and back yards because of the tropical trees and the tall, thick hedges. The complainant hadn't seen a thing. No one had been bloody or violent. The officials were wrong, I was sure of it.

One morning, I woke to see Ernesto and Jesus in the newspaper. They had visited Coral Gables City Hall to obtain, under the Freedom of Information Act, photographs and other evidence taken by police during a raid. I immediately phoned Ernesto. He had not been part of the Pinaldo invaded by the SWAT team, but he filled me in on everything he knew. Not only had the photos the police had taken inside the house disappeared, but when they approached the television stations all their video of the incident had been wiped, including the on-camera interview of Jesus immediately after the police left.

Talking to Ernesto helped me finally appreciate what it can mean to be a Lucumí priest in Miami. During the earlier ceremony, when the Eleggúa priest had instructed me to gather Ogun's sticks for protection, Ernesto had sat with a policewoman. She was an officer trained to recognize the legality of animal offerings. Little did I realize how precious her presence was that day.

Jesus recently observed to me: "The entire fiasco was cultural and racial bigotry on the part of the police department and the press. Nothing but a goddamned hillbilly circus. It continued for a month. The racist clowns came out of the woodwork like cockroaches from a shit pile, taking every cheap opportunity they could to say something disparaging about us. No surprise there. I've been through that many times before in my life, and many times since then. It's how I grew my thick skin. It's the only way to survive when you're a target for hate."

The only way to survive when you're a target for hate. Jesus said it well because he knew it intimately. It was easy to recall his parents' wrath when he told them he was gay, the derision in school, even for his name, "Jesus". He had subsequently lived through so much as a bronze-skinned, Latino gay man, who happened to be very spiritually gifted.

Jesus said that before the SWAT team halted the ceremony it had taken two days to prepare holy herbal waters used to cleanse Orisha stones and everything else in the house, including the walls and floors. Removing pollution from the initiation room reconstructed the environment in a pure way so that something new could be born.

The preparation of sacred waters and ritual removal of polluting energies from the home and surrounding garden was intense and time demanding work. Jesus took charge of the ceremony, insisting everyone cooperate to complete their tasks. He said that after they had repeated the cleansings, they sacrificed eight goats and forty-four fowl in preparation for the large dinner that finally followed the initiation.

Ernesto was not surprised that the people carried on with the ceremony after their frightening encounter with the law. Lucumí had withstood submission to the slave plantation system, atheism and Catholicism in Cuba, so it would survive this. At the same time, he commented that Coral Gables had sent twenty-eight police cars and a SWAT team to investigate the killing of a goat. By comparison, Sarah Palin, an advocate in Alaska for the barbaric practice of aerial gunning of wolves and bears, became the Republican Vice-Presidential nominee in 2008.

"It is easy to see," Ernesto said, shaking his head, "why the Olosha are suspicious of the police and feel that America is a country of hypocrisy when it comes to the issue of animal cruelty and welfare. The culture of Lucumí is one of survival and resistance. It doesn't give a flying hoot if people get arrested, because then it just goes more underground. Throughout the centuries, in Cuba, and now in Miami, believers have been unwilling to give up their practices, no matter the consequences."

PART 2

Cycle of Death / Rebirth

CHAPTER 12

Bloody Family Battlefield

> From the bloody family battlefield
> to have plucked the unbruised rose of individual consciousness,
> and to have found in this flower not isolation and self-absorption,
> but full union with God and the world.
> — Patricia Hampl

I ARRIVED FROM the southern hemisphere to attend my mother's funeral so jet-lagged I didn't know day from night. My brothers were at the gate exit. As I stood reeling with exhaustion, I could see my oldest brother was disturbed.

"I hate Carolee," he said without greeting, as if he'd waited to spit it out on me, his older sister.

"Why, I like her," I replied. At that time I had only met her once at their church, when she was very sweet to me.

"She's at home, sitting in Mother's chair," he said, all this at the airport just after I had arrived.

I was still wondering if Mother were really dead, she had arisen so often from heart attacks, strokes and hemorrhages over the years.

"Yes, she is definitely dead," my younger brother confirmed.

I pictured my slow, overweight father sitting in his lounge chair, mouth open, drooling and snoring in his white, sleeveless undershirt. His dentures often fell out while eating, and his CB radio squawked constantly in an annoying tone from the back bedroom.

"Carolee is a moron," my brother added. "And greedy. She's already eyeing all our stuff."

"No, I think you're wrong. She wants to be helpful," I explained. "And she's had a hard life." After all, she'd been nice to me.

"Wouldn't we want Dad to be happy, if they are attracted to one another now Mom has died," my younger brother said, always calm to my older brother's anger.

"Of course, that's very unlikely. But I think it's wonderful she wants to help," I said, finishing the conversation. Meanwhile my older brother continued to looked upset and tense.

My mother's illnesses were the only things that had drawn the three of us siblings together over her last ten years. We met in airports, hospital waiting rooms and critical care. We phoned one another in the middle of the night to deliver the worst news. We no longer knew what it was to come home and see one another without intense mother worry and exposure to the most hideous of modern medicine's interventions.

One of the last times I saw my mother she had thirteen tubes in her body, including the one that fed her. Both my brothers had worked at hospitals, and they patiently explained to me what was happening. They could make it seem normal and natural, even good. They could translate horror into terminology that seemed to contain, or at least neutralize it.

The day after my mother's funeral, I awoke at 6 a.m., walked quietly to the living room, and found my father watching a video he had made of my mother's last days in the hospital. It was pathetic, heart wrenching. I couldn't look at it so walked to the beach instead.

When I returned he invited me to go to breakfast at the nearby shopping center. We sat in a booth. He ordered sausages, ggs, biscuits, grits and toast. Grieving inside, thinking of my mother in her fine dress and makeup in the coffin the day before, I was having trouble eating. She had really died this time, after many false alarms through the years of her slow and crippling illness. I ordered oatmeal and toast. I realised my father had never invited me out to eat with him alone before. Mostly when I was home he stayed in the garage smoking and tinkering with his tools. When his sausages arrived, he ate two or three and then laid down his fork.

"Honey," he said. "I've been having an affair with Carolee. I couldn't do anything about it until now, until your mother died. That's why I'm telling you now."

Carolee was already a presence in our lives, practically living at our house. But I thought she was like a church fixture present at tragedy to help prepare canned food and lay out cold cuts for the grieving family—which is what she was doing, as well as cleaning the sink and vacuuming. And sitting in my mother's chair.

My cold insides went colder. Suddenly, I was cut off from all emotion and feeling, frozen. How do the mind and voice still work in these situations? My parents were "Boots" and "Tudy," names they invented for one another in high school; they were the two lovers who were never parted. Or so our mythology went. No matter they had struggled all their lives to "bust the overhead", as my father used to say. No matter that my mother had become incurably ill ten years earlier, and then an alcoholic. Like all children, even one fifty years old, I believed my parents were above the fray of betrayal and deceit. My pot-bellied, denture wearing, hard of hearing father could not have fallen in love with a younger woman. More to the point, could she with him? But there he sat telling me it was so. And more, he wanted me as his confessor.

"Honey," he said, "I'm so glad we are having this talk. I've always been able to tell you anything."

"Tell me how long you've been seeing her. Did Mother know?"

"It's been about two years," he replied.

My mind brought up a calendar. I thought of my exhibition my parents did not attend while he was with her; I thought of my mother's bypass operation while he was with her; I thought of all the events over the past two years when he was with his new woman, fooling us all, and fooling my mother.

"I needed her for love when your mother was sick," he mercilessly went on.

It was the day after my mother's funeral. We might have spoken of that momentous ceremony, consoled one another, remembered Betty as wife and mother. Instead, he wanted to talk about his own life and the perils he had undergone during his illicit affair.

He said, "One night when we were all playing cards, Mother saw Carolee put her foot on my foot under the table."

"'Leave my husband alone! Stop playing footsie with my husband!'

your mother said sharply to Carolee. From that night on your mother knew about us. I can't tell you how guilty I've felt. The guilt's been terrible."

The whole scene flashed through my head. How it would feel to see a younger woman put her foot on your husband's foot when you are just home from hospital, shaky and weak, but playing cards with people you imagined were friends? How much energy would you have to use to interrupt the card game? Would I have been a coward and ignored it, to excoriate my husband later? Had everyone just gone on after that as if nothing had happened? What did Carolee say?

I wish I had asked him for the whole scene, but I was in shock. Maybe Carolee giggled and my father said it was an accident, or he wasn't even aware of it, or that she was just repositioning herself in the chair, you know, all the lame excuses people give when caught red-handed.

I kept reviewing everything for the past two years, when I had often driven the three hundred miles between my home and my parents, summoned for each of my mother's crises. I was running home to solve what I now saw was the unspeakable heart injury no doctor could heal. I thought about how my mother would know everything at that moment when she saw lover's foot upon lover's foot, and feel suddenly exposed, sick and vulnerable. I thought about their fifty-two years of marriage. I thought about how my mother was already totally dependent on my father for her life and care, unable to live alone with her heart condition. She couldn't kick him out. Her Christian religion forced her into silence and into chaos. She told neither my brothers nor me, who could have come to her aid. So, from that moment on, she lived in internalized hell. Afraid of embarrassment, afraid of loss of face in her community, afraid of abandonment, she told no one.

My father loved Carolee. No wonder my mother had worried constantly about where my father was. Everything seemed to fall into place now that I knew my father, and the southern woman, Carolee, had stepped through the trapdoor of romantic love, betrayal and deceit. They had held hands during my mother's funeral. My father's eyes glowed even when he wept. It hadn't made sense then. Now it did.

At the same time, I thought about how my father did need support and love after all he'd been through with my mother. I thought about how neither my brothers nor I wanted to care for him. What could I do anyway? Besides, frankly, the old man had always intimidated me. I thought I must show him support, even though I was in shock and my heart broken. I decided to support him. I would take on my mother's grief, her betrayal, yet say nothing, just like my mother had done.

After congratulating him on his good fortune to have found love, I asked, "Are you going to get married?"

I nearly choked on the question. To say *marry* the day after my mother's funeral was bitter herb for me. But I probably sounded all right to him.

The timing of his announcement of love was so selfish and hurtful, I felt he must be unhinged. Hours after putting my mother's body in a vault, he was pushing me to the limit. My father, who sat each night in his lounge chair saying "Amen" after everything the right-wing fanatic Rush Limbaugh said, was a self-centered patriarch, a status conferred on him by white males who dominated white women in church, state and family. I saw once again how his insensitivity had surrounded me as a child. And now he was doing it to me again.

I saw much, but said little. He wanted to get all the forgiveness out of me he could before I disappeared back to the southern hemisphere.

"I haven't been able to do anything about it until your mother died," he said, referring to his forthcoming marriage, which would take place six months later, almost to the day. "Now I think we will. I just hope I can make her a good husband. She can get very depressed, Carolee can."

"Well, good luck to you both," I said, unable to swallow another bite, "I'm happy for you." Poor Carolee, already depressed before the wedding!

I didn't rant and rave at my father. I didn't denounce him for his betrayal. Neither did I jump to defend my mother. Nor did I mention how much his words had hurt me.

Later, I asked myself why our one breakfast alone had to be this one? It was because that was the way my father was. He didn't want to see me or talk to me unless it was to forward his own agenda. He didn't even consider that I loved my mother, and that what he was saying and doing would hurt me deeply. It didn't matter to him. It was his way or no way.

Later I told Carolee how nice it was to have her in the family, telling her how much calmer she was than my mother. We were riding in the car on our way to a restaurant. As a coward, I wanted to make everything all right. In my shock I dimly imagined that she could take my mother's place and everything would go on like before. Here was my father driving the car; here was Carolee sitting in my mother's seat; here I was in the back, the child. I wanted to validate her, flatter her, because I needed my mother. I was an adult child in deep shock, unable to grieve because my father demanded celebration. I was freezing up inside, glaciations overwhelmed me, my own new ice age.

After we arrived back from the restaurant I immediately went to the bedroom. I sat on the bed. I realized I had eaten very little in the days I'd been there; my pants were already loose. There was no chance of going forward here. I had to escape. I could hear my father whispering to Carolee through the thin walls, no doubt reporting our conversation. They were in his bedroom, my mother's bedroom, the day after her funeral, and any noise they made was too much for me in the adjoining room in the little Florida bungalow.

I found my ticket back to the Southern Hemisphere in my bag. I picked up the phone and changed my reservation to the first available flight back, which was in two days. I finished on the phone, left the bedroom, and sat on the sofa in the television room. My father and Carolee were sitting there together on matching lounge chairs, their feet elevated. It seemed like my mother had never lived there, although she had only been dead a few days.

"I've just talked with Air New Zealand and my return flight was changed to the day after tomorrow," I told them, ducking the truth that I had changed my ticket myself.

"You mean you're not staying a week?" my father asked.

"That's right, I have to leave in two days because my original flight was overbooked," I lied.

My father seemed annoyed and startled. Carolee looked stricken, because she knew the truth.

Good, I thought, *I'm getting out of here. I'll carry this terrible situation with me, far away, and hope it will disappear. I do not want to witness their union any more. This is all the confession I need.*

Somehow, I existed for the next two days, unable to cry, unable to talk or eat, alone, confused and sleepless. If there were ever a time a daughter needed to talk to her father, it was that time, but he had never talked to me or been interested in my life. My mother was the parent who raised us. My father wanted me to look at some of his photographs. I couldn't. My whole view of his marriage and our family had been too shaken-up.

I heard him praise an uncle who'd had two wives. One day he left my mother's sister for his other family. Suddenly, without warning. He left a short note that cruelly stated, "I have to go to my family." It turned out he had another partner and two children living in a caravan park nearby.

My aunt saw his note when she came home from work. She made him tapioca pudding every day, because she thought he had to have it for his ulcer. After a beat or two, she walked to the refrigerator, opened the door and pulled out that morning's bowl. Tapioca is a lot of trouble to make, double boiler style, the way my aunt did it throughout her marriage. She carried the tapioca outside and threw it onto the lawn.

CHAPTER 13

My Mother's Ghost

> I was just nine years old when I started milking. I got up at six every morning to milk and milked again at five in the afternoon.
> — Betty McCandless Hoch

TWO YEARS PASSED in the Land of the Long White Cloud (New Zealand) before I found myself back in the little house in Florida my mother had bought and decorated forty years earlier. The small, single story, white brick suburban house sat next to an old two-story frame home with outside verandas top and bottom, the sort where people used to sleep before air conditioners sent people indoors to live.

A planter around the front entrance of our family home usually trailed Mom's bright red geraniums. The back garden was surrounded by tall bamboo that sang in the ocean breezes and was often full of migrating birds, like robins and painted buntings, whose sounds filled the thick groves with unending buzzing, chirping and whirling. But just for a few days, then they were flitting away north again.

I had come a long way to visit Dad and Carolee. As soon as they picked me up I could tell something was different. My father wasn't happy anymore or joking around like he usually did. He was windless and tired, falling asleep on his chair as soon as we returned to the house.

His new bride, Carolee, told me to use the spare bedroom next to theirs. She said she had meant to clean out a couple of drawers but hadn't had time. I found the room had miscellaneous stuff stacked on every surface, the overflow melting out the closet. One twin bed with a quilted cover was visible, the other piled with clothes. The room's ceiling was low, creating a claustrophobic and unpleasant effect. Carolee had moved the furniture she inherited from her mother to her new home. She had placed it around the rooms next to my mother's furniture, so there were two of everything: two sofas, two dining tables, many extra lamps and end tables, assorted easy chairs, chests of drawers and piles of knick-knacks. Dad had been ill for a while, and both of them were unable to decide to let some pieces go. If second hand sale furniture is a style, they had perfected it. They had tolerated this arrangement for two years.

Carolee showed me the bedroom next door, where my parents had slept, the one where she and Dad spent their nights together. My parents had slept on single beds in the small room. Those beds had gone. In their place was an antique four-poster bed, very handsome, probably valuable—once, when it was in fashion. The bed's four carved, wooden posts were mahogany, thick and sturdy. The bed was higher off the floor than average, in the style of the older four posters which raised sleepers above the lower draughts. The space under the bed was used for storage.

Carolee would tolerate my father's snoring for a while after they had gone to their bedroom for the night. However, after an hour or so she would leave the bedroom and visit the kitchen for her first dose of pills to treat her headache.

I could hear Dad's snoring from the living room when he was sleeping in the bedroom, the volume was so high, the sounds explosive. My mother could not sleep because of his snoring, and Carolee was the same. Poor Dad, I doubt he wanted to keep his wives sleepless and constantly irritated. Hard to get through the day without sleep at any age, or a really quiet place to relax, but there was none here. Silence was an empty repository for CB radio, washers, driers, dish washers, vacuum cleaners, air hoses and, especially, television news and evangelical, right wing radio commentary. A herb for male impotence lay on the shelf near the headache pills, testament perhaps, to a difficult intimate life. No sex, no sleep, illness, and a house that looked and felt like a basement jumble sale.

Hours after arrival, I began to feel terrible. It was vertigo, which I had never experienced before. When I went from lying down to sitting, the whole world dissolved in long, blurred, black and white drips, dropping down like wax from a candle. After sitting up, I had to remain stationary for minutes with my eyes closed, before gingerly reopening them, hoping I would find the world back in place. After that, I was nauseated. It terrified me so much I wondered if I would ever be normal again.

I had planned to be at my father's house only a few days, but this new development left me feeling helpless and scared. I cancelled my plans and fell into a stasis of vertigo and exhaustion. There was no sleeping in the airless bedroom next to them, with two televisions blaring in their bedroom and the walls paper-thin.

Their televisions were on until long after midnight and started again before dawn. They were addicted to television, its noise and the anxiety pitch of network media, especially crime reports that shaped their world view. They were too paranoid to walk outside their house. To me the neighbourhood seemed quiet and benign, yet Carolee criticized me when I returned from the beach, because I hadn't locked the house when I left.

However, the noises coming from their room were not the only reason I couldn't sleep. I couldn't sleep because the ghost of my mother was haunting the house. She was there to take her revenge on us for betraying her. She was still in her beloved home, where she had spent her dearest hours thinking of fabrics and tiles, flowers, and her precious china. Now she was angry. Very angry. As well as confused and unhappy. I could feel a heaviness in the air, a fist behind the grey clouds.

"Get that woman out of my house," my mother had demanded of my uncle, my father's brother, on her deathbed.

"Now I know what she meant," said my uncle, after I told him about Carolee. He was the good cleric uncle who had moved to California.

"I wish she had told me," I said.

Mother had known about Carolee's desire to capture my father two years before she passed away. She told me that Carolee wanted to have everything she had. I hadn't understood. First Carolee came to live in my mother's home while Mom was in hospital, dying. Then she moved in with Mom's husband, who was now her husband.

Who could blame my mother if her spirit was still around to punish Dad and Carolee? And me as well?

Up until the week of her death, my mother was still decorating her house. The last thing she bought was a porcelain mask with feathers surrounding the face. It still hung in the bathroom, reminding me of her last painful days. When I noticed it, I also noticed Carolee had put her bathroom items things next to it.

"That was the last thing your mother bought," my father said when he saw me looking at the mask. "In her last days. I never denied her anything."

"She had her own money," I said tartly. I thought I should bring a little reality into the picture.

My mother was everywhere, in everything, as I moved around the little house. The place was so alive with her I felt she was still in her bedroom. Despite Carolee's furniture, the house was Mother's entirely, every colour, every decoration, every plate. She made each of the new choices about carpets and drapes, tiles and wallpaper.

Whenever I came home, after a long hug and kiss, she would tell me I looked wonderful, and we would stroll around looking at the new things in every room, holding on to one another. I would feel excitement and anticipation during these walks, discovering a part of myself in my mother's home. The last stop in our rounds was always the kitchen, where I would find, when she was well, delectable desserts and dishes made just for us. We remembered her chocolate chip cookies filling the cookie jar to the brim, soft, moist and delicious. Lemon cream pie, apple pie, pecan pie, fresh strawberry shortcake, fresh sliced peaches, and a refrigerator filled with greens were her gifts to us. Shortly after arrival we would sit down and my mother would serve us coffee and her home baked treasures.

A few days before my father died, my youngest brother asked our father what he remembered of our mother.

"I remember her meals," he smiled. "Every night when I came home from work, I looked forward to sitting down at the table."

My mother treated my father as the patriarch, although for most of their married lives she worked full time and made more money than him. My father was limited in his left-brain intelligence. For the whole of their marriage, my mother handled all their financial affairs, including balancing the bank account. Yet, she served him like a prince at the table and worked two jobs—her daytime job at the hospital and her job at home, cooking, cleaning, ironing. She did all the social calling and writing too. My father never phoned or wrote me until my mother died.

"Now your mother is dead, I realize I never knew you children," my father lamented. "I let it be her job to contact you and tell me what you were doing. Now it's too late." He was right.

When I came home to my mother we shared news of our lives and hers around the table for an hour or two before unpacking. My father would join us to eat, but in a few minutes, he would begin fiddling around with his video camera, find something he must do in the garage (often it was to have a cigarette), or in the bedroom where he kept his CB radio. He would disappear, and for the rest of the trip I would only see him at the table. It was my mother whom I really visited, and she with me.

In his new marriage my father was still the patriarch. But it was plain that Carolee was going to rebel. She had no idea before marrying him that my father was as limited as she was both in money and intelligence. At church he looked good in a suit, was an elder (in a dying congregation of eighty people), and looked after the facilities on the weekend. Now she was home with him all the time she discovered he expected her servitude at meals and around the house.

"Carolee is a great cleaner," he explained seriously. "Why, she gets right down on her knees to scrub the floor."

"Carolee," I heard him say before dinner, "I think it best if you use the sink in the kitchen to brush your teeth and wash your face at night. The hot water doesn't have to travel as far as it must to get to the bathroom and we'll save money."

"No," I heard her reply. "I won't do that."

"Why not, honey?" my surprised father asked.

"Because I don't want to,' was her reply.

He treated her like his daughter, of course,

Carolee's initial friendly attitude towards me turned to suspicion and distrust as soon as she married my father. The crowded drawers and lack of food in the house were early signs on this first visit.

Soon my father was having a talk with me. "I want to tell you that I have replaced you as the executor on my will," he told me.

"Oh, why is that?" I asked.

"Carolee wants me to use her nephew who is a lawyer. Why, he's almost like family," said my father.

"Where is he now?" I asked.

"In Orlando." It was a large city a hundred miles away.

This new family member, lawyer-nephew, never visited, called or wrote my father during the course of his brutal final illness. At that moment, while I was digesting this latest insult, Carolee called us to dinner, my first with the two of them.

"I made chicken salad for dinner," she said.

In her slow southern accent, the words sounded more like, "Aah maid chikun sal-ud fur dinna."

We sat down to the table where each plate had a leaf of iceberg lettuce lying on it. Carolee was dishing up her chicken salad from an aluminum bowl onto the lettuce leaf. It looked grey and unappetizing.

I sat down and picked up my fork, ready to cooperate with her cuisine even though I was a vegetarian.

"What is in this?" I asked after one excruciating bite.

"I brought home my left-overs from the Kentucky Fried Chicken that your dad and I had the other day. I combined them with some Granola that came as a sample in the mail and some mayonnaise".

"I'm not very hungry," I said, causing my father consternation. Carolee didn't like anyone not eating her food, but I was out of there and on my way to the beach.

The chicken salad said it all. My warm-hearted, funny, great cook mother was gone, and her sacred home, her private chambers, and her thousand precious choices, were all trampled under the chaos of my father's fast marriage and his new wife's clutter. The walls of the hallway leading to their bedroom had previously been lined with our family pictures. Now Carolee's family pictures were there too, like hijackers who had come to stay. I wanted the shout: Who are these people? But I stayed quiet for my father's sake. It was his house now. And hers.

Carolee not only had terrible insomnia, but also anxiety, depression, headaches, neck-aches and bowel problems. With my vertigo and my father's mounting illness (he had a catheter and severe bladder pain), and

Carolee sleepless, we were weakened further by guilt reinforced by the fear of communicating with one another. I lost touch with my life. During the two weeks I was with them, I spent a lot of time in the living room, rocking in my mother's chair, looking at old pictures and thinking about her.

I didn't wonder that Carolee couldn't sleep, because by that time I knew the willful spirit of my mother was there. She floated in the living room and down the hallway to my bedroom like a cool breeze around my shoulders, a wrap of death. No one in that house would rest until my mother did. The expanding dark hole that her heavy energy occupied would sicken and swallow us.

The last night with my father and Carolee I finally found the courage to cut my bonds and leave. Paralyzed by guilt and fear, sick with vertigo, I knew that nothing could change for me, no matter how long I waited. I would not get well in my mother's house. No one could, because my mother was still there. That last night, I knew it was either go or die. I lay in my mother's living room, under her organ bench, because my stepmother's furniture took up all the other floor space. I began to cry quietly, but uncontrollably, curled into a fetus, reliving the agony of birth into and out of my natal family. It was three in the morning and never had I felt more homeless, soulless and lost.

My options, dizzy and car-less, were few. My closest friend lived fifty miles away. I looked up her number in the phone book and wrote it down, waiting for 7 a.m. to roll around, the earliest possible time I thought I could phone her. Even under the organ bench, I could hear my father and stepmother in the bedroom down the hall when they awoke. They were up with headaches and pills. And more crime reports on channel two.

"Damn immigrants, damn feminists, damn criminals," my father shouted in the distance. If hell is a state of mind, here it was.

At 9 a.m. my friend Susan and her boyfriend Robert, a magician and club bouncer, were outside the house in her BMW. Without prior notice, and without packing, I told my father I was leaving. He wanted me to stay (apparently he had some further humiliation in store for me), but it was time to go. Robert was in the living room when my father stood between the door and me. Robert took my father by the arm and moved him aside. Then he escorted me to the car.

I sat in there while Robert returned to the house, went into my bedroom, packed my clothes, and carried out my suitcase. My father and Carolee watched in astonishment. They had never seen anyone move so quickly. The whole escape took under five minutes.

I swore I would never visit that house of decay and death again. But a few weeks later our family karma continued in evil decline. My father phoned me early one morning in Miami, just after I had become healthy and happy again, with awful news.

"Good morning, honey," he said, as if we were the best of friends again. "I have bad news for you."

What other kind did he ever deliver to me? I thought.

"Your brother was hit by a car last night, riding his motorcycle home from the races. He's in intensive care with severe head injuries. They don't expect him to live."

"You're joking," was my immediate reply.

"I wish I was," he said, "but it's true. He went out of here without his full helmet. He was wearing one of those half helmets. I told him it was dangerous, but he wouldn't wear the full one."

"What are you talking about?" I demanded, seeing through his attempt to somehow say he deserved his accident. "Tell me where he is and what is happening to him."

"He's at Halifax Hospital. He was operated on last night and is in a coma."

"What about Brenda?" I asked. Brenda was my brother Jeffrey's wife.

"She was on the back of the bike but is okay. She's taking care of him in intensive care because she's a nurse. But we're not talking to her. Carolee doesn't like her. And to top it off," my father continued darkly, "Carolee and I had an accident on our way home from the hospital last night. She's in a neck brace. Someone hit us from behind."

Now I was certain my mother was taking revenge on us all. Dad, Carolee and Jeffrey had each been injured by vehicles which struck them from behind. They hadn't see the dangerous vehicles coming. Destiny had knocked them all off the road. Dad and Carolee were in neck braces, and my brother was in hospital, unconscious. I was grateful not to be there.

But I still had a troubled feeling that my Mom had caused all this harm. It was like being in a thick family stew with the heat turning up.

After another long drive, John and I arrived at the familiar hospital. Brenda came out of the room Jeffrey was in to talk to us. She looked terrified and exhausted.

"I'm so glad you're here," she said. "I don't know if he can pull through this one."

"What happened, Brenda?" I asked.

"We were riding down Highway 92 and stopped at a light. A car hit us from behind and left us on the sidewalk. Someone else got the license plate. Jeff's helmet flew off and his head hit the pavement. He had a 90% hematoma covering his brain, which the surgeon relieved last night."

"Can we see him?" I asked.

"Yes, you can. But do you want to? His head is the width of his shoulders and he's badly cut up."

"You're right," I said. "I can't take that. We'll stay out here."

Brenda's mother arrived from her home down the coast and took a room at the hospital. We booked a room at a local motel and stayed a week. During that time my father came with Carolee to the hospital every night. They sat uncomfortably in the waiting room for an hour or so, needing their own healing after their car accident. Brenda came out and saw him there a couple of nights later, and he got up to talk to her.

"I brought the clothes you asked for," he said, handing her the clothes she had left at the house so she could change after three days in the same bloodstained gear.

"Thanks," she said.

"I just want you to know," said my father, "that if Jeff makes it out of this you can't come to our house for his recovery. Carolee won't have it."

My father was a genius at bad timing and making painfully blunt statements. He hadn't learned how to pad life with equivocating feelings, like, "I'm so, so sorry," or "This is a tough situation, and I wish I didn't have to tell you this," or anything similar.

A week later my brother was out of intensive care and on his way to Michigan for rehabilitation at a brain center. It was a miracle he lived. But would he recover his memory and his life? It was time to call Ernesto and take care of my mother before something else happened. My brother in Las Vegas was still out of harm's way, but no one was safe in my father's house.

"Ernesto, hola! Que tal?"

"Muy bueno. Hey, hello!" I heard the familiar deep voice reply.

"I need a reading badly," I said.

"Get over here," was his reply.

CHAPTER 14

Preparation

> Despite the absence of a direct causal connection between the ritual and the desired outcome, performing rituals with the intention of producing a certain result appears to be sufficient for that result to come true.
> — Francesca Gino & Michael I. Norton

I DROVE LIKE A MAD WOMAN down US1 to Ernesto's house, which greeted me like an oasis of heart in a desert of materialism. Ernesto understood the bigger questions of life. He would know immediately if my mother's spirit was still in her house, unable to make further progress after her painful death because of her husband's betrayal. For a moment the part of me that is a skeptical academic appreciated the jump I had made in believing what I felt and experienced rather than what others expected me to accept.

When I arrived at his home Ernesto and I hugged for a long time. I was conscious of how small he was, very thin, not tall, with a narrow frame. I was a giant next to him. I savored the familiar smell of his aftershave. As usual he looked immaculate in a pressed white guayabera style, long sleeved shirt and pressed dark slacks. He was never barefoot, always in polished shoes, his hair was perfectly coifed and his nails were shining and trimmed: an elegant Cuban man.

His home felt disciplined to me, as if dark and light energies were balanced and held at bay. Ernesto's was outside the Miami vibe of traffic and money, drugs and sex. I was moving circularly when there, not linearly, coming back to where I belonged, my cycloid, the point on the circle, creating its own arc beside an infinite number of cycloids on the circumference of the circle, also creating their own arcs. I wanted to know more. The road to self-knowledge is the only journey we can make. There is no end, but plenty of corrugations, diversions and uphill climbs.

Ernesto had known about my troubles because I had seen him at an initiation when I returned to Miami. There we talked about my family and he shook his head in sympathy. He was busy with his new child of the Orishas and could not talk to me for long. I danced my heartache to the music of the drummers who celebrated Ana Maria.

Soon I was alone with Ernesto, ready to tell him everything and seek the advice of the Orishas. Within ten minutes of sitting in his office I had described the disruptions, illnesses and accidents that had happened to my father, to Carolee, to my brother and to me from the time of my arrival at my Dad's house.

"Ernesto," I said, "I think my mother's spirit is still around our home, causing trouble, unable to leave. My father and Carolee upset Mom's funeral by holding hands in church and looking dewy-eyed at one another. There was no grieving time for Mom. Her husband and family denied her respect and love."

Ernesto was listening intently. He asked me to go on.

"Everyone saw my father and Carolee holding hands while the minister spoke about my mother," I said, listing this as the worst offense on the day of her funeral.

"Tell me about Betty," Ernesto asked.

"Betty was a woman no one could ever forget," I replied. "Her funeral was crowded with people. It was standing room only. The overflow went out the door. Many women were there whose babies were nursed by my mother at the local hospital. They told me stories about how wonderful my mother was to them and how they would never forget her. She was someone they all could trust, who brought joy into the room. One woman told me Betty brought a book my friend Anita and I wrote to the hospital. She left it on her desk to show everyone who came by. I never knew she even looked at my book!" I cried and told Ernesto how I never knew she paid attention to what I was doing. It was too late now.

I thought Ernesto must wonder how we Anglos could leave our families so far behind us and yet expect to have happy outcomes. His own family lived a stone's throw away in Miami, and they talked on the phone constantly, sharing everything. His mother had been his mentor and guide to the spirit world from infancy, and his brother was his partner in religion and in business. He was inside his family dynamics in an intimate and intense way, while I was outside mine, conflicted and hurting. Family fractures tend to preserve us in the patterns of behavior and thought present at the time of the fracture. I was beginning to see how important it was for me to heal the fracture I felt with my mother.

"Did anything else happen on the day of her funeral?" Ernesto prompted me.

"I couldn't mourn her, Ernesto. I couldn't even cry for her. I choked on my grief, hid it inside. I had to handle the lunch afterwards at the house, be there for mom's friends and relatives, and my father and brothers. The day after the funeral was when my father confessed his adulterous affair, conducted while my mother declined in a nursing home, alone."

"How long has it been since she passed away?" Ernesto asked, calm and non-judgmental. He had heard many similar tales in his practice, and much worse.

"Almost three years," I said.

"She's hung around long enough," Ernesto commented. "If she is still there. Let's take a look."

He touched the cowrie shells to my forehead, then threw the shells many times. Finally, he handed me a shell and a stone to hide behind my back.

"Right hand," he said, as he took the stone from my right hand.

"Left hand,' he said, and found the shell there.

Once more, I traded the stone and shell between my hands behind my back. I was already feeling relief that the Orisha would help me order my life again.

"Right hand," he said. The stone again. "Left hand," he asked, which held the shell.

"Okay," said Ernesto, "We have an answer. Your mother wants a ceremony. Here is what you have to do."

He proceeded to give me detailed instructions. We made a time to meet a few days later at his house.

"Don't worry," he said, "we can help her move on."

I thought about the reading the whole way home and well into the night. I could hear the waves of the Atlantic from my window on the Key, and watched the moon come up. My mother was angry, but not with me, not really. My father's affair with Carolee trapped me inside its web as much as her. We were both hurt by it. I had created suffering for my mother, and for me. Now it was time to heal my relationship with her. I owed her proper mourning and a ceremony for just the two of us, which would erase the miserable day of her funeral.

Ernesto had explained a lot more about the Dilogún reading before I left. I put it together in a way that made sense to my life. The sign that appeared in the reading was called *Oya and her Masks*. Ernesto explained that Oya, one of the great Orisha of the Yoruba, wears nine different masks. These disguise her when she encounters death and departed spirits. One of her many roles is the transporter of one's soul when it separates from the body and moves through its spiritual journey. Oya witnesses our death and escorts our soul into its new spiritual reality. That is why she is associated with the cemetery. Oya accompanies our body to its resting place, and she returns our soul to its original spiritual home. This is why Oya brings peace. The deity of death, Ikú, provides the service of ending material suffering. However, it is Oya who brings peace. In my mind, I saw the porcelain mask with the wide black eyes my mother bought at the end of her life staring at me in her bathroom. Was Oya waiting for her then?

Oya meets the egun, the spirit of the dead one, and directs it forward into spiritual peace, which allows the newly departed to continue on her spiritual evolution. Oya talked about my mother, Betty, in the reading. Betty had not gone forward into her own peace. She was stuck in the conflict surrounding her family on Earth, yet she had no place there.

Ernesto said the ceremony that we needed was *The Ceremony to Cause Peace*. I loved that phrase. Where else could I find a ceremony in fractious Miami to cause peace? Causing war is easy. We all know how to do that. Giving in to our rancor, our irritation, our arrogance, and going into conflict and combat with perceived enemies, is second nature to us all. However, cultivating and creating peace is something we have to practice and work hard to achieve. It takes a conscious effort and the will to drop a lot of ego protection, justification and blame. It is not a natural inclination for most of us, who think winning is destroying our enemy. At the very least, we all want to be right. Conceding mistakes or letting the other person have the victory does not come naturally. Not many of us even know that it is possible to bring about peace, or that peace is a better victory than war. We think peace should be a state that occurs without our effort.

"No," Oya said, "peace is something you do actively. And it is time to cause peace for Betty and for you." The powerful Orisha had spoken.

On the morning of the ceremony, following Ernesto's instructions, I prepared nine of my mother's favorite foods. While I was shopping for the ingredients the day before I had felt in touch with her in a tangible way. I could remember her desires and her tastes, and saw her eating and cooking, serving us food and enjoying a meal out. I remembered her enjoyment of eating together at family gatherings. I remembered the days she spent preparing feasts for all of us, which I seldom appreciated as much as I should have. It was only after her departure that I discovered no one loved me as my mother did. The absence of that love was a vital organ gone missing.

We were living on Key Biscayne, in a condominium by the beach. From my kitchen I could see and hear the water. It was there that I cooked for Betty.

First, I prepared a choice piece of prime rib for her. I was a vegetarian for thirty years and even refused Betty's turkey at Christmas a couple of times while I smugly drank carrot juice. That carrot juice never loved me as Betty did. Now I honored her tastes and prepared what she liked the best. Could I only be thoughtful when someone was dead, I wondered? My tears began to flow. I put the fillet in the grill and cooked it just the way I knew she would like it, a bit rare on the inside, nice and browned, nearly blackened on the outside.

Next, I made a turkey sandwich from the best turkey and filled it with lettuce, tomato, mayonnaise and sprouts. She had started to use sprouts at the end of her life. I salted everything well, just as she liked. I remembered how much I criticized her for it. I was such a critic, so uptight, so hard for her to love. I wanted her to be healthy, but I came off like a morality squad, lecturing from a moral high ground.

It was curious how the cooking for my Mom brought up so many of the issues I had with her. My mind swung between my cooking and our relationship. I don't think she was that happy with me at the end of her life. Or maybe with anyone. She and my father died alone.

Switching back to the turkey sandwich, I made potato salad with mustard, onions, mayonnaise and celery, the way she taught me when I was a little girl. We used to take that potato salad to her family reunions where there would be a couple of hundred people. I loved it the way she made it with the potatoes so well cooked they were mushy. The taste of soft warm potato mashed in my mouth with mayonnaise brought back the warmth of the summer sun in Pennsylvania where I grew up and the thrill of the first swim in icy summer water.

Then I sliced big, ripe, juicy tomatoes, the best I could get in Florida, where the tomatoes are mealy and tasteless compared to the vine ripened ones Betty and I raised in our garden when I was a child. The tomato reminded me of my Aunt Lucille, who was a fabulous cook. Every summer we visited her just as the tomatoes in her garden perfectly ripened, and we had a hamburger barbecue with homemade ice cream. Uncle Bob would arrive home from his volunteer fireman job (his other family, in fact) to turn the crank handle on the ice cream. Oh, the taste of that fresh ice cream with peaches as ripe and sweet as the tomatoes!

I added a banana salad to the feast, because my mother loved bananas, or at least she ate one for every breakfast, to get potassium she said. Then I cooked some green beans, as another memento of our garden in Pennsylvania. Chocolate chip cookies baked as I worked on the other dishes, which included big juicy prawns and sauce, fried egg sandwiches (she loved these at midnight when she couldn't sleep), and finally I added a lemon meringue pie.

The chocolate chip cookies stopped my tears and made me feel like I was arriving at my mother's house after a long trip away. Of course, I had bought bottles of her favorite Chablis and prepared coffee. It was the one thing she kept asking for, even while the tubes were in her stomach, the one thing she never stopped craving after her strokes. Like all of us, coffee gives hope with a fast rush. I often joked with her that we wanted coffee more than we wanted God. She actually laughed and agreed.

After three hours in the kitchen I had prepared nine different foods that my Mom loved. They were foods that had moved her. Some, like beef, butter and sugar, I had argued against. I was certain those foods weren't good for her, and I hassled her when I could. If only she were still on Earth, I would have joined her in a feast featuring these delicious foods.

I had learned my lesson, which I still couldn't put into neat words. Something about being a stuck-up prig came to mind, alongside the too-late-now mantra of mean, cool kids like me. Well, it *was* too late. The best I could do was celebrate her memory and evoke her spirit with a group of like-minded friends.

I arranged each of her foods on a brand new, white ceramic plate. The plates were shiny and clean when I carefully placed my offerings on them. The turkey sandwich was so tall and thick I had to cover it with plastic wrap to keep it from falling over. There was lettuce, onion, tomato, cheese slices, mustard, mayonnaise and many slices of turkey. I wish I had thought of adding bacon, because she would have loved that, too. I placed her grilled prime rib on one of the shining white plates. I added mashed potatoes made with cream to the steak plate, salting and peppering both. I wanted to run my index finger through the potatoes which I had arranged in a spiral, creamy and inviting. I resisted and was sorry later.

The nine different dishes I'd prepared for Mom sat around me like a banquet in the small, white kitchen in our little apartment by the sea. I would have liked to tarry for a few minutes, but I was almost late, and Ernesto's house was well over an hour away.

I covered and stacked all my plates on large trays so I could carry them to my car. Then I carefully showered, washed my hair, and dressed in white, including my underwear, which was new, as Ernesto had instructed. I watched myself in the mirror as I put my elekes, my beaded necklaces from the Orishas, over my head. I took a Polaroid photo of myself, camera-covering my face with necklaces resting on my white dress. The colours of my beads intertwined. They were strung in different arrangements of colour, according to the specific path of the Orisha appropriate for me. These were the vibratory frequencies of the five most powerful Orishas, protection I carried with me. It was the first time I had worn them out of the house.

I was conscious of my appearance, dressed all in white with the elekes around my neck, as I descended on the elevator from the floor of my apartment into the parking garage. A Latino rode with me, and I was sure he knew I was involved with Lucumí. He pretended to look the other way. Everyone in Miami has a subliminal recognition of the practices. Many misconceptions and superstitions surround Lucumí. Some believe it is a dark path, stuffed with cursing and sickeningly bloody animal sacrifice. Numerous people in Miami know that dressing in white and wearing beaded necklaces and bracelets is likely a sign of the faith. I could see why so many Orisha followers kept a low profile.

I stopped at a florist's shop on my way to Ernesto's home. The smell of the flowers was strong in my car as I crossed the bridge over the sparkling blue Biscayne Bay. I had a long wait at the intersection before turning onto South Miami Avenue, which runs along Biscayne Bay to Coconut Grove. The traffic was slow; someone had their car hood up and was blocking part of the road.

As I waited, I realized I was stopped in front of the Catholic Hermitage of the Virgin of Compassion. She was Caridad, from Cobre, Cuba. The sanctuary of the Hermitage houses the symbol of Cubans in exile—a doll-like representation of Caridad, who unites the Miami exile community with their families and friends in Cuba. This sacred doll is a likeness of the Virgin Mary in her epiphany as saviour of three fishermen, two Native American brothers and a black slave. This was in the Bay of Nipe, off the coast of El Cobre, near Santiago de Cuba. The name Caridad means Charity. You can feel an almost palpable maternal healing energy near her shrine in Biscayne Bay.

Caridad's festival day every September attracts tens of thousands of people to her hermitage in Miami, the largest pilgrimage site in America. The Lucumí say the Virgin of Compassion is a manifestation of Oshún, the beautiful, golden orisha of sweet water, and that Oshún was the one, not the Virgin Mary, who saved the fishermen from drowning. A river runs out to sea where the Virgin appeared, which is why the Lucumí say the Virgin is really Oshún, because it is Oshún who is connected with rivers. Since the arrival of the Cuban refugees, whether one is a Lucumí devotee, a Catholic, or both, Caridad represents the divine power of compassion that brings people safely over the sea from Cuba to Miami. People joke that Caridad was the first rafter, because her image appeared to the three fishermen on a wooden tablet.

When the Catholic Church built Caridad's shrine in Miami on Biscayne Bay's sparkling waters it sought to create a sacred pilgrimage place that could lure people away from the "superstitions" of Lucumí. However, although the Hermitage attracts hundreds of thousands of pilgrims every year, limiting belief in Lucumí has not been very successful. A local Catholic clergyman was quoted as saying there are many congregants from his church who belong to the "baptized multitudes," yet who visit the "ministers of Lucumí" looking for "good luck, health, protection and predictions about the future."[11]

The Catholic priest's words made me laugh as I waited in bumper-to-bumper traffic, stuck in front of Caridad's shrine. Seriously, who wouldn't want the things the priest referenced—good luck, health, protection and future knowledge? Heaven is a long way off, and meanwhile I have problems in the real world, problems that are Lucumí's specialty. So here I was, journeying to a ceremony officiated by a minister of Lucumí. I was one of the "unbaptized multitudes" looking for healing and protection, as the Catholic priest had feared.

I drove through the crowded village of Coconut Grove onto Old Cutler Highway, which was lined with the last old trees left after the developers had finished. It was noon and the sun shone straight down through these giant banyan trees arched over the road, mottling it with leafy shadow. Old Cutler brings back memories of Florida before it was filled with malls and condominiums. Those of us who are Miami natives try to stay off expressways, keeping to back roads like Old Cutler, where there are still giant trees and no billboards. I drove over the lacy shadows, the colossal deep green Banyan trees arching over my head. I felt elevated by the tropical beauty that still thrills me on a perfect Miami day. The sky was cloudless and cerulean blue, and the air warm and humid.

Old Cutler kept me off US1, the ugliest highway in America, an unending ribbon of strip malls. Ernesto's house was at the southern end of Old Cutler, just across the US1, near an historic district of older homes and Key West style shops.

Then I remembered why I was making the journey south to his house. I remembered my mother and tried to concentrate on her and my mission to create peace for her. Today's ceremony, blessed by blue sky and harmonious weather, would go well, I thought.

At the same time, I remembered the conflict with my father. He was unwell, and my heart filled with ambivalent feelings about him and his new marriage. My brother Jeffrey was still recovering in a head injury center in Michigan. I had not seen my youngest brother in years because he belonged to the Jehovah's Witnesses and could not participate freely in our family.

My natal family was deeply wounded and breaking apart. I became less sure of what I could accomplish with the ceremony to bring peace to Betty. I tried to think of her and of healing my relationship with her. One thing at a time.

CHAPTER 15

Peace Meal

> It isn't enough to talk about peace. One must believe in it.
> And it isn't enough to believe in it. One must work at it.
> — Eleanor Roosevelt

AFTER I ARRIVED at Ernesto's we immediately went to his backyard, without lingering over conversation or coffee as we usually did when I came for a reading. The Sun, high overhead, signaled it was time for the ceremony, which would begin when the Sun made no shadows.

I carried my trays of food, flowers, and my bottles of wine from the car and placed them on the long wooden table used for al fresco dining under the veranda roof. The veranda looked onto a large garden filled with palms and other tropical trees. A terracotta fountain surrounded by Mexican tiles adjoined the veranda, water flowing over its lip onto a water garden. The sound of falling water intimated tranquility and timelessness.

Three others were waiting for me: Nydia, Ernesto's wife and my madrina, and two priests, Jesus and Blue. I greeted each in turn. They had experience in Lucumi ceremony and were there to assist Ernesto in the ceremony and to help me. We waited by the side of the table where, in addition to my food, Ernesto had added other items he would need.

He picked up a piece of soft white chalk from the table and stood in front of each of us. One by one, he drew a white circle on our foreheads. The circle took in the third eye and curved upward to the hair line. I looked at his handiwork, seeing similar circles uniting us in sign and symbol.

In front and to the right of the veranda was an outdoor bathroom. It stood on a pad and was raised, making it an extension of the veranda. Its door was closed. Ernesto walked to the bathroom and opened the door. I could see the concrete floor and the small, white curtained shower inside the room.

Ernesto bent down to the floor and with the chalk in his hand, he first drew one spoke, then several others, all radiating from the shower and out the bathroom door towards the four of us standing on the veranda.

He then asked me for nine white candles, which I had packed at the bottom of one of my food bags. I handed them to him. He carefully placed the candles into paper cups and set them between the spokes of the chalk circle at different distances from the bath, lighting them as he went. They provided a flickering pathway to his work.

Ernesto took a large white enamel basin from a storage closet and placed the basin inside the shower stall on the floor. He stepped outside to ask me for Betty's wine. I found her Chablis and spent some moments opening it before I handed the open bottle to Ernesto. He carried the bottle into the shower, knelt beside the basin, and took a small piece of bread from his pocket, placing it on the bottom. With his other hand, he poured a little of the Chablis on top. This was the initial libation made to Betty (Elizabeth), an opening of the ceremony to move her spirit into peace and away from us on Earth.

I remembered reading in the I Ching that the initial libation of a Taoist ceremony preceded the actual sacrifice or ceremony. Its purpose was to begin the transformation, deep in feeling, that moved people from chaos to peace. My mind quickly evaluated how that was happening in this simple Lucumi ceremony. Our ebó (sacrifice) for Betty had been announced by the libation poured by Ernesto. It could now proceed.

We were taking part in a ceremony that didn't require animals to die. It needed no blood to be efficacious. Instead, the actual meaning of the ebó was the time, energy and concentration we were all giving to Betty's spirit and its evolution to a higher plane. The idea of sacrifice was much deeper than the popular press could imagine. The ebó in its most personal and transformative meaning required that one give up something important in order to initiate a change.

Betty needed attention, love, care and commitment from me. She needed to know that I loved her as a daughter and wanted only to assist her spiritual ascension. I needed to know that Betty could go on and be happy in her life after death. Perhaps she would choose to return to Earth soon. However, Betty was still stuck in chaos, the limbo of not living and not quite dying, still trying to affect her family life, not accepting her fate, and not acting positively. Now we saluted her with the wine Ernesto poured into the bowl and told her we were beginning a ceremony to assist her evolution into the next phase of Death.

Ernesto returned to the middle of the veranda, pulled a chair out from the table, and sat down. He signaled I should stand on one side of him and Nydia on the other. Jesus and Blue were in front of us. Ernesto had a long silver staff decorated with birds on the top, the ancestor's staff, which he held in his right hand. Its bottom rested on the floor.

He began to tap the staff on the concrete veranda tiles, creating a tempo for the chant in Yoruba. My Yoruba is almost non-existent now, but I could understand he was addressing the spirit of Betty and saying that I, her daughter, Judith, was here. Ernesto chanted Betty's name many times, until it became a hypnotic refrain.

The ancient chant went on, and as it did I felt myself growing calmer and steadier. The chant felt deep, old and full of the presence of spirit. I was amazed at the way Ernesto had transformed from my friend into a priest of stature and mystery, without donning fancy robes or sequestering himself behind an altar. He was simply sitting on a kitchen chair, dressed like a very urbane Miamian, yet as he sang his whole being changed. His concentration was completely on the ceremony, and his singing was beautiful. His voice was very appealing as he maintained a tempo flawlessly in counterpoint to the words.

While Ernesto chanted, Jesus slowly picked up, in turn, each of the nine white plates piled with my mother's favourite foods, and touched them to my shoulders, feet and crossed hands, starting with the steak and potatoes. Eight more times he performed this ritual, as I offered him the top of my head, my shoulders, hands, feet. Some of the dishes were still warm from cooking; all had been warmed a little by the hot Miami Sun.

Jesus took extra time touching each dish to my forehead, the back of my head, and finally to the very important crown chakra. The orí (head) receives special attention in Yoruba ceremonies because the orí contains the soul or destiny of a person.

After touching me with the plates to capture more of my energy signature, Jesus then carried each platter to the shower, leaving them just outside. He then took them one by one to the edge of the white basin. There he lifted each platter over the bowl and ceremoniously scraped its contents into the white basin. I watched as he repeated this with all the foods I had prepared: the prime rib and mashed potatoes, the turkey sandwich, the fried egg sandwich, the salad, the grilled cheese, the mashed potatoes, the potato salad, the lemon cream pie and the chocolate chip cookies. This was a banquet for a queen, all mysteriously disappearing into the small bath at the other end of the spokes and candles.

Until that conglomerating occurred I had imagined us dining on part of the food, at least. Now it was piled together, like a feast for a wild animal. Jesus resembled an alchemist, bent over his experiment, teasing spirit from flesh. What had taken a day and a morning to create disappeared in a few minutes into the maw of the enamel bowl.

Meanwhile, Ernesto was chanting. We accompanied him. Nydia, Blue and Jesus joined Ernesto in calling Betty's egun (spirit) to come to the feast and partake of her ceremony. We had chanted for about fifteen minutes when I finally felt my mother on the veranda beside me. The air was thick and my eyes saw everything through a slight mist of tears and emotion. All of Betty's culinary desires collapsed into that moment, the history of the foods she loved, and the foods she fed her family. I felt the love that bound us made public.

She was there for just a moment. I held her in my heart. If I could have had her back, I would have. I wanted her. I loved her then as much as ever. Then the moment passed, quickly replaced by a feeling in my heart that she was gone. It was an empty feeling, but a feeling that was entirely different from how I felt while I carried her mighty grief inside my heart, or while I was preparing her feast and recalling so much of my life with her. I knew I didn't want her to leave, but I had no way of keeping her with me. As I let her go, a giant space opened inside me; while I had kept her betrayal within, she had prevented my own going forward into life.

Sometime after this, while I was lost in deep feeling and thought, Ernesto gave a signal to Jesus, who walked over to the bath again and picked up one of the empty plates lying outside. He walked to the basin of food and stood over it with the plate. He produced a hammer and suddenly struck the plate in his hand. It smashed into several pieces and fell onto the food offerings. He repeated this task with the remaining white plates. He had to strike each plate several times to completely break it. One at a time, they fell in pieces on top of the food in the bowl.

The sound of the breaking china was quite jarring after the soothing chant. *There is no going back* that sound said to me. It was over. The broken plates dramatically illustrated that my mother's life on Earth was finished and our physical bond broken forever.

Finally, we shut the door. The bathroom had felt alive to me with the light of the candles and with the large bowl of food mixed with the broken china. I imagined that Betty had gone home after our party ended.

Ernesto invited me into the house, where we had a drink of water while he lit a cigarette and made Cuban coffee. I watched him smoke and drink the thick black brew as I had done each time I visited him. I wished that I could join them in the smoke and the coffee. It looked so convivial. I often had arguments with Ernesto about smoking. It was almost sacrilegious for a Cuban not to smoke. More than a token of their stolen identity, Cuban cigars were coveted in Miami, which was their actual place of manufacture. Cuban hadn't produced many of them for years, another victim of the failed state.

We chatted for a while, very casually, as if we were only a group of friends who happened to meet. Before I left Ernesto instructed me to wear light clothing for nine days, then return for another reading.

As we talked Blue went outside, opened the bathroom door, walked in and entered the shower stall. He put the food and broken plates, the entire contents of the libation and ebó, into a black plastic garbage bag.

Ernesto looked at me and gestured toward Blue and the bag. "Take that bag and throw it in a dumpster on your way back to the Key," he said.

"Okay. Just any dumpster? Should I do anything else?"

"No," he replied. "That will be enough. Just get rid of it fast."

Get rid of it fast! After the slow-paced afternoon, now I had to hurry. I put the heavy bag into the trunk of my car and started to drive. I went up

US1 instead of turning onto Old Cutler, because I knew I would quickly pass shopping malls and dumpsters. I had only driven a block or two when I saw a dumpster sitting behind a bakery. I turned right, into the parking area around the dumpster, and stopped in front of it. I got out of the car, opened my trunk, reached in and picked up the weighty black garbage bag full of the foods I had prepared early that morning. Now they were intermingled, their spiritual content gone, the new white plates broken into shards for the trash heap.

I returned to the island through the heavy traffic on US1, crossing the long bridge in a very different frame of mind than the one I had departed with that morning. There is often a "ritual let down" period in the wake of a very concentrated ritual ceremony. The *Ceremony to Create Peace* had begun with the reading at Ernesto's, progressed with shopping, matured in the kitchen, where my memories and summoning of my mom began in earnest. The ceremony at Ernesto's had passed quickly and now the magic was over for a while.

    I began nine days of dressing in white clothing and remaining in a state of consciousness that was as peaceful and serene as I could manage. Each of those nine days, I tried to think of my mother and to consciously let her go. She had come so close to me at Ernesto's house, then she departed. It was time to go on with my life.

    I liked to imagine that Betty met the Orisha Oya, two strong women in the same profession, on the afternoon of the *Ceremony to Cause Peace*. My mother had birthed infants into the world, and Oya birthed people out of the world. I thought they would like each other and I wished I could hear their conversation. My mother no longer needed to roam the cluttered hallways of the house she lived in while alive, unseen and unwanted. She no longer needed to exact her vengeance on husband, children and new wife. Her destiny on the Earth was complete. She needed to go on.

    Later, I discovered that this Lucumí ceremony to bring peace has a counterpart in Tibetan Buddhism. A Tibetan monk told me that if a spirit is living in a half-life like Betty, unable to evolve, the spirit or ghost is "trapped in the bardo." If a family has too much grief or anger, or if a ghost does not want to leave her possessions on Earth or let go of her family, the deceased may hang around in the bardo and try to communicate with the living. In all cases, too much attachment is at the root of the problem.

Soor is the name of the Tibetan ceremony used to call the deceased spirit into the presence of enlightened people who urge it to go on to higher planes. The Soor is the last supper fed to the ghost, the smoke eater, in order to free it from attachment to the earth. Attachment, my mother's and mine, was certainly at the heart of our problems. We both had too much emotion, too much anger, resentment and grief. Neither of us could let go. Attachment had trapped my mother in the bardo and me in stagnation.

By hosting a last supper for the ghost, the Tibetan monk and the Lucumí priest both bring peace to the living and the dead. The last supper of Christianity, where Christ meets one last time with his disciples, and Mary washes his feet with costly oil, is poignant and touching. The Last Supper is a final feast with a dearly beloved person after a special communion of food and drink. Betty and I parted after our last supper, which, while binding us together, celebrated our final goodbye.

CHAPTER 16

The Tornado and the Crossroads

> I believe that generally, men are still afraid of the dark, although the witches are all hung and Christianity and candles have been Introduced.
> — Henry David Thoreau

I ATTENDED A YOGA RETREAT on Sanibel Island, where I could practice yoga and gain perspective. A friend taught the class, the kind where you tie yourself into twists and sitting postures, with straps wound around your legs or arms to bind you in the pose. It's not my favorite, I have to admit. I prefer a moving yoga routine. However, the supported postures allowed me to relax my breathing, which had been short and tight in my chest. Between sessions, John and I jumped in the ocean and walked the beaches. Sanibel was known for its shells and nearly pink sand.

I was there three days, almost forgetting the sad, bad stuff, when the phone rang in the morning, before my class began. John said my father was on the phone. I had given him the number before leaving Miami, not thinking he would need to use it.

Oh no, I thought. *In my whole life with my father, nothing good has ever come off a phone call from him.* I picked up the receiver.

"Hi, honey," he began ominously, deceptively sweet as always. "I'm sorry to have to disturb you there, but I just wanted to tell you the doctor says I have bladder cancer. He wants to operate right away."

I knew he was sick; no one with the limited amount of breath he had could be well. But I hadn't expected cancer. I didn't know that cigarette smoking causes bladder cancer, especially in men. None of us can ever believe her parents are vulnerable to the scourge of cancer. But here it was. It was real. My father's time was limited. He was already home with a catheter, unable to pass water by himself, with the pain growing daily.

We returned to Miami and I decided I needed to talk to Ernesto again. Through all the years I knew Ernesto I had never needed frequent Dilogún readings. My life had gone on pretty much according to the goals I set myself, and the Odu confirmed that when I very occasionally visited him for a reading. Now I felt like my life and health were out of control.

Much had happened since my return to South Florida. I was flooded with emotion. From the moment I returned the trip was about my natal family, my mother's unhappy ghost, my brother's accident, my stepmother overturning our family dynamic, and my own contraction and ill health.

In addition, my youngest brother was in Las Vegas, stuck in a limbo state between membership in the Jehovah's Witnesses and leaving them entirely. I had barely spoken to him in twenty years, but I now needed his help with our father. My other brother was still in hospital. His doctors didn't want him to hear disturbing news. I was the only child present to deal with my father's illness.

"Ernesto, what's going on?" I asked him.

"Come on over later in the afternoon," he answered, "and we'll take a look at it."

I drove to Ernesto's house in the Redlands, passing slowly through the Grove and down Old Cutler. I knew the drive so well I could go into a trance, half in the world of cars and highways, half in the world of my own troubles. I couldn't leave my dark thoughts alone. I felt weak and helpless, and was creating more loss and pain in my own head, the worst kind. I felt the giant banyans as I drove slowly under their patterned shadows, tattooing my body and my car into a single organism on the highway.

I knocked at the door. Natalia, Ernesto and Nydia's cocker spaniel, knew me and did not bark at my arrival. She stood up, looked out the door, wagged her tail, then lay down again to a long tropical nap. I could hear Spanish music playing in the backroom and assumed Ernesto must be listening to a CD.

I knocked again, harder this time. There was no reply. Finally, I walked around to the back of the house. The veranda, the shower room and whole backyard were quiet, as if sleeping. There was no sign of our recent peace ceremony for my mother, or any of the other ceremonies held over many years in the lush, palm-lined garden.

Suddenly the back door opened and Ernesto put his head out. "Get in here," he said. "I didn't hear you knock."

We stood in the kitchen while he made his Cuban coffee and smoked a cigarette. He always had so much happening, people coming for his advice, political irons in the fire in Hialeah, and obligations to his children. His son, Ramon, had received scholarships to Tulane and MIT and had chosen Tulane, my own alma mater. New Orleans was the place I met Vodou. I thought of Ramon walking the same streets I had walked at his age.

Finally, after talking for a half hour, we walked back to Ernesto's consultation room. He had changed it since I'd been there last. Now his room was simpler. There was no Lucumí altar or offerings, just a small curved desk, some shelves holding up books and a couple of African icons, and a large statue of the Buddha with a candle burning in front of it. A picture of Ernesto in African shirt and hat on the front page of the Miami Herald was framed on the wall behind the desk. I thought how much more ecumenical Ernesto had become in the years I had known him. And how much his philosophy now revolved around finding peace. The Buddha was his central image. Lucumí was like Hinduism: it could absorb everything with resonance.

Ernesto's computer was up and running. He opened it to the Dilogún program he created to keep a record of his client's readings.

"Okay, Judith," he began. "Let's see what's going on now. We know that your sacrifice for Mom was received and that the Orisha are beginning to channel fortune to you on Earth. But let's read it again and see what is happening around you."

The shells touched my forehead and Ernesto began to throw them onto the divination mat on his desk. Again and again he mixed and tossed the shells, waiting for the sign to become clear. Finally, he handed me the stone and shell. I accepted them and juggled the two between my left and right hands behind my back. Yes, no, yes, no, yes, no. The shells were answering questions Ernesto posed to them about the location, nature and context of my relationship to the universe.

"This one's clear and straightforward," he said when the process was complete. "You have the blessings of your ancestors. You know Judith, that is always where I find your blessings. The sign that is coming up for you is called, *Victory Over Strong Enemies*. Another name for it is *The Tornado and the Crossroads*. Welcome back to south Florida, Judith!"

"Shit," I said, at a loss for any more descriptive word. "That describes it so perfectly. This tornado has just about wiped me out, and I'm at a crossroads. What better way to describe the loss of my family? What do I need to do? What happens now?"

"This Odu deals with one who is on a long journey, but with no specific direction. This journey has been bitter and sweet. You've returned now to the same place you are from. This is a destiny journey for you. It was in your file that you would return now and face this situation."

"I wish I could see the contents of that file and not just recognize it in retrospect! Why do we have to walk blindly into the things that are our closest destinies? Ernesto, what does this have to do with my family and the things that have been happening to me?"

"This odu predicts potential enemies," he explained. "I would call it the return of the black witches. This is a situation where witches, evil spirits, come down and possess people in your family. This odu also deals with the unknown aspects of life: the unseen, the grave, the inner depths."

"What do you mean by witches, Ernesto? You don't mean what I mean by witch, do you, a good person who heals with herbs and incantations, and who honours nature?"

"No, Judith, if that is a witch then that is not what I am. I am talking about the earthbound witches that the Yoruba world tells us about, those evil ones who possess the people who need illness and accident, death and destruction, to wake them up or to destroy them."

"So, they perform a service in a way and are part of the overall plan, our over-all destiny?" Powerful witches, aiye, were rumored to be behind very successful Yoruba business men who paid for their protection services, as well as the destruction of their enemies.

"Absolutely," answered Ernesto, "they give us our wake-up calls. Sometimes it's too late."

"What about me in all of this Ernesto. Why am I here?"

"The evil witches have been working in your family, causing disturbances, ill health and bad fortune. You've been pulled back in as a neutralizer. Shocking things are happening to your family because they're not listening, and shocks are happening in different ways. You are the mediator. You help them wake up."

"I hate that role," I said.

"Don't worry," he said. "You get to go far away and not play this role very often any more. In fact, the reading is suggesting that you should always live far away from your family members, or they will pull you into their lives where you don't belong."

"But for now I'm here. It feels like I'm right in the middle of everything, but I'm so uncertain about what to do," I said. "I feel I'm responsible for my father, yet I can't stand to visit him. Something did possess him after he married Carolee. She sucked the laughter right out of him. He was never a perfect father, nor was I a perfect daughter, to say the least, but he did tell lots of jokes and laugh readily. Now he seems dead before he's gone."

"You needed to depart from your family. Now it's time to get back into things and have your victory over your strong enemies. It was time for you to be pulled back to the United States. I can't tell you what you have to do to solve this, to neutralize it. Just remember that you are not responsible for it, but that you have to be strong and defend yourself. Don't let the witches convince you they are right. It is indicated that the Orishas will bless in heaven whatever you choose to do."

"So I don't need to do anything else, no more ebó (sacrifice), no ceremony, no nothing?" This was bad news as far as I was concerned. I wanted a fast, easy, solution that would lift me up and move me forward.

"No," said Ernesto. "As you know that would be far too easy. You have to figure out what to do. But you do see the outline of the situation now. What would hurt your fortune at this point is not being able to stay focused in one direction, to become chaotic. This is a test of your will. You must choose what to do."

"What a return to Miami!" I lamented.

CHAPTER 17

The Bed of Destruction

> Now we shall explain what it is we call Oya ...
> (She) Tore his house to shreds as he sat comfortably,
> Swept up all his money, all his clothes, everything ...
> What sort of thing is this?
> We looked around. Nothing to be seen.
> Aha! What sort of an invisible housecleaning?
> — Judith Gleason

A COUPLE OF WEEKS later John and I prepared to return to the distressed home of Farrell, my father, and Carolee, his wife. My father's cancer was causing him horrendous pain. Every few minutes he cried out. He was waiting for surgery, however his surgeon was vacationing for three weeks. Cruelly and heartlessly, he had abandoned his patient, my father, leaving him without adequate medication when he was clearly declining rapidly. I tried to find another surgeon, calling everyone in the phone book. I couldn't find one.

One doctor prescribed some painkillers, but they didn't work. All they did was block my father's digestive system. Whenever he tried to pass urine the pain took hold, making him first groan then shout in agony.

The day John and I arrived from Miami an ambulance simultaneously parked in the driveway beside us. He'd had a manual faeces extraction at the hospital, a treatment for his constipation. The paramedics unloaded my father and carried him on a stretcher into the house. They shifted him onto his bed, then said goodbye.

It was like receiving a tortured prisoner from one of Saddam's jails. It appreared the hospital procedure had added to my father's suffering, leaving him incontinent, unable to walk, and in even greater pain. We were unprepared and unable to cope with the physical, mental and emotional consequences of the disease. But we had no one to call on for help.

My father became weaker from crying in pain. He could no longer get out of bed on his own. He was continuously restless and uncomfortable. He couldn't sleep or rest. When the pain came, he wanted either my husband or me to be at his bedside, holding him, stroking him, talking him down. Although I phoned doctors constantly, took him to emergency rooms in the middle of the night, and had him conveyed in an ambulance to visit doctors in their offices, no one prescribed any pain medication to dull his torment. The most heartless comment came from his family physician, when he saw him on one of our emergency room visits.

He looked at the chart and said, "Well, Farrell, you've lived past the life expectancy for men and can't expect much more. You've been a smoker, too. Bladder cancer is caused by smoking. It's lucky your surgeon went to Vegas. Your cancer's spread and you would never have recovered from the operation." *Boom! boom!* and he left the room.

Maybe bluntness and the truth were best for my old Dad, who operated like that himself in life. But to me the doctor appeared cold and unsympathetic. He was the son of the man my parents went to for treatment most of their adult lives, the same doctor who repeatedly told my mother that smoking and cancer had not been proven to have a causal link.

Meanwhile, I tried to do my best for my Dad with techniques I had learned from yoga relaxation. But I wasn't equipped to work with this level of illness and trauma. My father was way beyond yoga therapy. I soon exhausted myself and was left unable to sleep.

My father's condition required constant tending by several people. When I had visited him a few months earlier, he had been breathless and tired. Now he was completely dependent on John, Carolee and me.

We were all frightened. Many unspoken and difficult emotions swirled between the four of us. I was angry with my father and felt abandoned by him. I had trouble feeling compassion for his situation. Yet as his oldest child, I was expected—or I expected myself—to take charge.

My father's new wife was a stranger to me, but she was present at every moment. I had lived in many different hells with my parents, and this was the culmination. Everything was brought together now, the consequences of addiction, the television news, the emotional abandonment, the betrayal of family and love, their false morality and religiosity, their hatred of everyone different, and the realization that my brothers and I had been torn apart by our parents and had no relationship with one another.

I was with my husband, but he couldn't imagine my mental nightmares or what it was like being a member of my family. Carolee had to bear me in her house. I had to bear her in what I still thought of as my mother's house. My father lay in pain, in his own excrement, in the middle of the world he created.

Although I could leave through the front door and not return, the mental and emotional damage would remain with me. There was no doubt in my mind that the evil witches Ernesto had spoken of had come to Earth bringing this horrific degeneracy and suffering. But I could not agree with Ernesto that I could be a neutralizer. In fact, there was almost nothing I could do except call my brother and ask him to come and take over. His training with the Jehovah's Witnesses had equipped him better than me to deal with the terminally ill. He would cope well and was not, I thought then, as damaged by our family as I was.

My father was stoical when I was a child, so to see him in such a state was unbearably distressing. He usually ran away from me when I was home, to the garage, to the car agency, to the store, and later, I knew now, to Carolee's house. He was never interested in my life, not in any real way that would have taken his time and energy. Now he wanted me by his bed, holding his hand, and negotiating with doctors.

"I need you every minute," he cried to me.

"I'm sorry Dad, I can't be here for you every minute," I said, broken and bleeding inside. "I'm tired and not feeling well myself. John and I need to return to Miami."

My conflict with this man extended far back into childhood. He had worked to put bread on my table, but was rarely present for me. He had criticized me, ridiculed me, forbidden me and beaten me. I could only remember one Christmas when I was eight that he played with me, when he pulled me on my sled over the snow, up and down the little terrace at the side of our house. Even at the time I knew that it was over too quickly. We could have shared that beautiful night for longer minutes together. I remembered that sled ride with my father like an icon of the perfect father/daughter relationship. For years and years I returned to it as a memory of love and laughter between us. For those minutes, my father had cared enough about me to take me for a sled ride in the dark night over the glowing white snow.

I couldn't honestly tell my father how angry I was with him for abandoning my mother and never getting to know his children. My concerns and feelings seemed so petty compared to what he was suffering. Maybe if he survived there would be time to clear my feelings with him. However, that never happened, just as it had never happened between my father and his parents, the strict Germans who treated him harshly.

I guess that's why my father repeatedly abandoned me, especially in his last years, taking me from his will as executor, ignoring my life and work, making me his confessor, criticizing my mother in front of me, and telling me he had not married my mother for love. In his distorted view, he was doing me a favor, making me tough, showing me what life was like, subtracting love and intimacy and adding gut wrenching denial, fear and repression.

My father lay in the antique bed that Carolee had brought to the house, a carved four-poster she inherited from her own mother and father, who slept in that four-poster in their last years of painful cancers. Carolee had cared for them both until they died, at which time she inherited their furniture. The heavy, wooden posted bed was a fond reminder to her of her parents. The bed was also a symbol to Carolee of her womanhood after the death of her parents, when she married, for the first time, my father, when she was in her late 60s. Now her husband of two years lay in that bed of pain, dying as her own parents had done, from the same illness.

Carolee's parents' bed was the first piece of her own furniture she moved to my mother's house after Mom's death. How could she not see the terrible irony? I wondered. The bedroom was the one my father and my mother shared for forty years, the one that Carolee and he shared on the day after my mother's funeral, when I heard their intimacies through the thin walls of the house.

Carolee's bed occupied the middle of the room. It looked out of place in the block Florida bungalow. That bed loomed large in my mind as a symbol of Death. My father was its third occupant to be dying of cancer. I could barely stand to look at it. We tried to keep my father comfortable, but it really wasn't possible.

On the second night of his greatest pain we heard my father screaming and shouting at the top of his voice. We all remained stiff with horror while the awful noise continued. Soon the screams resolved into a splintering crash. It sounded like the bed had exploded and fallen through the floor.

We rushed into his room. Dad was lying on the floor next to the bed. His hands held pieces of the bed posts. He had grasped the posts above his head and jerked them from their supports. The frame of the bed had collapsed, lopsidedly, to the right, throwing him off, the mattress under him also lurching onto the floor.

Seeing the four-poster fallen down, with my mother's picture still on the wall above it, I realized part of the evil was neutralized and could go no further. Objects contain our emotions too, and this bed knew it was time for it to fall. So, it did, under my father's weight and force. In falling, it said to all of us that the marriage was over, life was over, our family was finished. The bed of death was finished, too. It doesn't bear thinking about the magnitude of his pain as he pulled the bed apart.

Perhaps I had returned to be the mediator, the neutralizer. But all I could do was to hold myself together until my youngest brother finally arrived from Las Vegas. He helped me organise to have my father admitted to a teaching hospital.

The nurses there were very kind, tending him day and night. But the treatments he was given were very painful and did not work. However, my father wouldn't stop them, because he felt he would be committing suicide. I still can't bear to think about the surgeries and radiation that he received, nor his crying and pain. Nothing can prepare a family member for what goes on in a teaching hospital where methods are tried that are not considered elsewhere, in order to experiment with the last days of the terminally ill. None of this can be healed by simple, folk ceremonies.

When he was only a few days from death something happened that showed we do live in a universe which cares about our evolution. When my father was first admitted to the teaching hospital in Gainesville, the second bed in his room was empty. The next day the nurse wheeled in another patient who climbed into the empty bed. The man was black. A few minutes later his wife and children joined him by the side of his bed. His wife was a lovely woman with an outgoing personality. She said hello to all of us, then began to take care of her husband's needs behind the curtain the nurse drew between us.

Carolee looked at my father and they both rolled their eyes. It was their nightmare to share an intimate hospital room with negroes, as they still called people of darker skin colour. Brought up in the old south, the only black people Carolee had known were helpers in her house. I said nothing, thinking that it was too late to change them. I had fought my father about his racial prejudices all my life, but it was too late now. I kept quiet and resolved to get to know the new couple who were joking and laughing behind the thin curtain.

The next day, the doctor in charge of my father's treatments stopped by to talk to us. We stood around my father in his bed.

"There is nothing more we can do for you," the doctor said to my father. "The cancer is all through you."

I asked the inevitable question that everyone in this situation asks: "How long does he have?"

"Days, perhaps a few weeks at the most," the doctor answered. "The body is not far from death. We must find a suitable place for him now. We can't do any more for him here."

Until that moment, the doctor was reluctant to say Farrell would die quickly. Now it was certain. It was impossible to wish life for him with all the bags and tubes and support that his life of agony and misery required. There was nothing, no part of life, which was possible for him to enjoy. Carolee, my brother and I began to cry. So did my father. Hearing our crying, the wife of the man next to my father came over to us. She began by hugging me, then hugged the others in turn, including my father. She asked us to all join hands.

"Dear Lord," she prayed. "Help this beautiful family to accept the death of their father and husband. We know he is going into your care and that he will be cared for with your compassion and grace. Please ease his pain and suffering, and let him accept his own passing into your light and love. Let this family know how much you love them. We offer grateful thanks to you for bringing us together at this important moment. Amen."

When she finished her deeply healing prayer, she hugged us all once more and walked back to her husband's bed. Her words, *thank you for bringing us together at this important moment*, resonated in my mind for weeks.

Neither Carolee nor my father said a word about the colour of her skin again. They cried together and thanked her for her prayer and concern. They were able to receive the love that the woman brought, and to see, perhaps for the first time, the unity of all people. At least that is what I like to believe, after weeks of having listened to them in front of the television news, cursing in fear and loathing. At the zero hour, some of their hatred and fear were neutralized, replaced by love. The caring and gracious woman's prayer united us in love and caring for my father. She was a shining light, an angel, who my father and Carolee would not have chosen if they'd had the opportunity. Instead, fate chose for them that day. From then on, Death's presence was acknowledged.

A few days later, my father died in a nursing home near his home. His two or three days there were pain free, according to my younger brother, who traveled with him and stayed with him there. The nursing home director put some little drops in my father's mouth, which immediately stopped the pain and allowed him to sleep for the first time in days. I understand that American hospitals must now give cancer patients adequate pain management, but when my father died that was not the case.

My brother rang me in Miami, on what would be my father's last night, and surprised me by saying Dad wanted to talk with me. When I heard his voice it was coherent, and he could talk clearly, without moaning. He sounded like himself for the first time in weeks.

"Hi honey," he said. "I love you and I want you to have a good life." He repeated this many times.

"I love you too, Daddy," I said over the phone, guilty that I was not by his bed like my younger brother. I had returned to Miami, exhausted from the anguish, empty and lean. Two friends were with us for dinner, but my mind kept thinking of them and my food cooking in the oven as I spoke with my dying father. I felt the same impatience with him and wanted to get on with my life. How silly, in retrospect. It was my father's last hours and I could not think only of him. How can I complain about his lack of attention to me? Was I any more compassionate and caring than he was?

"Your brother is so good to me," he went on. "Thank you for all you've done for me." With the pain erased, he could think clearly. He recognized his life was nearly over.

"Daddy, I love you so much," I repeated again, "Thank you for everything you did for me in my life."

Strangely, there was nothing else to say. This loving phone call replaced the bad ones.

That night my brother awakened us at two in the morning. My father had died quietly in his sleep. I envisioned his spirit passing from the Earth, held in the wings of angels. I know my father had a tender heart and soul. The next time around, when we meet, we will appreciate each other better, I am sure. If there is an afterlife, and notions of reincarnation are true, I am sure that my father and mother will also have much to do together, in whatever planes of existence they may be traveling now.

Life and death hold endless surprises, scores of which we would never want if we were given the choice. Salvation comes in numerous forms, many of them accessible through prayer.

CHAPTER 18

Tree Adimú on Key Biscayne

> Indigenous people go to that unseen energetic place to try to repair whatever damage or disturbances are being done there, knowing that if things are healed there, things will be healed here.
> —Malidoma Patrice Some

ERNESTO HAD A SUGGESTION to help me start breaking out of my self-made cage. "Take an offering at noon to the tallest tree near the ocean. Spend some time quieting yourself and do whatever inspires you."

The next morning I donned my elekes (beaded Orisha necklaces) and went early to buy succulent fruits: mangos, paw-paws, bananas, pineapples, watermelon. I added Cuban yams, cassava and sweets to my shopping cart. After checking-out, I loaded my purchases into my backpack before walking out of the freezing store into the steaming Miami heat. I unlocked my bike from the stand under the windows where I'd left it. It was just after eleven, a clear, celestial sky above, on a typically scorching Key Biscayne summer day. I rode my bike out of the parking lot and down the boiling sidewalk. The fruits and vegetables jumped in my backpack when my tires rolled over the cracks in the pavement.

At the park entrance I stopped and paid the entry fee at the gate, then pedalled onto the bike trail, turning south toward the end of the island. The hot sun baked my shoulders and the back of my neck. Young Florida native trees, such as palmetto palms and live oaks, quickly enclosed the bikeway. Cicadas crackled from every tree. With pleasure, I noted that I could no longer hear the drone of Miami traffic. Leaving behind crowded Crandon Boulevard, Key Biscayne's main street, I had also left the island's condominiums, houses, shopping centers and hotels. When I crossed the boundary into the park, I felt the gradual transition from a human, manufactured world to a wild, natural one.

I pedalled halfway around the loop track, which circles the island, before I stopped my bike at a likely spot. There I dismounted. The still air had cooled me a little while I was moving on my bike, but now it covered me like a thick, hot blanket. I laid my pack on the trail and hid my bike behind some thick coco plums heavy with delicious red fruits.

Picking up my pack, I stepped into the young forest, leaf litter shuffling underfoot. I looked up at the cloudless firmament, searching for the tallest tree that was nearest the ocean. The sea lay to the east not far ahead of me; I could just hear the lapping of waves. After the recent hurricanes, which had toppled the old non-native pine trees, the park staff had replanted the land with young natives. They hadn't grown large enough to produce a shading canopy.

In full sunlight the undergrowth, not inhibited by shade, had grown thick and tangled. Only a few steps into the forest I had to stoop down to get below the impenetrable three- or four-foot-tall growth. I proceeded by crawling on my hands and knees, observing narrow trails forged by rabbits, raccoons, possums and other small mammals. One or two rabbits darted off as I pushed my pack in front of me beyond another low hanging shrub.

I kept craning my neck, trying to spot a tree which could shade me and serve as a focal point. I moved slowly, carefully assessing each place, standing up, then stooping down again, moving slowly on animal trails toward foliage that looked more substantial.

Finally, I reached a taller live oak tree, high enough to stand under. I straightened and brushed the leaves and stickers from my hands and knees. I placed my hands on the tree's trunk. I felt happy and somehow at home, so sat down under the oak tree's small shadow.

The ground under the leaf litter was sandy, the grasses a bit sharp. I set my pack beside me and closed my eyes for a few moments, softening my face and listening to my breath. Cicadas crackled in the heat, while ants crawled on my legs. Otherwise, there was only the hot silence that comes over Florida at noon, when humans stay indoors. At midday the light is so intense in Miami it erases sharp edges, colours dull, and shadows shrink. Perspiration was running down my face and back. It was August, the hottest month, and the intense heat exacted surrender. I sat back against the oak, trying not to move a muscle while the songs of the cicadas, their distinctive double clicks, reverberated around me.

After a few minutes I untied my pack, reached in, and removed the candy I had brought for Elegguá. I moved away from the shadow of the tree to a place where two animal trails joined, a natural crossroads. I lay my sweets in the center. Then I returned to the tree, stooped down to pick up my pack, stretched its opening wide, upended it, and allowed my fruits and vegetables to tumble out. I arranged this natural bounty around the base of the tree trunk until I felt the produce looked attractive and appealing. The live oak had scaly silver bark and dark waxy leaves, and the oranges, reds and yellows of my offering stood out in contrast.

When I had finished, the young tree appeared to spring from a cornucopia. She was about ten years old, the age when trees in Florida start to thicken and spread a crown of leaves that shade the ground. She had strong, young energy. She reminded me of the tree of knowledge in the Garden of Eden. But, thankfully, there were no vengeful male gods to fill me with terror and command my subjugation.

I noticed I cast no shadow when I placed my offerings. I could feel the Sun graze my head through gaps in the leaf cover, but it stood so directly above me that my body had no umbra. Even after this small exertion, I needed to sit down and cool off. I sensed the tree was quite female, calm and wise. I took a few minutes to relax myself thoroughly with long inhalations and long exhalations, while I tried to send my breath to the small crippled place inside, where I still grieved for my father.

A few minutes passed without healing inspiration. Then, almost without warning, my heart began to pour out its sorrow in songs and words. After a long while, I felt emptied and much better. I leaned my forehead against the tree. I could feel the tree's freedom from every concern. Her peeling, grey bark radiated a lustre that dazzled my eyes. I touched her, once again laying my hands on her round trunk. I wanted to hold her, to unite myself with whatever ancient purpose evolved with her on Earth. And I wanted that purpose and mine to be one.

The thought occurred to me that the live oak and I were sharing this zenith of a summer day on our little island park off the coast of Miami. Forever, this experience would entwine the tree and me. We were both witnessing the day, alive and present, together, touching one another, as the heat pressed us on all sides. The searing temperature was a world apart from air-conditioned apartments, which were nearly thirty degrees Fahrenheit cooler, located on the other side of the park gate. The broiling temperature kept other humans from visiting the forest. Alone under the tree, I was imbibing oxygen, freedom and inspiration. At that moment, I understood clearly that real Florida lived here—in the forest, under the tree, in the sizzling light, because the spirits of the land were here, embodied in the trees and in the earth.

I thought about the ancestors of the land, the Tequesta Indians who lived here centuries before me, who had preserved the beauty of the island and loved the bounty of the sea, creating large shell mounds, which grew enormous and became new natural islands. I thanked them for honoring the land with their lives for so long, and for adding to, rather than subtracting from, our lovely, wild world.

It's hard to explain, but I felt comforted knowing I was related to a much wider family, including the native peoples of Florida, as well as, I concluded, every human who had lived, stretching back to the first ancestors in Africa. They were my ancestors, too. Then I talked to my biological ancestors, to my mother and father, to my grandmothers and grandfathers, and to those who came before them. I explained why I was here. I spoke from my heart.

During my prayers I was conscious of the tree, the feeling of her bark, the smell of her resin, and the cushion of her fallen leaves on the sand. I thought about how the words *sacred grove* resonated with my soul, because trees are the most ancient life forms. There are ancient kahikatea trees on our land in New Zealand, whose own ancestors were young when dinosaurs lived under their limbs. I also knew that the ancestral line of the small oak I had embraced was at least sixty-six million years old.

That's why I'd had to come: to discover the Tree of Knowledge, also known as the Tree of Life. We have been entwined from the beginning: vascular plants' DNA contained the promise of the human even hundreds of millions of years ago.

Sitting under the tree that day I found it impossible to separate birds, insects, wind, sky, animals, earth, sun and rain. Worshipping in a grove puts a human being in the way of everything in nature. The activity unites the person with the wisdom inherent there. Many poets and mystics have seen beneficent, spiritual beings in or around trees. In Nigeria, the Yoruba once worshipped the Orisha in sacred stands of old growth trees, until these giants were destroyed by missionaries and colonial administrations. Rogue loggers and development projects now threaten to destroy the remaining stands.

Earlier in the morning, just prior to preparing to visit the Key Biscayne park, I had read an Orisha pataki (story) about the Yoruba Tree of Knowledge. I've adapted this intriguing story and will tell it now because it summarizes the profundity of ancient trees.

A long time ago, when the world was full of wonders, the young god Ogún was the favourite son of his mother Yemmu and his father Oddudua. Ogún was young, strong and handsome, and his mother had eyes only for him, ignoring her husband. Oddudua spied on his wife Yemmu and his son Ogun every day, his eyes narrow, angry slits as he watched his son and his wife getting closer and closer to one another. Like all lovers, the mother and son were oblivious to the rest of the world.

One day, Oddudua's worst suspicions were confirmed when he discovered Yemmu and Ogún in sexual embrace. Any human would fall in a rage at this spectacle of mother and son's love-making, but the god fell into something worse. In Oddudua's case, it was a silent and ominous pause to see what the incestuous mating would produce.

A few weeks later, after she was sick in the morning, Oddudua rubbed Yemmu's swelling belly. He knew she was pregnant. Nevertheless, with the patience of a god cognizant of what he would do, he waited until the child was born. Finally, Yemmu went into labor and delivered Ogun's healthy brother/son, whom she named Orúnmìlà. Only seconds after the first cry from the new born, Oddudua burst into Yemmu's room, stood over her, and coldly, cruelly, ordered her to bury her incestuous love-child alive. Where was Ogún, the favourite son of Yemmu, the new born Orúnmìlà's father and brother? We don't know.

Her new infant in her arms, Yemmu immediately acquiesced to her powerful husband's demand. However, unknown to Oddudua, her mind was not on her son's death; it was on his salvation. Therefore, she conceived an excellent plan to save Orúnmìlà.

Yemmu wrapped her child in a cloth and carried him on her back into the dark forest. She walked until she approached an ancient iroko tree (chlorophora excelsa) with a mammoth canopy. Suddenly her steps halted, stopped by an unseen force. Yemmu sensed in her soul she had found divine protection for her infant and need go no further. Without delay, she carried her baby son under the thickest branches, where she knew he would be protected from rain and sun, and she covered him with earth and humus, as if she was planting a seedling in the rich, leaf covered soil. She buried him only up to his neck, like a tiny shoot whose head remains above the earth growing toward the light, while its roots go downward into the dark soil.

Life turns everything up and down. For many years Oddudua believed Yemmu's and Ogun's son was dead, and life went on as before. Yemmu knew otherwise, because she regularly snuck out to the iroko tree where she had left her child. There she saw a miracle.

Instead of dying, Orúnmìlà was alive and well, transformed by the sagacity and nurture of the Tree, which had become his mother and teacher. While buried in the Earth, he had learned from the Tree the secrets of the incredible Oracle of Ifá. Orúnmìlà had grown older and exponentially wiser. Far from disabling him, his arduous apprenticeship under the Tree of Knowledge made him the first and greatest babaláwo (diviner) of the Ifá oracle. Soon, people came from everywhere to have him read their destinies and find remedies for their misfortunes. Life became much happier for everyone with the wisdom of Odu. Many people arrived to study with the famous diviner while he was still buried in the Earth under his master teacher, the iroko tree. And that was only the beginning!

The Orisha in this story, Oddudua and Yemmu, are passionate and full of destructive rage, while they commit incest, adultery, child abandonment and murder. Nevertheless, they unknowingly created a positive situation where Ifá divination, the treasured jewel of human wisdom, could be born. The gods manifested the most negative cultural excesses possible, before nature rebalanced life with the superlative acumen of the oracle. The Tree gave people an interpretive code for living virtuously in culture and society, thus turning the whole situation to fortune. The extraordinarily auspicious being who achieved this wonder was an old iroko Tree filled with the entire corpus of the Ifá divination system (from which the Dilogún is derived). The Tree's teachings centered on the virtues of self-knowledge and moderation, the very qualities missing in the Orisha world at that time.

Reading this story I was reminded of Odin, the Norse god, who like Orúnmìlà also received an important teaching from a sacred tree, Yggdrasil. While hanging upside down from Yggdrasil Odin spied divinatory runes* lying in an abyss. Like Orúnmìlà, Odin had no food or drink during his incapacitation, and was exiled far away from his family and friends.

As I considered these stories, it dawned on me how often trees are associated with profound human knowledge. A tree in the Jewish and Christian traditions is at the heart of the Garden of Eden. The Tree of Life is also the central symbol in the Kabbala, which uses a tree as its map of creation. When artists pictured the first god recorded in written scriptures, Inanna of Mesopotamia, they depicted her as a pillar or tree trunk. This divine symbolism expanded through the Middle East and Mediterranean for thousands of years. It continues to be used in the present day.

When I thought about it, I decided time devoted to quiet sitting beneath a tree can yield unexpected personal and cultural treasures. It might even change the world. Many ancient cultures, whether they prayed to one god or many, acknowledged trees as having the power to elevate human consciousness and receive messages from spiritual dimensions.

A tree was responsible for the spiritual elevation of the Buddha. Prince Siddhartha, after years of searching futilely for enlightenment, finally sat under an ancient Bodhi tree, also called the Bo tree, a type of strangler fig related to my beloved Miami banyans, sacred to the Lucumí. One legend says in the very first week he gained his elusive enlightenment; his mind rested, and he knew bliss. Then, in acknowledgment of the Bo Tree, he gazed at it without moving his eyes for seven more days. After that, Siddhartha was ready for his mission as the Awakened One.

---

* Alphabet characters, the basis of ancient Germanic languages, used in divination.

Today that same Bodhi tree's descendants, propagated from the original tree, shelter monks in meditation in Bodhgaya, India. It is possible to view these contemporary monks on YouTube, still quietly meditating under the spreading Bo tree descended from the very one that sheltered the Buddha.

The banyan tree is also sacred to the people of Wangari Maathia, the Kenyan Nobel Prize winner, who during her lifetime was responsible for the re-greening of many parts of highland Kenya by planting millions of trees. When Maathia was a child in her home village the banyan tree was protected, because her people knew it conserved fresh water (in fact, they considered it a source of water), knowledge that was obvious from the many springs and creeks near strangler figs. When she was an adolescent at boarding school colonial administrators cut down the giant trees. On her return home Maathai found her village was a desert. Crops had failed, and people were malnourished for the first time.

While reading Maathai's book, *Unbowed: One Woman's Story*, I recalled a visit to Mossman Gorge in Far North Queensland where there is an Aboriginal owned, tropical forest. A local native man guided me through the forest near his village. There he invited me to sit under a spreading banyan—their church, he called it—while exchanging songs.

As a child, like most children I loved to climb trees. I instinctively loved the forest where I adventured every day after school with my dog as companion. When we are without guile, we recognize what is true. That day in the park on Key Biscayne, just across from downtown Miami and the towers of Brickell, I imagined I could communicate across the globe through the tree that was my companion. I could feel her organic knowledge traveling from one sentient being to another, from root mass to root mass, and under the oceans.

At that moment, I intuitively understood how Ifá was lodged in the great iroko tree. I thankfully received the ashé the young live oak pumped into me that afternoon—I can see her now, leaves glistening in the Sun. Somehow, she helped fuel what came next.

CHAPTER 19

One Night

Seed, Summer, Tomb.
Who's doom—
To Whom?
— Emily Dickinson

A LMOST TWO WEEKS LATER I returned to New Zealand. On my first night at home I slept alone in my yoga sanctuary, thinking about my father and his passing, a white candle burning for him constantly on my altar. His illness was a hard picture to erase; it lived in a deep place inside me. I kept seeing his suffering, my own inadequacy to stop it, and my inability to love him unconditionally. The space he had occupied in my life felt empty and raw.

About three o'clock in the morning the phone rang on the table beside my bed. I waited for my answer message to come on, but it rang and rang, maybe ten or eleven times. Our voicemail was set to five rings. Why hadn't it answered the call? Finally, impatient to stop its noise, I sat up in bed. I lifted the receiver and held it to my ear.

"Hello?" I said softly.

"Honey, don't worry about me anymore. I'm in heaven."

Then the caller disconnected. The line went silent.

It had been my father. He had spoken clearly and concisely, determined and strong. My father's spirit had found a way to communicate with me, to let me know he was alive in some other dimension and capable of using the phone for a few seconds. It was the single best phone call I've ever received.

I immediately accepted his spirit had made the call. I slowly replaced the phone in its cradle and examined my confusion of feelings. As I did, I paced around my yoga studio, the implications of the call sinking in.

How could my father who had passed away weeks before have phoned me in the middle of the night at my home in Waitaha? I picked up the phone to check it. Yes, it was still working. There was nothing odd about the dial tone. I wished I'd had time to say something. Would I have asked, "Dad, is it really you?" It would have been smart to say, "Describe exactly where you are!" What is death? Is there an afterlife? But I was certain I had heard my father's voice.

No voice said it better than Mary Shelley's: "Many things will appear possible in these wild and mysterious regions, which would provoke the laughter of those unacquainted with the ever-varied powers of nature."[12]

I had to move. Donning my jacket, I went outside to look at the stars in the clear night sky. As usual, the southern firmament appeared crowded with celestial light. Stars, galaxies and whole universes twinkled and turned in the dark phase of the Moon. The next night would bring the new crescent and the changes of another month.

The chill night air caressed my cheeks. I held my jacket close around me as I sat on the edge of the veranda looking down on the silver, star-lit field and river in the valley below. The night was still, except for the morepork, a small owl, calling its partner with two haunting notes. In a few seconds, a clear reply returned from the forest below, to my left. The feral melodies touched something inside me and my sense of ego disappeared.

The natural is always full of the supernatural. The Divine communicates with us all the time. Manifestations of the supernatural are everywhere, Many transcendental experiences take place out of doors. A verse from the *Yoga Sutras* describes what I was feeling: "When awareness is clarified, the reality of the Self is revealed."

For a few minutes I was the night, the shining field, the dark forest in the distance, and the cool, katabatic wind blowing down the mountain. I knew if I walked to the river I would see the luminous light which had followed me for many years. It would feel heat behind my back; but when I turned I would see only darkness and a question: What was following me? Sometimes it felt like car headlights shining warmly on my back and glinting off my shoulders, but I could never see the source.

The river lay at the bottom of our land, a black ribbon through the valley. The luminosities on the river wanted my attention. It was almost time to bring it all back home where my answers lay buried in the land.

CHAPTER 20

Stephen's Pea

> It is the muted voice of the dying embers
> Which enchants this heart of mine.
> This heart which like the covered flame
> Sings as it is consumed.
>
> — Toulet

ONE FROSTY MORNING before sunrise I lit a match to the newspaper inside the tepee I had built of twigs gathered from the forest. The flame caught the paper, flowed around it, blue and yellow, until the paper was ablaze. People use the word "licking", and that was what the fire did: a graceful licking. It sent itself forward and back a while, up and down, not giving itself away until the entire tepee was invisible inside the flames.

The living colours of the fire, oranges, reds, yellows and sometimes blues, transformed themselves, again and again, like a palate in motion. I understood the ancient Vedic fire worshippers. Fire and human evolution went hand in hand. We never find Homo sapiens without fire. Human beings lived without many things, pottery, metal, the wheel, offensive weapons, permanent houses, but they never lived without fire. It made food palatable, it warmed and cleansed. It was the center of life. And still is.

Sitting by the fire at night, transfixed by its brightness and its song, may have been the first reverie of the human race. Through this reverie creative insight was awakened. It is an irony that when we concentrated on the external object, the flame of a fire, we elaborate our own internal capacity for imagination and visualization, spirit journeying and shamanism. Fire offers a wonderful example of how the inside is in union with the outside. Who cannot be lured by the flame? We are mesmerized by a burning fire. When we gaze at fire we ordinarily do not think of fire. Instead, we dream of many things, or we voyage in a weightless trance. But we did not think about fire. Nevertheless, the fire fuels our fascination, because life is fire: a brilliance and radiance that sent us out in all directions, wherever we need to go.

Yet while life has these characteristics of brilliance and radiance, at the same time, like watching fire, it is very difficult to witness life directly without falling into a long reverie, from which we only emerge as the log is consumed. My radiance attracts your radiance, and on and on we follow our passions and our bliss, and continue to evolve and learn, taking all positive turns, which sometimes turn negative, following ancient paths while working out relationships. One day, we awaken as if from a long sleep, and find we are 60 or 70 or 80. A lot of life has passed; we were helpless to stop it.

Ancient spiritual practices like yoga teach us to look at radiance, the brilliance that is life. Yoga in its oldest form, which we glean from the 3,000-year-old collection of Vedic hymns, appears to have been the practice of disciplined introspection, or meditative focusing. Samkhya philosophy—with which yoga philosophy is closely identified—says that unless something is inherent in you, you can't experience it. Yoga turns us from our vigil at the external hearth to begin a study of the properties of our own energetic fire within. The German Indologist Georg Feuerstein says that traditionally when a person—usually a male—decided to study yoga he approached a master of yoga with fuel in hand, the fuel stick signifying his readiness to be consumed by spiritual practice.[13]

I have had metaphysical crises in my life, during which I thought of nothing but my desire to perceive and understand the nature of my own life. There were times when my eyes in the mirror looked like the strange luminous orbs of some alien creature whose nature I could not fathom. What energy fuels this light behind my eyes? I wondered. What engine fires my voice? Or breathes my breath when I'm asleep?

I wanted desperately to see the Face of God. I demanded again and again that I be able to see it. My crying out for knowledge reached a time when I felt abandoned and could take no more.

One night I began to long for an experience of the Divine, to know

God, as I called this longing in those days. I stared into my eyes in a mirror for hours, watching my face go through contortions of every description. Finally, I wound up with a gruesome one-eyed fish staring back at me. It's unlikely, I thought, that's what God looks like. I gave up and looked away.

Before I started to look in the mirror, I had been reading a book by Northrup Frye on literary symbolism. This book had fallen from my lap to the floor, but when I became engrossed with the mirror I hadn't noticed it had done so. Now I did. The book was open to a page on which the sole sentence I had underlined was, *God has no face.*

Surely, I had read that. How else could it be underlined? How quickly I forget important stuff! I'd had my answer, but hadn't believed it until the mirror showed me the truth.

When I was a teenager I would lie awake at night trying to imagine Death, wondering where I had been before I was born, struggling to penetrate the darkness inside my head. How deep and black it was. And yet, I thought, so lovely. We were taught to fear the colour black at church. Satan was black, evil things were black. Yet I knew I loved it.

Years later, I ran across this traditional Bengali song, which reminded me of my first memories of the Great Dark:

> The black bee of my mind is drawn
> to the blue lotus flower of Ma Kali's feet,
> See how black is made one with Black.

What I really wanted was an experience of God. One day, when I was sitting in my Hindu Studies class, I received an answer. My Indian professor was rotund and dark. He was dressed in a long formal black robe, because we were at an English University. But he had a face that could beam. He was talking about how yoga taught you to experience God inside yourself. God was essentially an energy which everyone could experience by calming down, going inside and merging with this universal spirit. That day, as he said that, his face beamed and his radiance was unmistakable.

Everyone else looked bored. I was transfixed. I stored this away at nineteen and knew I would find out what he was talking about when the time was right. At the back of my mind, while reading the endless books and articles which provide the common ground of intellectual thought, I believed that someday I would study yoga seriously. And I knew that my life had been touched by the divine, an inner fire that fuelled my search. Each day, I looked for proof. I still do.

One year I joined fourteen others and travelled with a shaman from Australia up to an isolated mountaintop. Our purpose was to search for our spirit animals during long drumming sessions extended over seven days. While our souls journeyed to fabulous places, the weather covered the mountain with fog. Rain fell for a week. When it finally stopped raining, the mountain was an island surrounded by a ring of water. There was no access. So another week passed, on the mountain, with the drums. We lay on the floor with our eyes closed and visualized a long tunnel opening into the Earth while we concentrated on the drumbeats.

One day, after about five minutes of listening to the drum, I suddenly fell into a steep vortex with cascading water, like New Zealand's famous Huia Falls. I rode the water until it turned into a long, dark tunnel. I fell rapidly down the tunnel. There, to my surprise, I spotted a giant bear below me, looking up with big eyes.

A second later I tumbled softly into the bear's arms. Somehow I knew she was my mother bear. The soft giant grabbed me in a great hug, like the crushing hug of Luis/Elegguá. But the bear's hug had no words and was deeply nurturing. After a few minutes of her cuddling, she rose up with me in her arms and started to fly above a beautiful verdant world. After a long look flying around the strangely lit terrain, where I saw camps of people with bonfires and flocks of animals, the drum called me back.

I returned, exalted. I definitely felt as if I had found a piece of myself in a real inner dimension, and that I was a valuable person protected by the bear, despite all my faults. Well, despite everything. It was a strong enough vision that I remember it clearly, as if it happened yesterday, or even just now. I can still feel the deep, luxurious texture of my mother bear's arms around me.

That night I had a dream that illumed what I experienced with the bear, although it was quite different and the bear wasn't present. I was riding in a jeep with men dressed in military uniforms holding machine guns. They were standing up on both sides of an open tray on the jeep, four on each side. I was in the front seat with a driver. At first, we were driving through snowcapped mountains, then we were travelling past large religious temples.

We passed a Christian church where priests and ministers waved from the garden. The men with the machine guns in my jeep fired on them and they all fell down dead. We drove on to the next stop, a Buddhist temple, where monks with bald heads and brown robes chatted out front. As we passed the monks, once again the men in my jeep fired their machine guns and killed the holy men. Their temple, which had stopped the rounds of bullets, began to crumble into rubble. Next, we passed a Jewish temple with the same result: the temple crumpled as the rabbis died. In the dream I felt something like guilty horror, yet maybe guilty satisfaction too.

"All patriarchal religion must disappear to make way for the new. In the new world, men will not dominate women or religion," said a voice.

Since that time I've felt that all institutional religions were doomed to fail, because their separation from nature, which reveals the supernatural, was complete. They had dumbed themselves down through pride and discrimination. At any one time, for instance, the Catholic priesthood is missing 50% of the spiritual geniuses who might be part of it: women.

The religion of nature, of animism, is fully inclusive of everyone. Who is born or lives outside of nature? The answer is, no one.

Yesterday I read an important article buried in the second section of the morning paper. On the front page I saw the usual stories about murders, politicians and fires. The startling, earth-shaking article was small and hidden in the back section. The title of the article was, "Pea." It began with a quote: "The whole universe was created from something the size of a pea." The article was on the ideas of Stephen Hawking.

I plant peas in my garden, hard, wizened, olive-green things the size of a small nut. Can he mean *a pea*? I wondered.

Hawking went on to say, "The pea expanded in less than a fraction of a second to near the present size of the universe."

"The Seed contains all!" said Stephen in conclusion.

The original seed of life expanded in less time than it takes to blink, into everything we know, and do not know, which we call our universe.

Each time I read those words, I blinked. "The Seed contains all!" Yeah? Nah! If you repeat that sentence enough times you begin to get a feeling for the absolute absurdity, irony, impossibility, of Stephen Hawking's theory. Finally, my little mind reduced it to an idea: an oak tree from an acorn.

It is one thing to imagine the physical universe expanding and creating all that we see, and another to imagine our egos contained in that expansion, along with our karma, and our destinies, too. The visible and invisible things that I had pondered over as a kid: how did a pea manage that for all of us? Can individual destinies, destinies that were not even at the micro-organism stage, have been inside that pea? Were they there, inside, before the pea expanded, waiting for billions of years before coming to fruition in you and me? Can we believe this impossible idea?

I know that when I plant a pea, I get a pea plant. There are no exceptions to this rule: all the plants look the same, yield the same fruit, grow and behave in the same way. No amount of food or water will change its life span, its fruit, its habits of growth, its colour. Is the pea that created everything, everywhere, in the whole universe, like that? Are our ideas, mythologies, crazy lives, strong feelings, successes and failures, pains, deaths, sufferings, betrayals, jealousies and angers ... is everything in there? Is free will an illusion, after all?

The Orisha had warned me to chuck away all the things from my childhood that were anchoring me to my past, but I couldn't find a way to do that for a long time. Like Stephen Hawking's pea, perhaps these seeds contained everything at my birth, and it was my destiny for them to grow out of me. From my soul, these seeds grew to become a life that could hurt me, just as my father's life hurt him and my mother's life hurt her. Lucky for me, there were many seeds of happiness waiting to germinate when the evil ones had lived their lives.

If Stephen Hawking is correct, my own life, my family, every experience, Laura, Nydia, every feeling and every thought, were in The Pea before the beginning of time and space. Can I imagine them all sucked backwards in an ever-decreasing dark stream until they all disappear into a little green pea that rests ever so gently in Stephen's remarkable hand? Yes, I think I can.

Ah, it is restful to watch that happening, like a video on rewind. Time and space, all relationship wound back up, awaiting the primeval friction that will set them on forward again. I find there is never a good place to start or end, because of the tendency for things to seem finished, but then sputter, begin again, and reappear in another form. There is no beginning, middle or end in life, because something always starts again, seldom from the beginning, even if I believe that it has. Time is warped and speeds up or slows down for me according to the perceptions of my own life. Time doesn't exist except in my memory of my own past life events, which I have ordered and filtered, along a timeline I remember.

Physicists say time isn't fundamental. If it was we would remember the future, which has more entropy than the past. Everything in the next moment, and beyond, is unordered, not under my control, not on a timeline. Especially my demise.

My life is apparent. I have my birth certificate with my time, place of birth, and parents' names. My birth shrank all available times, places and people to a microcosm of specific facts. My death is not shrunken yet, it is still large, not small like my birth.

CHAPTER 21

Lightning, Eels And Black Bean Soup

> Time is a river which sweeps me along, but I am the river;
> it is a tiger which destroys me, but I am the tiger;
> it is a fire which consumes me, but I am the fire.
> — Jorge Luis Borges

THE DEATH OF A PARENT is often the first death a person experiences, when still feeling far away from the time that black curtain will drop on their own life. But in the midst of every person's life there unfailingly arrives a showstopper: Death. Homo sapiens die and know they will die. Our species has known about death for a very long time.

Birds do not know they will die, at least they don't appear to. But for humans like me, despite the evidence of time on face and body, time will suddenly and surprisingly stop. We know that truth deeply in our souls. It is an irony that Death is such a whopping big subject, yet we actually know nothing about it, especially not the time we can expect it or how it will arrive. When I think about Death, it makes me laugh—because, why not? Only those who suicide control the time of demise; but they still know nothing about it.

I once decided to read as much about death from a spiritual perspective as I could. I saw a book that intrigued me, poems written by Zen monks who were close to death. Composing them was a traditional practice. I read the book from cover to cover, twice. I was disappointed to discover the monks didn't know what death was either.

African religions certainly can't explain death, but they offer hope for life past death via ancestral practices that involve identifiable essences surviving human demise. It's an essence that can communicate with living people. I've experienced communication with departed people. To the people who say it was my mind creating the communications, I say, of course it was. In every way my mind was involved, through the layers of time and experience, training, expectation and interpretation. It is my mind, my particular mind, that creates all things in my life.

For instance, sometimes I wonder if the messages from Nydia Pichardo, which arrived soon after her shocking death, were the creation of my mind. The interpretation of them surely was, and is. But did I cause the events somehow?

Nydia died suddenly and violently. Her death was fitibo, a fate prophesized by a Lucumí diviner when she was a teenager in Puerto Rico. This was after an automobile accident left her unable to walk. She told me about the fitibo prophecy not long after I first met her, three decades ago. I had forgotten it completely it until she was gone.

I found out about her sudden death via social media, a few hours after her passing. A post on Facebook read: "I just heard that Nydia Pichardo died today."

I had never seen a post like that conveying such a brutal truth about a friend's hours' old death, a friend alive and well the day before. Healthy, looking forward to a retirement pension in a few years, to travel with her husband, to watching her sister's new twins grow up, Nydia nevertheless died without warning on a fine winter day in South Florida. Fitibo had claimed her. Her death was irrevocable, sudden and mysterious.

From one day, one hour, to the next unknown moment, dark-haired Nydia Pichardo disappeared from our world of form and light. Nydia left the planet instantaneously, in Miami, on a clear blue-sky day, while on her way to her dentist. Thanks to the mind-boggling miracle of the scientific technologies we have to communicate worldwide, a few minutes after reading about her death I watched a newscast from Miami showing her cataclysmic end.

Just a year before I had spent her 60th birthday with her in Miami at an Italian restaurant, where we laughed and laughed, whispering candors to one another. We felt like a family with the other six people at the table, folks we'd known for many years. I thought we had transcended time and would always be together. That is how I remember Nydia now, laughing and drinking red wine and eating freshly made pasta. However, on the day of her demise the Miami newscast showed her body strapped to a gurney, covered completely, while being loaded into an ambulance. I looked and looked at that gurney, knowing the covered and strapped shape was Nydia's, but also disbelieving that it could be her.

I could also see from the drone video the long route the truck had taken to reach her. It had been marked by traffic cones. The big truck, 4,100 pounds of metal, had left the crowded six-lane Bird Road on an out-of-control right angle. Managing to miss other cars, trucks and buses, it crossed through a strip of vegetation, then traversed a wide footpath, narrowly missing a line of palms while thundering on. The murdering vehicle, its route and existence unknown to Nydia, strolling toward her dental appointment, then broke through a tropical planting of palms and continued to swerve right. Finally, it crossed another wide pavement, before smashing 120-pound Nydia into a concrete block wall, a few feet from the door of the dental office where she was booked for a check-up.

It was immediately apparent that the truck had to take one single, specific, long and curving route to hit Nydia from the back, shattering her against the concrete wall. It had to take that exact route, at that exact moment in time: perhaps ten seconds later she would have been inside her dentist's office.

The newscast showed a pot-bellied, maybe fortyish, man sitting on the planter by the wall near where he had killed Nydia. He was the driver, still drunk, a multiple offender it turned out.

This was the second time Nydia had been struck by a vehicle. The first time was a car wreck in Puerto Rico, when she was a teenager. Her family was active in Lucumí. During divination, as she lay paralyzed in her hospital room in San Jose, the Orisha talked to Nydia:

"We will give you back your life now. We shall see to it that you walk and dance again. This will be in exchange for your life's service as a priestess of Shango. To reciprocate, this is the situation we will set up for you. You will live many more years and fulfil many of your life's goals. Then, sometime in your future, the same fate of fitibo that paralyzes you now will find you again and take your life."

Nydia happily agreed to these terms. She did walk and dance again.

But she lived with the prophecy and never forgot it. She said goodbye to Ernesto every morning, as if it were her last day. She served the Orisha with all her talents, unstintingly, devotedly, tirelessly. Her home was a refuge of spiritual peace and power, her kitchen the studio for *Nydia's Miami Kitchen*, her much loved YouTube cooking show.

I had other deep losses that year, another friend having suddenly frozen in the mountains, and my dearest Laura finally vanquished by cancer. Nearly every human being feels the same about death. There is no getting used to it. A blank emptiness appears when a loved one is gone. I am shocked every time it happens to someone close to me.

Each of us awakens during and after our first observed death, because there is nothing more enlightening than the death process. Yet it's always a surprise. Because I, like everyone, think I am immortal, and most of the time love my life, lush nature, delicious food. Hey, I'm having a great time in the beautiful Holocene on Planet Earth. What? It's going to be over? It all looks so real and permanent!

After Nydia was obliterated, I felt I had the mark of transparency, a being without boundaries. I became introverted, deeply pondering and remembering. I was not looking for messages from her. I had been her distant Lucumí godchild. I had wanted to know her better. Now it was too late. I was still guilty about not turning up for her enough. It was Ernesto I'd worried about, because of his cigarette smoking.

I felt ragged and shocked even as I pondered these trivial thoughts in bed at the end of the day, before my mind finally closed, and my soul slept. I lived like that in the empty hole Nydia had left for two days, awakening and going to sleep, floating through space, thinking of living on Europa, a smooth, young Moon circling Jupiter. Under its glaciated surface I would hang in cryptic waters, blind, holding a moment of the past suspended.

During an evening of this existential transparency, two nights after Nydia had passed into spirit, I was standing by a full-length window looking out on the dark sky, mountains and sea. I felt an equivalence between the infinite blackness inside and the blackness outside my body, the creative darkness from which everything goes and comes.

Suddenly, on the horizon, literally from one moment to the next, I watched lightning strikes from the top of the sky to the bottom, down past the drop of the turning Earth where they disappeared. The lightning increased its number of strikes, faster and faster, so fast it made me doubt my eyes. Dazzling yellow-white light pulsated behind the sand spit across the bay. The lightning barely waited on the thunder, which finally cracked the firmament, then they both performed simultaneously.

One diagonal bolt of lightning streaking across the night sky branched into scores of smaller zig zags shooting down to the Earth. These bolts were uncountable. Every bolt was different, comprised of electric zig zag lines arranged into branching rivers and deltas, multiple tributaries like arteries and veins in a heart.

I've never seen lightning that filled the sky above the horizon, striking fast, multiple times, an electrical dangerously high voltage chaos. I was oddly elated by the lightning, through something like a musical harmonic connection, a pulsating resonance. At the same time I felt uneasy, because the wild is unpredictable. I stayed by the window in a reverie for a long time after the show had ended. A few hours later, after midnight, I wondered if I had imagined the epic nature of the supernatural display.

The next morning, on the front page of the local paper, I read there had been 100,000 lightning strikes the night before, the most ever recorded on New Zealand's South Island. Hundreds had witnessed the unusual display, never seen before on our island. So I hadn't dreamt it.[14]

The night before I sensed Nydia in the lightning, which had started as I was standing by the window, absorbing the news of her death. If I'd been in the shower or reading a book, I wouldn't have seen it. Intriguingly, Nydia was a priestess of Shango, the powerful Yoruba divinity who manifests in lightning and thunder. Lightning is the force of destruction, blasting apart what must change, melting even the Earth with its temperatures five times hotter than the surface of the Sun. I thought of Nydia during the lightning. Perhaps now her essence was in a realm where she could fathom the immense dominion and genius of Shango.

The Orisha represent fundamental natural principles and laws. The God of Lightning, in this case Shango (it could be Thor or Zeus or Indra), would seem almost childish to non-animists. Yet lightning is essential to life on Earth. New research shows that lightning was as important as meteors in creating the perfect conditions for life on Earth to emerge.

When lightning strikes the Earth's surface it creates a rock called fulgurite. Fulgurite contains a type of phosphorus that can be broken down in water. Phosphorus is essential to life. In contrast, the phosphorus present on the early Earth's surface did not break down in water, making it useless for the evolution of life. Fulgurites delivered exactly what the Earth needed 3.5 billion years ago.[15]

The early meteorites brought liquid water, amino acids, hydrocarbons and other organic matter to fuel the Earth's complex evolutionary pathways. When meteorite numbers decreased, lightning provided a usable form of phosphorous essential to life, neatly packaged in a mineral it fabricated from heat and earth: fulgurite.

Shango is symbolised by lightning, each appearance of which is marvellously sudden, intense, dangerous. The fact that the lightning signified Nydia's death to me was a synchronicity, a meaningful connection based on my own life. The truck had struck Nydia like lightning, at a force and speed no person could survive.

I poured a glass of wine for Nydia and put it in the corner of the table, in front of the big window where I had witnessed the incredible lightning extravaganza, which had appeared out of nowhere, like the beginning of life on a magical planet. It harkened back 3.5 billion years, messaging me that there was nothing more important than the phenomena I had witnessed. Honestly, that glass of wine I poured for Nydia should have been a vintage bottle worth millions of dollars to give honour proportionate to Nydia's sacrifice.

I was starting to think of her accident that way, as a sacrifice. Death comes quickly and without forewarning, taking what it needs from the unsuspecting victim. The Orisha had needed her at that exact moment. Perhaps she was a sort of fulgurite, providing exactly what was needed by spirit to protect life on Earth. Nydia, I said, thank you, thank you for inspiring me, for letting me know you. When a channel is open between myself and a departed friend it feels like a wounded blessing.

The next morning, John and I walked along the river early. The dew was still wet on the grass, while the newly risen Sun made tree shadows long. The tree's wet leaves sparkled with gold. We stopped at the sacred pool at the top of the stairs on the river path. Something had caught our eyes.

As we looked into the pool we saw a large eel, four to five feet long, lying on the shore of the sacred pool, in not more than a foot of water. The early light made the water translucent green-gray. The eel's supple body was quite dark in the water, curving and effortless, moving slowly as we watched it. We were both surprised, because this was the first eel we had ever seen near the edge of the sacred pool's riverbank during all our decades of walking by the pool several times a week.

No doubt eels have been there when we weren't. But this large eel was there at that moment, at that exact place in the sacred pool, so it felt natural for me to see a conjunction of two things: our time and place of observation and the eel's appearance. They were simultaneous.

It was a synchronicity for me, because I bestowed the eel with meaning that was personal for me, similar to the way I had recognized the meaning the lightning had held for me. It was another sign to me that Nydia's essence was present and could communicate through natural beings.

The eel here in Aotearoa New Zealand might be said to be a taniwha, a water dragon, with powers to both bless and curse. I wrote about taniwha in my book, *Prophecy on the River*. A young woman gave me her drawing of a taniwha and an eel after reading it. Eels are particularly important to Māori culture. Before the colonial invasion Aotearoa was literally full of eels, freshwater and saltwater. They had over a hundred names. Māori raised eels in special ponds where they grew for decades, beloved pets and a substantial source of food. Now eels are quite rare in most streams and creeks. Lucumí is an indigenous religion of nature. Nydia would have had deep understanding of the Māori respect for eels. She would understand the eel was a message to me; she had read *Prophecy on the River*.

After the eel departed, John and I walked on quietly. After we arrived back home, we went upstairs to change. I walked through John's office and saw that his computer screen was lit. When I stopped to look at the screen a YouTube video began to play, unbidden. I was astonished to see it was *Nydia's Miami Kitchen*, a popular YouTube show in which Nydia presented the typical foods of the Caribbean, especially of her home, Puerto Rico, and Cuba, where Ernesto was born. I hadn't seen it in months. At 8 a.m. John's computer was showing the start of Nydia's cooking show, as if it were the most natural thing in the world. John had never watched it, and had definitely never played it on his computer. Nevertheless, there she was, teaching us how to make black bean soup, a classic Cuban dish, starting with the dry beans that are soaked overnight then cooked the next day. She prepared the sofrito, adding cumin, white wine, vinegar, bay leaves and oregano to the thick brown gravy.

It was enthralling. The entire episode played as if it was the most natural thing in the world. There was Nydia filming in her kitchen at her home in South Miami: it was eight minutes of seeing her just like the last time I saw her, when we celebrated her birthday. The lightning, the eel in the sacred pool, and now her YouTube channel, spoke to me, hinting that Nydia's essence was nearby, communicating.

The next day I prepared Nydia's black bean soup, leaving a bowl of it for her at the sacred pool where the eel had appeared. All of this despite her death being so raw and new. Somehow, our conversation was still on-going.

Soon after these signs, Ernesto and I chatted for an hour, both of us feeling the opening into profundity that death brings, his broken heart not even beginning to mend. *Death rules* are two words that define our existence. Those words sit heavily on our chests when we wake each morning, especially after losing a beloved friend like Nydia. Her manner of death revealed the random, even chaotic, art of destiny. Every person has a destiny. When we are in alignment with it we inhabit our skin in a different, more confident way. In that sense, on the day she was crushed by a drunken driver, Nydia was in perfect alignment with her destiny of Fitibo.

I am arrogant. I love to be in the know, to feel cool and detached. But, like everyone, I am stopped by mortality. I am silent, without tools, because there is no tool, no real preparation, no real understanding, no deep comprehension. Of course, there is acceptance, after a long while. But more than that Homo sapiens cannot say, because death is a void. We are all cancelled, nullified, leaving an empty shell behind.

Even saying that is too much. The person is gone, and the pillow which once held a lover's head holds the beloved no more. Unfortunately, there is no making a Faust's pact with Death to ensure you always arrive home safely, where you have your favourite foods and your own warm bed.

As far as I know, no one anywhere has outwitted Death.

Still, the majority of humans live from day to day as if they were immortal. I know I do. I take some comfort in the existence of spirits who survive death. But that still doesn't make me overly keen to die and find out what happens. Few of us know anything about spirit that is personal, real, and not tinged with fear.

We say that we have a spirit, which may leave our bodies at death, and we may hope our spirit survives us, because we feel we are more. But we are uncertain and so use the word spirit in a few different ways. Other meanings include a person with spirit who is enthusiastic, or when we call an excited person spirited. Horses can be spirited animals. We have school spirit, but we can also drink spirits, or have spirits in a cannister for our small camping stove. Spirit can be the atmosphere of a place, the way a person feels and thinks, and can also mean passion or guts. Spirit is a chameleon, like the word time: the more we look at it, the more it conceals itself and changes the way we see it.

Laura, my now departed friend, once said she couldn't give thanks and offerings to her ancestral spirits because none of them had cared about her. Neither did she care about them. Not long after that, Laura saw a Jamaican painting in which a handsome African woman, wearing a white head tie and matching pagne, had numerous luminous, cloud-like souls pressed up against her body, from head to foot. The woman in the painting was preparing food without the slightest knowledge the translucent entities were touching her like soft bubbles up and down her body. They touched her gently, laying their cheeks on her, smiling.

After that, Laura cultivated the idea that spirits cared about her well-being, spirits that had been with her since birth, not her biological family members. She nurtured her new orientation by offering them food and candles, employing herbal cauldrons buried in her garden, and other actions Ernesto recommended to her.

I've had experiences which have convinced me Homo sapiens' spirits can stay near loved ones after death. How this works I have no idea. Many people remark on their mental and emotional states as deeper, more present, that they feel an intense unqualified significance, when they sit by the bedside of someone who is dying. Death-on-its-way is an altered state of consciousness that detaches, internalizes, and stuns. Everything stops for Death.

I've come to think of Death as an entity which has its own time and space, walking a road which intersects with each person on the inevitable crossroads. Lucumí calls Death Ikú, an all-powerful being with superhuman powers. Ikú performs a service for us by destroying our bodies and moving us into another realm. There, the Lucumí say, Orisha Oya will take us further. The living know nothing more than that.

We die, and will maybe then find out more. But we have to die to discover if we do find out more. Futile tautology. Astrophysicists like Brian Swimme[16] say we are each, every one of us, the center of the universe, a universe in expansion, where no energy is created or destroyed. So, what dies? And what about the immortal, omniscient, omnipresent Power?

The Yoruba call the highest evolutionary power of the universe, Olódúmarè. *If you say it is female you are lying; if you say it is male you are lying*, says the Yoruba proverb. It is a stupendous mystery, without gender. It is the source of all ashé, all life forces, all power. Power also collects in living forms like water, rocks, wind, trees and the sky from Olódúmarè, the Source. This is an example of animism, which considers a vital essence exists in all things that is bestowed by the Creative Power. Does Death overwhelm this Creative Power in end-of-life excitement? Die and see.

Time disappears the moment you let it, like now when I contemplate Nydia's and Laura's deaths and their places in my memories. Around me is quiet, except for the singing of birds and a feeling of uneasiness about the wider world. I've lost a lot of my dependence on linear time, an extraordinary feeling in a culture whose mantra is *no time to waste*.

The experience of Nydia is now a memory, but not her black bean soup, which is present and delicious. At the end of life food transcends time more than prayer. Food brings back our friends, our mothers, our families, our favourite places. Food, filled with spiritual essence, in turn calls to spirit, the essence of a deceased loved one, who may choose, if we're fortunate, to answer.

CHAPTER 22

Angelita

*Sometimes, the strength of motherhood
is greater than natural laws.*
— Barbara Kingslover

THREE DAYS AFTER my mother's funeral, after my father had revealed his two-year affair with Carolee and declared he intended to marry her, I flew out of Miami. I changed planes in Atlanta on the way to Los Angeles. There the hurt caught me. All of a sudden my abandonment felt real. I had lost my mother one day, and my father the next. I was fifty, but I felt like five. I bought a frozen yogurt and cried into it.

"Please universe, I have run out of faith," I prayed. "I am exhausted. I no longer believe in anything beyond what I see. I am lost and no longer believe in miracles or in love. Please restore my faith and bring me a sign. Please let me know my mother is all right."

I had arrived in Los Angeles exhausted and empty. Luckily, I could depend on my yoga practice. I could stretch and strengthen, breathe into my body, mind and soul, and flow would come again. I hid my tired body behind a large column in a corner, unrolled the mat I always carry, and slowly I began sun salutes, breathing, eyes closed. While I was coming up into cobra, laying on the ground and looking up, a young girl appeared in front of me.

"You know a lot!" she said in an eight-year old's sweet voice.

"What do you mean?"

"What you're doing now, is that yoga?" she asked.

"Yes, it is. How do you know that?" I asked.

"I take dance classes. I've seen it there. Will you teach me?" she asked.

By this time, I was standing upright and looking down on her smiling face. "Of course, I will," I said.

A student had appeared. I wanted to be the teacher working with this child's radiant being. She trusted me to teach her. I would learn more than she.

"Follow me," I suggested, as I began moving with my breath through the standing postures. I jumped my feet apart and slid sideways into trikonasana, the triangle. She copied me like a pro and matched her inhalation and exhalation to mine. I stretched my hand to the ground in front of my foot and lifted into ardhra chandransana, half-moon posture, legs L-shape, arms extended, balanced on one leg. The young girl did the same, no questions, no hesitation, no imbalance.

She was quiet and deeply into her pose, but watching me intently. I'd never seen a child with such deep concentration. She had shining black hair to her waist, flashing black eyes, and a determined expression. But when she laughed it was like the sound of the bells I ring for relaxation posture at the end of my yoga class, pure, clear, relaxing.

For the next hour she mirrored me in all my postures, even handstands, headstands and splits. Suddenly, the visit to my father and my soon-to-be stepmother no longer sat on me like a heavy weight. Instead, I was new and excited. The beautiful young girl had wide-open groin muscles so could do a perfect split. She could sit in lotus posture and perform handstands. I wasn't teaching a child, but rather had a partner igniting my energy, making it easier for me to do the poses too. I sharpened my routine, did more. I forgot my sorrow, grief, depression, self-pity.

Suddenly, I looked at my watch and saw more than an hour had passed. My flight was boarding just around the thick column where we were doing yoga, down a long gate. Few remained in line. I laughed when I saw I would be among the last to board. I had never been late for an airline flight before or failed to hear boarding calls. Everything felt light and a little silly. But a thought crossed my mind. Where were her parents? I felt slightly guilty, but had no time to find them.

"I have to board my flight now, darling," I said, "and you must go back to your parents." I realized I didn't know her name.

I looked into her eyes and said, "Sweetheart, what is your name?"

"Angelita," she whispered, "Angelita is my name."

"Thank you, Angelita," I said, "I am much happier today because of you."

I bent down and we hugged one another. Before I was ready to let her go, Angelita turned and ran toward the concourse away from my gate.

Then, I was in departure fervor. I rushed to the attendant guarding the gate, presented my ticket, and entered the plane, the last passenger to board. I took my seat on the aisle, in my favourite bulkhead row, no one in the middle, a good-looking quiet man silently reading a book in the window seat.

As I settled myself, a realization dawned. Angelita. The little angel. The young girl with the flashing eyes was an angel, or at least acted as one toward me. How else explain my completely altered mood. I had not slept for three nights. I had been grief stricken, weak and depressed just an hour or so before. Now I was on top of the world. I was so refreshed that I needed no sleep and read an entire novel during the first nine hours of the trip. Was Eleggúa part of this energetic mystery appearing to me in his child avatar, I wondered?

At about four o'clock in the morning New Zealand time, a couple of hours before landing, I still felt radiant, without a thought about my father. I was dressed in my mother's black knit pull-over with fancy gold braiding. I combed my hair and applied deep red lipstick.

Unexpectedly, the chief flight steward was standing by my seat. I looked up at him. He was about forty years old, with dark hair and smiling eyes. He leaned over a little and asked, "Have you ever been on a flight deck?"

I was intrigued by the question. For a moment wasn't quite sure what he was asking.

"Do you mean have I been in the cockpit where the captain is flying the plane? No, I haven't. Why do you ask?" I said tentatively.

"Because I wondered if you would care to visit the flight deck upstairs?"

"Would I? Absolutely. Yes!" I more or less exclaimed, trying to keep my voice down as people were sleeping all around me.

"I thought you would," he said. "Let me go and call the captain." He turned and walked to the galley and disappeared.

I was stunned, too excited to think. I watched him pick up the phone on the wall of the galley and speak a few words into it. He replaced the receiver and walked back to my seat.

"Follow me," he said, and turned to his left, walking down the aisle to the forward galley. There we turned left and walked down the opposite aisle until we came to winding stairs leading to the first-class cabin. I had always wanted to see what was up those stairs, the stairway to heaven, as I recalled calling them, many times as I passed them going to my economy seat.

The steward disappeared up the stairs. I raced up not far behind his black polished shoes, fearing he might change his mind and send me back to economy if I wasn't quick enough. By the time I was at the top he was opening the door to the cockpit and gesturing for me to walk inside.

Inside the door was an arc of neon light, purple, green and orange dials with glowing numbers beneath a curved window that looked out on the heavens. An enormous full moon was positioned in the sky just above the horizon. Moonlight glazed the western sky from top to bottom and sprinkled itself over the black water far below. It was exquisite.

My willing eyes were filled so deeply by this profound sight I could feel the vision throughout my body. A world of amazing loveliness had existed undetected just meters away from me in my economy seat, where a tiny window had embraced just a tiny portion of the night sky. And not a whiff of the Moon.

The high night sky flew by at eight miles a minute. Only a little glass separated that rushing moonstruck night from the calm interior of the cockpit. My tongue couldn't move. I was paralyzed as I recognized the divine universe so often out of sight and so unknown.

The pilot rescued me. "I was just like you the first time I saw it," he said. "I have never stopped being thrilled by the miracle of this sight."

"You mean you always feel like I do now? Like fainting, like shouting, like leaving my body?"

"Oh, absolutely," he replied. "Nothing could ever stop me from making this flight. There would be no more fighting in the world if everyone could see what we are seeing now. Sit down behind me," he instructed. "Put on the seat belt and ask whatever you want."

"Thank you. I'm stunned. The vastness, yet the intimacy, with the Moon in our faces, the gold, the black water and sky. I will never forget."

"Then it was perfect that the steward invited you up, perfect that it was you he chose," said the captain.

"I know, I know." I was gushing now, I couldn't stop myself.

Then I fell quiet and didn't speak for a long time. Time disappeared as my body rushed through space, my whole being absorbing moonlight, stars and dark matter.

I was concentrated and humbled. My mind stopped chattering; my voice was silenced. I wanted to fly through space forever. I could not imagine how this splendor could be improved.

My awe increased over the next thirty or forty minutes. The great white Moon gradually turned orange, while it fattened, appearing larger and larger. Eventually, this shamelessly magical, full orange Moon slowly slipped down the outside of the globe, leaving colored light in its wake, until it disappeared from view into the orange black sea.

Now cadmium orange light was glazed across the ocean where silver moonlight had rested earlier. At the same time, the eastern horizon was glowing. Within ten minutes a white-yellow sliver appeared on the eastern horizon: the Sun was rising. As it rose higher, pink shot through the gray lacy sky and across the charcoal sea.

At first, I thought the Moon was rising again. But no, nature was co-ordinating its wonders. It was the mighty Sun. As the Sun appeared, suddenly the lights of Auckland emerged in the middle of the horizon, midway between the vanishing orange Moon and the awakening white-yellow Sun, which was changing the color of the sky from black to gray and blue.

The southernmost Polynesian island was touched by moonlight and sunbeams at this early period of day. I could see a large white cloud stretching down the middle of the North Island. Aotearoa, the Land of the Long White Cloud, was living up to its name. I was home.

The pilot turned around to face me.

"I'm sorry, but you'll have to go back to your seat now. I'm not allowed to have a passenger up here when we land. I'm so glad you got to see this. Not many people appreciate it the way I do."

I returned to New Zealand in a way I could never have imagined. Slipping between the hemispheres on the flight deck of a Boeing 747, viewing the most transcendentally beautiful sight I had ever seen, the curving

Earth, the rising Sun, the again setting full orange Moon, the gray opaque and wrinkled sea. It was as if I had come from another universe to visit this new, magical one, filled with joy, with ecstasy, with sheer pleasure.

To one who flies in the air and looks down, there is nothing ugly on Earth. Never had I been so purely happy. Only a few hours before I had cried in the Atlanta airport that I no longer believed in miracles. Then Angelita joined me while doing yoga and my gloomy miasma lifted. Hours later, I sat behind the captain, looking out on an Earth of such splendor I could find no words to adequately describe it.

"The universe supports our attempts to be better," the pilot said mysteriously as I left the cockpit, gushing my thanks.

A few weeks later, I finally came to see this day as a perfect example of a favorite Buddhist thought. We live a thousand births and deaths, every single day, because of the nature of mind, which is constantly fluctuating between happiness and despair. This day had been a good example. For twenty-four hours, my life had stretched between deep descent and pinnacled ecstasy, with everything imaginable and unimaginable in between. And it would again.

References

1. "Wole Soyinka on Yoruba Religion: A Conversation with Ulli Beier", *Isokun Yoruba Magazine* (Vol. III No. III, 1997).
2. Akinwumi Ogundiran, "A long view sheds fresh light on the history of the Yoruba people in West Africa" (in *The Conversation*, June 27, 2021).
3. Carl Jung, from the Foreword to *Richard Wilhelm's I Ching, , or, Book of Changes*, translated into English by Cary F. Baynes (Princeton University Press, 1977).
4. Luc Sala, *Ritual, The Magical Perspective: Efficacy and the search for inner meaning* (Nirala Publications, 2014).
5. *Animal Sacrifice and Religious Freedom: Church of the Lucumií Babalu Aye v. City of Hialeah* (University Press of Kansas, 2004), p. 94-5.
6. *Church of the Lucumi Babalu Aye, Inc. v. City of Hialeah*, Supreme Court of the United States, 508 U.S. 520, June 11, 1993, Decided.
7. *One Hundred Americans Making Constitutional History: A Biographical History*, edited by Melvin I. Urofsky (CQ Press, Washington D.C. 2004), p. 157-159.
8. Miguel Ramos, "La División de la Habana: Territorial Conflict and Cultural Hegemony in the Followers of Oyo Lucumií Religion 1850s-1920s" (in *Cuban Studies*, Volume 34, 2003), p. 48-50
9. *The Miami Herald*, July 1, 2007
10. *The Miami Herald*, June 17, 2007
11. Thomas A. Tweed, *Our Lady of the Exile: Diasporic Religion at a Cuban Catholic Shrine in Miami* (Oxford University Press, 1997), p. 47.
12. Mary Shelley, *Frankenstein or the Modern Prometheus* (Portland House Illustrated Classics, 1988), p. 19.
13. *Georg Feuerstein, The Yoga Tradition: Its History, Philophy, Literature and Practice* (Hohm Press, 1998).
14. "Thunderstorm watch: 100,000 lightning strikes across the country," Georgia Forrester and Tim O'Connell (*Stuff*, online, Dec 7 2019).

15 "Lightning strikes as a major facilitator of prebiotic phosphorus reduction on early Earth" (in *Nature Communications*, Vol 12, March 16, 2021).
16 Brian Thomas Swimme, *Cosmogenesis* (Counterpoint, 2022).

Glossary

Ashé	Similar to *kundalini* in yoga and *chi* in Taoist philosophy. Ashé is the universal energy of birth, evolution and enlightenment. It is heard in Lucumí greetings and prayers to affirm and invoke awareness.
Adimú	A small offering of food for orisha and/or ancestral spirits.
Babaláwo	Literally, the word means "father of mysteries" in the Yoruba language. The title refers to a diviner and priest of Ifá.
Dilogún	A shortened form of the Yoruba word *merindilogún*, which means sixteen. It refers to the sixteen cowrie shells used in this ancient method of divination.
Egun	The spirit of a deceased person.
Elegguá/Eshu	The prime mover of the universe, this complex orisha is a profound philosopher and translator of the Dilogún.
Ifá	The formal Yoruba divination system used by babaláwo, who divine with sixteen palm nuts or a divination chain.
Lucumí	The word Lucumí was a greeting used by the Yoruba people in Cuba to recognize their common ancestry. Now it refers to the sect of Yoruba religion that began in Cuba.
Obá	The Yoruba word for king, and one of the words used in Lucumí to designate a master of ceremonies.
Obá-oríaté	A ceremonial master of Lucumí and a master diviner of the Dilogún.
Obatalá	The wise and truthful Orisha who created the human body and who is older than the other Orishas.
Oshún	The orisha of sensuality and abundance, who in her later years became a profound mystic. Oshún is identified with sweet water in rivers and lakes.
Odu	The codified symbols and verses which are the fundamental elements of both Dilogún and Ifá divination.

Ogún	The orisha of metal, blacksmiths and the knife. It is in his name that a priest sacrifices an animal.
Oracle	The word oracle comes from the Latin word meaning to pray; it is also connected to the word for mouth. In this sense, the diviner, or oracle, is the mouth of spirit.
Oríaté	One who divines on a mat and interprets the Dilogún.
Orisha	The pantheon of Yoruba gods, or an individual member of that pantheon. The Yoruba say there are 401 orisha, divine beings with superhuman powers, but only a few are recognized in the Diaspora. The word is both singular and plural.
Orúnmìlà	He is the god of the Ifá divination. Orúnmìlà learned Ifá from an ancient Iroko tree.
Oyá	She is identified with the whirlwind and thunder. Oyá transports the spirits of deceased people to peace in the afterlife.
Padrino	The Spanish word for godfather, referring to the male who initiates a person into Lucumí and who guides that person's development in the religion.
Padrina	The Spanish word for godmother.
Shangó	The orisha of thunder, justice, resurrection. He was also a general and king of the Oyo Empire.

About the Author

Photo: Murray Hedwig

Judith Hoch's eyes were first opened to the world of spirit, music, and Africa's rich oral traditions while carrying out doctoral research in western Nigeria, where she lived for two years among the Yoruba people. Her undergraduate work had been at Tulane in New Orleans, where she first encountered Vodou, while her Masters degree research was among Cree people in northcentral Quebec. This research made her very aware of the negative impacts of white colonialism.

After receiving her Ph.D. from McGill University, Judith held faculty posts at two Florida Universities, where she taught anthropology and oversaw student research. She later became an exhibiting artist. During this period she exhibited widely, won a national competition, and gave numerous workshops to discuss her ideas and work, using her art to explore the depths of non-western spirituality and expose the holocaust of the European witch trials.

While living in Miami, Judith met a Yoruba priest, Ernesto Pichardo. He challenged her cultural assumptions around whiteness, and introduced her to Yoruba spiritual practices, including to her personal head Orisha, Elegguá/Eshu, the trickster. Judith also studied with the senior teachers of

B.K.S Iyengar for many years, teaching at a yoga institute in Miami, and near her home in Aoteaora.

Judith and her husband John first arrived in New Zealand in the 1980s, where they bought land, built a house, and planted native trees. There she was strongly drawn to Māori, and especially to Aroha Ropata, whose warmth, generosity and love of Bob Marley made her seem like an islander from the Caribbean, and very Miamian.

Judith passed away in 2022. *Soul Healing in Afro-Cuban Miami* complements her first memoir, *Prophecy on the River*. Both present a rich mix of travel, research, welcomed influences and personal exploration.

A note on this book: When Judith passed away she had almost completed revising the text. Part of her revision involved consulting with Jesus Suarez, clarifying the history of Santería practice and events that involved him. Jesus kindly completed that process during the text's final edit.

Support Attar Books

Small presses rely on the support of readers to tell others about the books they enjoy. To support this book and its author, we ask you to consider placing a review on the site where you bought it. Other Attar Books publications related to this collection are listed below. They may be viewed on www.attarbooks.com and are available from all online bookstores.

Prophecy on the River by Judith Hoch

Best Book Finalist: 2020 International Indie Book Awards
Book Book Finalist: 2020 Ashton Wylie Book Awards, New Zealand

"In *Prophecy on the River*, artist, anthropologist and environmentalist Judith Hoch describes her magical experiences with the people, land and history of New Zealand. Written in eloquent prose, this memoir tells how Hoch came to recognise in a very heartfelt and visceral way that her own spiritual rejuvenation, along with that of both indigenous Māori people and descendants of the colonial settlers, depends upon acquiring deep respect for rivers and forests, and appreciating the innate power of the natural world and its need for revitalization.

Hoch writes of her efforts, with those of her husband John, to repopulate a forest preserve adjacent to her home on the South Island; her encounters with ancient, majestic trees and with spirits that inhabit waterways; and her struggle with neighbours who despoil the land. Her story is compelling, the narrative flows easily, and the overall experience is both moving and motivating."

— Richard Schwartz, Emeritus Professor, Florida International University

In a rare meeting of the Afro-Cuban Lucumi and Aotearoa Māori cultures, Judith uses skills learned as a student of Orisha divination and mediumship to delve into the tragic events that historically impacted the land as she seeks a way to heal it. Guided by her Miami-based padrino, Ernesto Picardo, and working with her Waitaha Māori friend, Aroha Ropata, Judith connects with the land's ancestors and the spiritual forces required for her ecological efforts to succeed.

The Lantern in the Skull by Hugh Major

Best Book Finalist: 2020 International Indie Book Awards
Book Book Finalist: 2020 Ashton Wylie Book Awards, New Zealand

A camera previously in perfect working order, which inexplicably won't photograph a fetish in an African village chief's basement, provides the first stop on Hugh Major's engaging survey of experiences that hover intriguingly beyond the margins of the everyday. Using his own experiences as a springboard, he considers telepathy, psychic perceptions, psychedelic insights, artistic transports, near death experiences, and much else.

Hugh Major provides a timely snapshot of current research into "marginal zones of the extraordinary". In precise, jargon-free language, he indicates the territory being explored and outlines major directions researchers are traveling. There are numerous captivating, and surprising, discoveries along the way.

"*The Lantern In The Skull* offers an engaging meditation on consciousness, that clear light that seemingly lives inside your head, stubbornly resisting materialistic explanations. Author Hugh Major provides a clearly written and well-informed study of the increasingly critical need to see beyond a simple clockwork model of reality."

— Dean Radin PhD, chief scientist at the Institute of Noetic Sciences, author of *Entangled Minds* and *The Noetic Universe*

Of Hugh Major's *From Monkey to Moth: An Imaginal Evolution*

"Very readable, eclectic, full of wisdom drawn from experience. The ineffable is given shape with allegory, parable and metaphor. I so enjoyed it I went back several times to the sections that aroused a wealth of feeling."

— Joy Cowley, author of *Veil Over The Light: Selected Spiritual Writings* and *Navigation, A Memoir*

People of the Earth by Peter Calvert, Richard Bentley, Carolyn Longden and Trisha Wren

When Peter Calvert gathered a small group of meditators and set them the task of opening their minds to whoever arrived, he didn't anticipate the astonishing encounters that would result. *People of the Earth* offers a unique account of communications with spiritual identities normally invisible to us: deceased people lost between worlds, nature spirits who nurture the Earth's ecosystems, and non-human beings who "drop in" to see what is going on.

Through a sequence of intriguing dialogues between the meditators and visiting non-embodied beings, recorded during the encounters and subsequently transcribed, *People of the Earth* provides sobering insights to the relationship between the so-called living and dead, and insights into what is required of us spiritually to sustain the planet's ecological health.

"I have always considered the nature of our embodiment the most important unresolved issue of our civilisation. Peter Calvert and his colleagues have made an ambitious attempt to communicate with disembodied life forms. The fact that these dialogues are of varying clarity, alien credibility, and internal continuity is not as important as the acts of faith that generated them. The urgent truth is that we have to begin somewhere if we are going to explore tabooed portals, claim our place in the greater universe, and find the wisdom necessary to redeem our own world." — Richard Grossinger, author of *The Night Sky: Soul and Cosmos* and *Bottoming Out the Universe: Why Is There Something Rather Than Nothing?*

The Ecstasy of Cabeza de Vaca by Keith Hill

In 1528, a Spanish expedition was shipwrecked in the Gulf of Mexico. Eight years later only four men remained alive. One of the four, Cabeza de Vaca, later published an account of what occurred. Naked and enslaved, de Vaca was stripped of all he possessed, then underwent an extraordinary transformation. *The Ecstasy of Cabeza de Vaca* is Keith Hill's masterful retelling of Cabeza de Vaca's story. This is a heartbreaking account of courage and faith, barbarity and miracles, that encapuslate the extremes of human experience.

"A tour de force. A truly original and remarkable recasting in verse of the ill-fated Narváez expedition to Central America. Hill's humanizing of de Vaca is the ingredient that makes it so moving and once taken up, impossible to put down." – Alistair Paterson

"In a series of extraordinary encounters depicted in beautifully rendered action and imagery. Hill makes de Vaca's inner world spring to wondrous life. Natural, memorable and rewarding." – Raewyn Alexander

"An extraordinary effort of imagination. In New Zealand literature there's certainly no long poem like this one." – Roger Horrocks

www.ingramcontent.com/pod-product-compliance
Lightning Source LLC
Chambersburg PA
CBHW020340010526
44119CB00048B/543